AGEING MATTERS

Social Policy in Modern Asia

Series Editor
CATHERINE JONES FINER

In an age of globalization, this series is designed to help broaden the basis and the perspectives of international comparative social policy by introducing fresh countries and above all fresh perspectives on social policy into what has hitherto been very much a Western-dominated field. Topics to be covered include social care, welfare services, family structure, crime and punishment, pensions, housing, and healthcare in various countries including China, Taiwan, Malaysia, Indonesia and Thailand.

Also in this series

Social Policy Reform in China: Views from Home and Abroad
Catherine Jones Finer
ISBN 0 7546 3175 3

The Possibility of Social Policy: The Political Construction of State Welfare
in the Republic of Korea
Gyu-Jin Hwang
ISBN 0 7546 4261 5

Housing in the New Welfare State: Comparing Europe and East Asia
Edoted by Alan Murie and Rick Groves
0 7546 4440 5

Ageing Matters

European Policy Lessons from the East

Edited by

JOHN DOLING, CATHERINE JONES FINER, TONY MALTBY
University of Birmingham, UK

ASHGATE

Published by
Ashgate Publishing Limited
Gower House
Croft Road
Aldershot
Hants GU11 3HR
England

Ashgate Publishing Company
Suite 420
101 Cherry Street
Burlington, VT 05401-4405
USA

Ashgate website: http://www.ashgate.com

British Library Cataloguing in Publication Data
Ageing matters : European policy lessons from the East. -
  (Social policy in modern Asia)
  1.Aging - Cross-cultural studies 2.Older people -
  Cross-cultural studies 3. Aging - Asia - Case studies
  4.Older people - Government policy - Asia - Case studies
  I.Doling, J. F. (John F), 1946- II.Jones Finer, Catherine
  III.Maltby, Tony
  305.2'6'095

Library of Congress Cataloging-in-Pubication Data
Ageing matters : European policy lessons from the East / [edited] by John Doling,
Catherine Jones Finer, and Tony Maltby.
        p. cm. -- (Social policy in modern Asia)
  Includes bibliographical references and index.
  ISBN 0-7546-4237-2
  1. Aging--Cross-cultural studies. 2. Older people--Cross-cultural studies. 3.
Aging--Asia--Case studies. 4. Older people--Government policy--Asia--Case studies.
I. Doling, J. F. II. Jones Finer, Catherine. III. Maltby, Tony. IV. Title. V. Series.

HQ1061.A424415 2005
305.26--dc22
                                                                2004017827

ISBN 0 7546 4237 2

Printed and bound in Great Britain by MPG Books Ltd, Bodmin, Cornwall

Contents

PART I: THE CONTEXT

PART II: THE CASE STUDIES

List of Tables

List of Figures

List of Contributors

Seong-Hoon Bae is Deputy Director of the International Relations Team, National Pension Corporation, Seoul, Korea.

Professor Hsiao-hung Nancy Chen is Professor of Sociology, National Chen Chi University, Taipei, Taiwan.

Professor Sung-Jae Choi is President of the Korean Academy of Social Welfare, National University of Seoul, Korea.

Gordon Deuchars is Policy Officer, AGE Older People Platform, Brussels, Belgium.

Professor John Doling is Professor of Housing Studies at the Institute of Applied Social Studies, School of Social Sciences, University of Birmingham, UK.

Professor Catherine Jones Finer is Honorary Professor at the Institute of Applied Social Studies, School of Social Sciences, University of Birmingham, UK.

Li Kan is Visiting Research Fellow at the Institute of Applied Social Studies, School of Social Sciences, University of Birmingham, UK.

Professor Joe C. B. Leung is Head of the Department of Social Work and Social Administration, University of Hong Kong.

Professor Tee Liang Ngiam is Member of Parliament and a member of the Department of Social Work and Psychology, National University of Singapore.

Tony Maltby is Senior Lecturer in the Institute of Applied Social Studies, School of Social Sciences, University of Birmingham, UK

Tetsuo Ogawa is Research Associate at the Oxford Institute of Ageing, university of Oxford.

Professor Roziah Omar is Dean of the Graduate School, University of Malaya, Kuala Lumpur, Malaysia.

Professor Paul Wilding is Emeritus Professor, University of Manchester, UK.

Acknowledgements

Any endeavour such as this will have benefited from contributions made by many people. The smooth operation of the workshop, from which the chapters of this collection are drawn, owed much to the hard work and enthusiasm of Judith Lockett who – always with a smile – dealt with correspondence, booked rooms and transport, organized the paying of the bills, and generally made sure everything ran smoothly.

Our thanks are certainly given to the speakers from the six Asian countries who wrote and delivered papers in a spirit of genuine desire to share the experiences of their own societies, and were willing to travel halfway round the world to do so. Thanks are also extended to those Europeans who came and contributed to the lively and interesting exchanges of information and views. One – Gordon Deuchars – gave a paper, and those acknowledged below chaired sessions:

Dr Saadet Degar, Institute for Asian Studies, University of Birmingham, UK.

Professor Anne-Marie Guillemard, University of Paris-V Sorbonne and Centre d'Etude des Mouvements Sociaux, Paris, France.

Dr Maria Luisa Mirabile, Istituto di Ricerche Economiche e Sociali, Rome, Italy.

Dr Zsuzsa Szeman, Academy of Sciences, Budapest, Hungary.

Professor Phil Taylor, CIRCA, University of Cambridge, UK.

Dr Maria Theofilatou, DG Research, European Commission, Brussels, Belgium.

Finally, we would like to give thanks to the European Commission for agreeing to fund the APPLE project, and especially to Dr Maria Theofilatou who, as our Scientific Officer in Directorate-General Research, provided full support; she opened the workshop on behalf of the Commission and chaired one of the sessions, but most of all fully supported our efforts to achieve outcomes that, hopefully, will contribute, if only in a small way, to the well-being of Europe's ageing society.

John Doling
Catherine Jones Finer   *University of Birmingham*
Tony Maltby

PART I
THE CONTEXT

Chapter 1

Editorial Introduction

John Doling

This book is an outcome of the APPLE (Ageing Populations: Policy Lessons from the East) project, which was conceived at the University of Birmingham and supported by funds from the European Commission. At its heart was a workshop that brought together policy experts from a number of Asian countries with workshop participants drawn from policy-making and research communities throughout Europe. It encapsulated two main propositions: that economically advanced countries shared a common challenge founded in demographic developments; and that it should be possible for policy-makers in Europe to benefit from knowledge about how policy-makers in Asian countries were responding to this challenge

Common Challenges

All the economically advanced countries of the world are experiencing similar demographic trends, albeit from different starting points and at different rates. Falling birth rates, longer life expectancies and the breakdown of extended and nuclear family models are combining to present a number of challenges for national policy-makers, including the following.

- As the ratio of retired to working people shifts toward the former, who is available to work to provide the services (shops, banks, restaurants, hospitals) demanded by retired people? Will the present preoccupation of many of the economically advanced countries with labour surpluses be replaced by a preoccupation with labour shortages? To what extent will governments attempt to raise retirement ages in order to keep more people in the labour market? Will they encourage the immigration of younger people from economically less advanced countries, for example Central and Eastern Europe, India, China and Africa?
- How can the rising numbers of older people be helped and encouraged to take a larger role in society, using their skills and experience to remain as active citizens? What role can governments take in reconceptualizing the meaning of retirement and citizenship, towards an 'active ageing' approach? The encouragement of active ageing has taken on a key focus within international

debates (see, for example, OECD 2000; WHO 2001), but questions remain about the most appropriate policy responses.

- The changes to family structures caused by, for example, lower rates of marriage, higher rates of divorce and lower fertility rates pose questions about how to replace the support and care formerly provided through the family. Can the family remain the focus of the care of frail older people? If the state and the market are seen to be solutions, how will care systems be funded?

- As the ratio of retired to working people shifts increasingly toward the retired, how are pensions to be funded? Typically, in Western countries pensions for currently retired people are paid from the taxes paid by the present working population. What pressures will there be to reduce the level of pensions as a proportion of average incomes; to move from income for life to lump-sum pensions, and to encourage greater reliance on defined-benefit pensions? The favoured approach to date, supported by the World Bank, is for versions of the 'multi-pillar' approach, whereby the state regulates private forms of provision (see Bonoli 2001; Hughes and Stewart 2000). Yet questions remain about the ability of such privatized forms to match the adequacy, inclusiveness and security offered by existing social insurance schemes. Typically, in Asian countries there is more emphasis put on employee- and employer-funded pension schemes. What are the specific characteristics, advantages and limitations of these?

Learning from Asia

There has been considerable interest in the West (including Europe and the USA) in the economic, political and cultural dimensions underlying the dynamic postwar growth of a number of Asian economies and this is reflected in numerous publications available in the West. They range from social scientific studies to 'airport' management guides. For example, there is an established pattern of the importation to the West of Japanese business and industrial policy lessons.

In relative terms there has been much less interest to date in the social policy dimensions of their politico-economic systems. But there is evidence that this is changing: thus, the recent introduction in the UK of stakeholder pensions has been based on the example provided by Singapore's provident fund system, which itself was a legacy of the British colonial administration (see Blair 1996). The different conceptualization of retirement and the different relationships between the individual, the family, civil society and the state in Asian countries may provide the West with alternative models.

As argued in chapter 2 of this volume, the possibility of learning social policy lessons from the East has developed, partly as a result of an awareness, within the Asian countries themselves, that they will increasingly be facing many (Western-style) social problems. Predominant among these is probably that of how to care for and support people in old age, the issue coming to the fore as the combined consequence of declining birth rates, increasing life expectancies and the break-up of the traditional extended family. One result is that there are no longer such extensive child and family support mechanisms to provide care, financial support and a secure living environment; another is that older people in Asian economies are taking a less active role in their societies. These matters are increasingly being studied and discussed in workshops within the individual Asian countries, and although the deliberations and findings are sometimes published they are not widely accessible to Western researchers and policy-makers.

In addition, over the last few years there have been a number of publications that have examined social issues and social policies in individual Asian countries, frequently locating the discussion in a cross-national, comparative perspective (for example, Doling and Omar 2000; Jones Finer 2001). But these publications, while including chapters dealing with policy responding to ageing populations, are not solely concerned with that issue.

The APPLE Workshop

So, at the time when APPLE was being planned, there had been limited progress in systematically bringing together information about trends in, and policies regarding, ageing populations, that relate to all the major – that is, more advanced – Asian economies and that was accessible to researchers and policy-makers in the West. This was the inspiration for APPLE, an inspiration that was realized with the assistance of a grant from the European Commission under its Fifth Framework Programme.

The APPLE team had already identified relevant Asian countries and experts. The six countries – Hong Kong, Japan, South Korea, Malaysia, Singapore and Taiwan – are those with the highest GDP per capita, mainly based on flourishing manufacturing and service sectors (see the Statistical Appendix for relevant indicators). The latter was considered an important criterion since there are Asian countries (principally Brunei) which owe their prosperity to rich natural resources, but without institutional arrangements being developed as in other economically advanced countries. The economic similarities between them and the EU member states, therefore, probably make our six the most likely to yield relevant policy lessons.

The agreed plan was that the APPLE team at Birmingham – Doling, Jones Finer and Maltby – would make study visits to the six countries in order to obtain briefings about the major issues relating to ageing populations in each country and to identify which aspects would probably be of most interest to Europeans. The visits would also confirm the appropriateness of the Asian experts – a mix of academic researchers and policy-makers – to be invited to have direct involvement in the project.

The project focused on a two-day workshop held at the University of Birmingham at the end of March 2003. The programme began with a paper by Gordon Deuchars that outlined the policy challenges of ageing populations as seen from Europe, and the specific perspective of a non-profit organization representing older people's organizations across the EU. This was to be followed by six country sessions, each following the same pattern: a chair from a European country, one or two speakers from Asia presenting brief summaries of previously circulated written papers, a discussant from the project team, followed finally by general discussion involving all participants and spokespersons from the floor. The focus of each of these sessions was the challenges as seen from one of the six Asian countries and the relevance of their experiences for European policy debate. The final session was to be a round table involving all those who had chaired the earlier sessions.

In the event the planning and the running of the workshop was disrupted by events of global significance. War in Iraq commenced a matter of days before the start of the workshop and precautions imposed by a number of employers in Asian countries made it impossible for some of the speakers to attend. Some of the anticipated European participants also withdrew. Even closer to the start of the workshop the SARS epidemic became headline news. In terms of the number of participants, the workshop was about two-thirds of the size intended, but far from detracting from its quality this actually facilitated a more inclusive and participatory occasion.

The present book follows the pattern and objectives of the workshop: in summary, a recognition of the European agenda, an introduction to Asian perspectives and experiences, and the drawing of lessons from this last.

Chapter 2 reflects on the nature and meaning of policy lessons and transfer. In it, Catherine Jones Finer examines aspects of both the principles underlying policy transfer – including issues of from whom to learn and how to learn – and the history of lesson-learning and exchange between East and West. In chapter 3, Tony Maltby and Gordon Deuchars identify the main policy debates current across the EU as a whole and within its member states. Together, these two chapters provide a context against which to read the ensuing case studies.

The main part of the book consists of chapters about each of the six Asian countries involved in the APPLE workshop, each identifying aspects of the ways in which their governments and societies have responded to ageing of their societies. The specific emphasis varies from chapter to chapter. Thus chapter 4 on Malaysia, written by Roziah Omar, emphasizes the future of care, particularly in the context of the decline in the incidence and contribution of the extended family system. Here, there are important differences between the Malay and the Chinese ethnic groups: the former Muslim, still having relatively large families; the latter more economically advanced Confucian, with much smaller families.

Ngiam Tee Liang's chapter on Singapore sets out the main features of the Central Provident Fund. As in Malaysia, this is a legacy of the British colonial period, established as a mechanism to provide pensions, with each person in the scheme benefiting directly from the contributions made by themselves and their employers. Singapore is also interesting by virtue of the scale of government intervention in the housing system, one feature of which has been attempts to provide housing specifically designed in location and layout to meet the needs of older people and to encourage continued family cohesion via proximate housing arrangements.

Hong Kong now also has a provident fund system, ostensibly designed to meet income needs in old age. However, as Joe Leung argues, a major limitation of this is that it has only recently been introduced and it will not be fully functioning, in the sense of even notionally providing adequate levels of pension, until 30 to 40 years from now. In the meantime, the government is concerned about the erosion of the family as an institution providing financial and other forms of support for its older members. As in Malaysia, tax breaks are being used to encourage adult children to provide for their parents.

In Taiwan, as Nancy Chen shows in chapter 7, the appropriate role of the state with respect to pensions has been a matter of heated debate for some years. In practice, ironically, this level of political attention has never resulted in any decisive legislative conclusion. Hence the case of so far 'virtual reform' here reported. At the same time, the erosion of traditional family values continues to present difficulties for many older members of Taiwanese society.

According to Sung-jae Choi and Seong-hoon Bae, the family in South Korea is still the main source of support for older people. Indeed, they argue that the dominance of filial piety, ideologically and practically, has actively hampered the development of social welfare-based approaches. In this sense, Korean society has only recently begun to address issues of social concern in terms other than of family responsibility.

Finally, in chapter 9, Tetsuo Ogawa reports scrupulously and extensively on the key, ostensibly unique, policy approaches to aspects of ageing being taken up in Japan. If the European Union is to take note and learn from anything by way of Eastern experience then this, in his opinion, is where it should start.

The concluding two chapters (10 and 11) offer two different sorts of postscript. Having been involved in the workshop as a chairperson, as well as an active contributor to the general discussion, Paul Wilding has furnished his own concluding comments on the conference itself and thence on this book, with reference to ageing in East and Southeast Asia. The editors conclude by offering their own comments on the fruits of this exercise as a whole.

Finally, Li Kan's Statistical Appendix presents statistical information that allows for easy comparison between and within the Asian countries included in the APPLE project and the member states of the European Union. As usual, because of the definitional variations inherent in the different sources used, the statistics must be read with some caution. Indeed, it is for this reason that some of the quantitative information given in some of the chapters differs slightly from that provided in the Appendix.

References

Blair, T. (1996). *New Britain: My Vision of a Young Country*. London: Fourth Estate.
Bonoli, G. (2001). The politics of pension reform in Western Europe. *Benefits*, 31 (May/June).
Doling, J. and Omar, R. (eds) (2000). *Social Welfare East and West: Britain and Malaysia*. Aldershot: Ashgate.
Hughes, G. and Stewart, J. (2000). *Pensions in the European Union: Adapting to Economic and Social Change*. The Hague: Kluwer.

Jones Finer, C. (ed.) (2001). *Comparing the Social Policy Experience of Britain and Taiwan.* Aldershot: Ashgate.

OECD (2000). *Reforms for an Ageing Society.* Paris: OECD.

WHO (2001). *Active Ageing: From Evidence to Action.* Geneva: World Health Organization.

Chapter 2

Prospects for Pragmatism: Trading Lessons in Social Policy Between East and West

Catherine Jones Finer

Introduction

The 'APPLE' project was founded and funded in the belief that it was capable of generating useful ideas and information, on the key subject of population ageing, for policy-makers in Europe. This belief was grounded on a series of assumptions, themselves still the subject of some debate in comparative social policy:

1   that countries could actually learn from each other's experience in social policy, given a suitably structured framework of investigation and analysis;
2   more particularly: that the West (in this case Europe) might learn from the East (in this case Asia-Pacific) – an assumption running counter to generations of post-imperial policy conditioning, in both regions;
3   that any investigation of potential lessons to be learned (whether negatively or positively), via a project workshop formula, could, so we hoped, turn into a two-way process to the advantage of both sets of parties concerned – again in contrast to the record of East–West mutual misunderstandings, misconceptions and mistrusts which had gone before.

This chapter tackles each of these propositions in sequence, as a prelude to the substantive chapters and material to be presented in the rest of this book.

Taking Lessons from Abroad

A *lesson* is a programme designed to deal with a problem in one country by drawing on the experience of other countries facing the same problem. (Rose 1991: 2)

This is a deceptively simple definition of what remains a complex, contestable and chancy proposition. The very notion of being able, profitably, to take lessons in this way implies an understanding of the dynamics of social policy's formation, delivery and reception well beyond that evinced so far in comparative social policy. Fortunately, in practice, lesson-taking tends to be a much more piecemeal, eclectic, selective, subjective business than Rose's pure definition would suggest. As Dolowitz has observed (1996, 1999), policy copyists tend to pick and choose between particular items within a programme in which they might be interested; they may simply be attracted to a particular institutional arrangement for policy delivery, or to a particular ideological line in policy justification, or to the mechanics of 'attitudinal transfer' as a means of bringing their own publics around to a fresh way of thinking on key issues.

Then, again, there are *degrees* of lesson-drawing, or policy transfer, to be considered: from attempts at exact copying, at the one extreme, through attempts at emulation, attempts at 'cherry-picking' hybridization, right down to the mere garnering of inspiration from others' example. All of this constitutes good news for the chances of practical outcomes from the present East–West collaborative project.

Motives for Seeking, Taking and/or Offering Lessons

There is a pseudo-category of interest to be disposed of first. The sorts of arguments advanced by politicians (including local government politicians) and top bureaucrats to justify expenses-paid fact-finding trips abroad – or by such as labour union spokespersons to justify a levelling-up with selected practices elsewhere – have more to do with politics and the gathering of ammunition than with the possibilities and limitations of lesson-learning *per se*. Of the same ilk, and of no less significance, may be exhortations from the same sorts of people on the theme of whose policies, and which sorts, are to be shunned at all costs. Nevertheless, to the extent that all these receive media attention, they help shape and inform, as well draw strength from, shades of public opinion – as is of course their object.

Academic interest in studying the feasibility, etc., of lesson-taking may be presumed more disinterested in principle, since academic credibility is after all at stake. Yet even, or especially, academics can find the offer of choice invitations abroad enough for at least the suspension of judgement, when it comes to forecasting the likely practicalities of lesson-taking by where, from where – especially in advance of a high-profile research project or well-funded international conference proposition. Indeed, the very rules of funding engagement (e.g. those emanating from the European Union with regard to 'third-country' involvement) might delimit the range of fundable possibilities from the outset.

The European Union, for instance, generally prefers that, where the research to be funded involves a third country or countries, these last should normally be of developmental rather than outright competitive economic status – even where the prime location for EU-funded research may lie beyond the bounds of the Union itself:

> The structure is colonial in terms of the flow of money and also by the requirement that a European research institution be involved. More often than not the European researchers in the base institution take on the lead, or in Euro-speak 'coordinating', role

since they have a well-resourced infrastructure, internal expertise and multiple understandings of the nature of research and its findings. (Lewando Hundt 2000: 421)

Thus it is that the present project, involving a mix of the economically developed as well as the still-developing ageing environments of Asia-Pacific, constitutes in itself a breakthrough in EU research funding conventions.

Amongst the most genuinely interested in the matter of lesson-taking (and for that matter lesson exchange) for its own sake can be specialists actually on the job and in the field – from strategic levels of policy formation down to the sharpest end of street-level service delivery: forever in search of useful, usable ideas and feedback from elsewhere. For such people, however, it can be difficult to discern, from a standing start, just which ideas, practices and elements of feedback (negative as well as positive) are likely to be of workable use to them in their particular situation. In short, this is where academe is supposed to step in, as a form of theoretical and context-setting support, advice and (maybe) correction service (see the next section). Hence, in an inverse version of this strategy, the APPLE project's original decision to recruit a mix of academics and practitioners from each participating country to this East–West advisory project.[1]

Logically, there remains the reverse category of those who characteristically presume to bestow lessons on peoples and governments elsewhere, as was eminently true of the British Empire in its heyday. Such traditions can leave a long, long trail of self-fulfilling attitudes in their wake, on both sides. Nowadays, however, with the possible exception of the current United States of America, the governments of developed countries tend to be chary of telling other peoples what to do – not least because there tends to be some doubt nowadays, moral as much as political or economic, as to who is in any position to lay down the guidelines for anyone else. Far better to leave all such matters to the activities of non-governmental, international organizations – or better still, as is the argument of this project, to engage in processes of free lesson exchange.

Policy Transfer in General, versus Lesson-taking in Particular

Policy transfer is the blanket, all-inclusive category, embracing everything from spontaneous policy diffusion, through forms of policy imposition to (historically these are the rarest) forms of voluntary, conscious, selective lesson-taking from abroad. Specialists in the study of policy transfer tend to be more interested in monitoring and documenting the processes *per se* (academic inputs included), than in estimating or itemizing the chances of 'success', episode by episode. Albeit to varying degrees, there is bound to be something lost in policy transit every time. To adopt a gardening metaphor, policies transplanted into a strange environment tend to evolve different characteristics – depending on the degrees of change in environment – if they are to survive at all.

Policy diffusion stands rather for the spread of an idea than for the precise replication of its application from one country to the next. Witness the insidious, indiscriminate spread of the social insurance idea from Bismarck's Germany throughout western/northern Europe, from the 1880s up until the First World War

– and the immense variety of national social insurance schemes thus generated. Other forms of policy transfer have more often occurred as a result of lesson imposition rather than spontaneous lesson-taking. Colonialism has a great deal to answer for here (e.g. Jones 1990, on the subject of Hong Kong), as has the present generality of 'offers you can't afford to refuse' from richer to poorer states (with or without the backing of the World Bank). In just such an indiscriminate way, the World Bank encouraged the replacement of collective provision by private market provision in post-communist Eastern Europe, and the IMF was to encourage deregulation as an automatic component of its rescue packages proffered to countries in Asia-Pacific in the wake of the Asian financial crisis.

Lesson Identification as a Form of Academic Specialism?

Certainly it has the makings of such a specialism. In the words, again, of Richard Rose:

> Lesson-drawing addresses the question: under what circumstances and to what extent can a programme that is effective in one place transfer to another. Searching for fresh knowledge is not normal; the stimulus to search [comes from] dissatisfaction with the status quo. Lessons can be sought by searching across time and/or space; the choice depends upon a subjective definition of proximity, and epistemic communities linking experts together, functional interdependence between governments, and the authority of intergovernmental institutions. The process of lesson-drawing starts with scanning programmes in effect elsewhere, and ends with the prospective evaluation of what would happen if a programme already in effect elsewhere were transferred here in future. Lesson-drawing is part of a contested political process; there is no assurance that a lesson drawn will be both desirable and practical. (Rose 1991: 2)

But it scarcely has the makings of an exact science. The best we can do, for practical purposes, is to estimate probabilities based on desirability and feasibility (Rose 2003), on the one hand, backed up by considerations of cultural distance versus size of lesson.

Lesson-drawing, Rose insists, is about contingencies with regard to *feasibility* (under what circumstances and to what extent will a programme that works there also work here?) and *desirability* (which may be critically affected by a change in government, in the balance of power within a government or in the appreciation of national policy by civil servants with critical roles in the policy process) (Rose 2003: 12–13). This line of thinking generates its own two-by-two matrix (see table 2.1)

Add to this a related two-by-two set of considerations, relating the potential scale of such endeavours to the 'cultural distance' (political-social-economic) between potential teachers (or models) and takers (see table 2.2). Even within the north-western part of Europe (presumed relatively culturally close-knit) it has become customary to talk of different categories of welfare state regime (*à la* Esping-Andersen 1990), between whom there seems little scope for anything more than highly focused, specific versions of lesson-taking and possible exchange. Between East and West the scope would seem even more constricted.

Table 2.1 Feasibility and desirability of lesson-drawing

Feasibility	Desirability	
	High	Low
High	Doubly attractive	Unwanted technical solution
Low	Siren call: educational	Doubly rejected long-term?

Source: Rose (2003: 14).

Table 2.2 Cultural distance versus size of lesson: chances of success

	Extent of cultural distance	
Possible scale of lesson	Small	Great
	Great	Small

Source: Jones Finer (1998).

In short, there would seem more scope for the passage of little ideas – more akin to useful techniques or modes of policy delivery, whether statistical, institutional, rhetorical or inspirational – than for that of very big ideas regarding what society is supposed (by implication) to be all about. Eminently (for all that Tony Blair thought his Third Way to be a borrowing from the likes of Singapore), the West is no more minded or capable of switching to an Asia-Pacific Confucianist style of regulatory governance than is Asia-Pacific capable or desirous of embracing Western welfare statism.

Perceptions, Misconceptions and Counter-ceptions

Lesson-taking either way can be as much about perceptions as about actualities. In the present case, Eastern perceptions of the Western welfare state dependency disease have long been matched by Western perceptions of – at one and the same time – the collective unfeeling, *and* anti-individualistic, norms of the Asian economic miracle state. It can take time and patience to discover how far families and governments across these clusters of ageing societies, albeit situated within such disparate policy-making environments, may be up against comparable problems, with potentially an overlapping range of ameliorative solutions for their mutual consideration.

Nevertheless, the opposite – an apparent blanket enthusiasm for exploring other people's policies in a search for 'good useful ideas' irrespective of culture, politics or ideology – could potentially be just as (if not more) damaging for all concerned. Witness contemporary China's modernizing pursuit of so-called 'non-political' ideas on social policy delivery,[2] via its universities-backed study of Western systems of social security in operation from Nordic right through to North American democracies. If it works as intended, this could constitute the greatest exercise so far in policy design-and-delivery cherry-picking.[3]

Meanwhile, with regard to the countries of this particular study, democracy – even the show of effectively one-party democracy – evidently matters, to the extent that no elected government is going to be able (or willing) to 'sell' Western-imported policies (as opposed to useful techniques) indiscriminately to its electorate. Precisely the same applies to member governments of the European Union in respect of 'the East'. Hence the cumulative process of mutual East–West probing, bargaining and wheeler-dealing – only to be expected by realists in search of a realizable future – should there be a positive outcome to this and related projects.

'Tides' of Influence to Date between East and West

It was Gordon White and Roger Goodman (in Goodman et al. 1998: 3–24) who first drew widespread attention in Britain to the notion of there having been *tides of influence* between East and West over the second half of the twentieth century. Subsequently Doling and Jones Finer (2001: 293–306) set out to elaborate this idea, as outlined below.

Western Ascendancy, 1950s to 1960

The Second World War left the countries of Asia-Pacific in conditions of either defeat, demoralization and Allied (US) occupation in the case of Japan; or of simple ruin and demoralization in the case of the rest – in the wake of their 'liberation' from Japanese occupation. Modernization was seen as the key to recovery and economic development – and modernization signified westernization. The tenets of Confucianism – as variously interpreted across Asia-Pacific – were seen as antithetical to modernization, owing to their emphasis on a system of hierarchical relationships geared to the maintenance of an unchanging, unequal, deferential social order. The predominant Islamic culture of Malaysia was no less geared to the maintenance of the family – rather than the state – as the bulwark of social order.

So this is not to suggest that 'the East' ever embraced Western liberal values very profoundly or with enthusiasm. Welfare statism – so seemingly at odds with the East's own insistence on family responsibilities – was still seen as a Western disease (if not specifically 'the English disease'). Nevertheless, it was Western economic performances with which the countries of Asia-Pacific had to catch up, then compete.

But this was a form of competition – first from Japan and soon from the *little* tigers of Hong Kong, Singapore, South Korea and Taiwan – which the West, over this period, typically regarded as 'unfair'. These were countries of cheap (or soon, at least, cheap*er*) labour, whose governments seemed to evince little interest in taxing and spending to support Western-style social welfare provision on behalf of its workforce. It was to be a foretaste of things to come, whenever countries possessed of 'cheap labour' threatened to undermine the job security of organized Western workers. The latter's attempts to insist on comparable welfare protection standards for workers in competing countries were as ever presented in 'human rights' – rather than in nakedly protectionist – terms.

Western Welfare States in Crisis, 1970s to 1980s

These were the decades when – not merely in Eastern eyes – the 'chickens' of the Western welfare state were deemed to be 'coming home to roost'. The crisis was as much one of the welfare states' legitimacy as of their affordability, in the wake of the oil crises. The welfare state had failed to deliver an egalitarian, poverty-free 'New Jerusalem' (in the case of Britain) or even rock-solid social stability (in the case of Germany). Only in Scandinavia – with the exception of Denmark – were its credentials (and hence its funding) to remain relatively unchallenged for roughly a decade longer.

Japan and the little tigers of Asia-Pacific were no less vulnerable to the oil crises, but there was no temptation, this time around, to seek to emulate the Western example. Instead, Japan embarked on its programme for the re-establishment of a 'three-generation' Confucianist *welfare society*. In the meantime, the authorities in Hong Kong, Singapore, South Korea and Taiwan each set about constructing, in their various ways, their own reformulation of the ideal self-sustaining and self-policing Confucianist society, ostensibly from the grassroots up (i.e. from the family and the urban 'village' housing block), albeit under firm government direction (e.g. Jones 1990: 67–9; Jones 1993: 208–9).

It was from the 1980s that Western social scientists as well as politicians began to take the tigers' example seriously, not least in the light of what was seen as the latter's continuing superior economic performance.

'Swings and Roundabouts', 1980s to 1990s

Consider the fashion for *communitarianism* and 'back to basics' in Britain and North America, and for the pursuit of *social inclusion* across the European Union, as part of a drive to cut down on 'welfare dependency' and boost the sense of individual and family responsibility for ensuring popular well-being from the bottom up. This did not of course mean that the Western welfare states shrank to the social spending levels characteristic of Asia-Pacific (see below), but such policy moves were expected at least to slow rates of growth in governmental welfare expenditure. Clearest of all in its obeisance to the Eastern example was the initial idea of Britain's new prime minister Tony Blair, to render Britain a 'stakeholder society' – an idea apparently first elaborated by him, in public, on the occasion of an address to an audience of businessmen in Singapore (Jones Finer 1998: 170). As it happened, this was an idea more reminiscent of moralistic, individualistic Victorian Britain than of state-centred, capitalist, Confucianist Singapore; nevertheless, the idea that there might or even *should* be a two-way traffic in ideas had caught on.

Unfortunately, this idea was to be undermined straight away by the onset of the Asian financial crisis and the chorus of 'I told you so'-style comment that it occasioned among numerous Western observers. This time it was for Asia-Pacific, if not to learn from the Western example, then at least to put itself enough in accordance with 'Western' rules of world market behaviour to be able to comply with these, without too much further damage to itself and its trading partners. Nevertheless, once again, this was not an episode calculated to impress the peoples of Asia-Pacific with the innate superiority of Western standards of behaviour. On the contrary, as the views of loyal Koreans queuing up to pledge family heirlooms in support of their government's financial crisis made clear, this whole affair could be interpreted as a cynical Western plot to undermine the East Asian economic miracle.

Prospects for Pragmatism: A Free Trade in Social Policy Ideas and Practices between East and West?

The beginning of a new century ought, psychologically at least, to be a good time to start afresh. Extremes of ideological difference seem certainly to be being downplayed – consider, for example, Blair's Third Way (being neither socialist nor anti-socialist), Taiwan's (Blair-inspired?) 'New Middle', China's pursuit of 'socialist market capitalism', and the state-led/family-based forms of capitalism characteristic of Asia-Pacific's tigers in general. Plainly it is economic viability and competitiveness which is the be-all and end-all in today's global market, never ideological purity *per se*. 'What counts is results!'

Hence the search, in both directions, for mid-range useful ideas and techniques, somehow capable of adoption and adaptation, irrespective of sociology and ideology. Even so, old adages can die hard. It is all very well for the current leadership of 'socialist market' China to declare its conversion to the merits of NGO (even foreign NGO) activity with regard to the care of the elderly (e.g. Guan 2000: 120–2; Chen 2003: 227–8); and for Japan to institute a system of long-term care insurance for itself (e.g. Ogawa, this volume; Izuhara 2003: 395–410). The abiding question remains: how is the family to cope – or to be helped to cope – sufficiently to be able to retain its pivotal position in the ordering of social care and concern?

It is this very question which is of such supreme interest to governments in the West, with their ageing institutional support structures and their patent hopes of somehow being able to bring their own families – or at any rate communities – back in.

Notes

1   In practice, owing to the difficult political situation pertaining at the time of the workshop (see Acknowledgements, this volume), though with the distinguished exception of Seong-hoon Bae (Deputy Director of the International Relations Team, National Pension Corporation of Korea) it was academics rather than practitioners who succeeded in presenting papers at the workshop in Britain.

2   Despite the massive social upheavals resulting from its shift to 'socialist market capitalism', social policy could only 'come of age' in Communist Party China to the extent that social policy was deemed merely a matter of top–down programme design and delivery techniques, upon which academics could serve in a consultative capacity to government. There was never any question of examining modes of policy deliberation and formation elsewhere (e.g. Jones Finer 2003: 2).

3   However, the evidence to date suggests that such exercises have in the meantime also added to the local credibility problems of China's own policy-making systems (e.g. Jones Finer 2003: 2).

References

Chen, T. (2003). 'Social care and voluntary action in China: the policy of "societalizing social welfare" and its effects'. In Jones Finer (2003).

Doling, J. and Jones Finer, C. (2001). Looking East, looking West: trends in orientalism and occidentalism among applied social scientists. In C. Jones Finer (ed.), *Comparing the Social Policy Experience of Britain and Taiwan.* Aldershot: Ashgate.

Dolowitz, D. (1996). Towards a model of policy transfer: an examination of the British and American welfare-to-work systems. Unpublished PhD thesis, University of Strathclyde.

Dolowitz, D., with R. Hume, M. Nellis and F. O'Neal (1999). *Policy Transfer and British Social Policy Learning from the USA?* Buckingham: Open University Press.

Esping-Andersen, G. (1990). *The Three Worlds of Welfare Capitalism.* Cambridge: Polity Press.

Goodman, R., Kwon, H.-J. and White, G. (eds) (1998). *The East Asian Welfare Model: Welfare Orientalism and the State.* London: Routledge.

Guan, X. (2000). China's social policy reform and development in the context of marketization and globalization. *Social Policy & Administration*, 34, 1: 115–30.

Izuhara, M. (2003). Social inequality under a new social contract: long-term care in Japan. *Social Policy & Administration*, 37, 2: 395–410.

Jones, C. (1990). *Promoting Prosperity: The Hong Kong Way of Social Policy.* Hong Kong: Chinese University Press.

Jones, C. (1993). The Pacific challenge. In C. Jones (ed.), *New Perspectives on the Welfare State in Europe.* London: Routledge.

Jones Finer, C. (1998). The new social policy in Britain. In C. Jones Finer and Mike Nellis (eds), *Crime and Social Exclusion.* Oxford: Blackwell, pp. 154–70.

Jones Finer, C. (ed.) (2003). *Social Policy Reform in China: Views from Home and Abroad.* Aldershot: Ashgate.

Lewando Hundt, G. (2000). Multiple scripts and contested discourse in disseminating research findings. *Social Policy & Administration*, 34, 4: 434–47.

Rose, R. (1991). *What Is Lesson Drawing?* Glasgow: Centre for the Study of Public Policy, University of Strathclyde.

Rose, R. (2003). When all other conditions are not equal: the context for drawing lessons. In Jones Finer (2003), pp. 5–22.

Chapter 3

Ageing and Social Policy in the European Union: A Contextual Overview

Tony Maltby and Gordon Deuchars

Introduction

This chapter completes the introductory section by providing a contextual overview of the contemporary issues and debates regarding ageing populations in the European Union. Its purpose is to consider the central issues raised within the country case studies, forming Part II of this volume and offer a European perspective on such issues. It hence provides the context for these more detailed country analyses. Uniquely, it sets out a number of broad issues about ageing in Europe, drawing on the perspective of a non-governmental organization (NGO) called AGE,[1] working on these issues. A short chapter does not allow for any detailed analysis of policy across the large range of issues affecting ageing populations, and readers might like to refer to Maltby and Walker (2004) for a fuller treatment of European Union (EU) policy issues. However, our focus will be upon pensions and employment, two related and central issues and the focus of many of the chapters that follow. Before embarking on this analysis, the chapter provides a broad overview of the demographic issues pertinent to the discussion, followed by a summary of the role of the European Commission and the EU in formulation and implementation of social policy.

Background: An Ageing Europe

It is well known that Europe has a population in which the percentage of older people is rising rapidly, largely a result of increasing life expectancy and declining birth rates (see table 3.1). As Walker and Maltby (1997) indicate, this should be seen as a result of the triumph of successive social policy since 1948 (or earlier) and not, as many would have it, a cause of some anxiety and distress, although it is recognized that social policy may have not overcome all the challenges presently being faced by a worldwide ageing population. The key reasons for an improvement include enhanced general living standards, improvements in public health, the existence of general social security systems including pensions, and more generally the development of various models of welfare state. These social

policy measures have contributed to greater life expectancy and a decline in birth
rates across Europe, crudely represented by the slogan 'fewer babies, longer lives'.

Table 3.1 Projection of population over 60 (percentages)

Country	2000	2020	2050
Ireland	15.8	24	39
Netherlands	18.5	29	37
Luxembourg	19.6	28	36
Finland	19.8	30	36
Denmark	19.9	28	36
Sweden	20.2	29	36
Austria	20.4	28	40
France	20.7	29	38
Portugal	20.9	26	38
UK	20.9	27	37
Spain	21.8	28	44
Belgium	22.1	30	38
Germany	22.9	30	41
Greece	23.2	29	41
Italy	24.0	32	44
EU 15	*21.8*	*29*	*40*

Source: Eurostat.

It can be seen from table 3.1 that Ireland currently has the 'youngest' age
profile of the EU (15) countries and Italy the 'oldest'. This position changes in
2050 with the Scandinavian countries (Denmark, Sweden, Finland) sharing the
youngest profile with Luxembourg, and Italy still with the 'oldest' profile but
sharing it with Spain. Yet it is the growth in the proportion of those over 80 years
that is the most intense and in policy terms perhaps the most important. As Walker
(1999) indicates, within a five-year period from 2000 and across EU (15) countries,
this cohort will on average increase by 18.6 per cent. It will result in the average
age in EU (15) countries increasing from 38.3 years in 1995 to 41.8 in 2015 and by
2025 to 43.7. Only Japan surpasses this figure with its average in 1995 being 39.3,
and 45.9 in 2025.

The European Union and Policy Debate

Although social policy on social security (including pensions) and health care is a
national government not a European Union competence, since 2000 the EU
countries have adopted a common economic and social policy agenda, known as
the Lisbon Strategy. From March 2000 and the Lisbon summit meeting where it

was adopted (see http://ue.eu.int/en/Info/eurocouncil/index.htm), EU countries aimed at ensuring both competitiveness and social cohesion in their social policy.

The ageing of the population in Europe, and the policy response, was identified as one of the key common economic and social challenges to be faced at this macro-policy level. This was largely a result of the demographic imperatives outlined above and the focus of the media upon it. Yet the issue is viewed primarily as an economic cost to broad societal aims (e.g. cost of pensions, cost of health and long-term care, the perceived negative impact on productivity of having proportionately fewer young workers) whereas it is clear that older people have much to give to society and can make valuable contributions at most stages of the life cycle.

The Lisbon Strategy was adopted in a period of economic upturn and many of the targets, including those on employment, now look optimistic. However, it still represents a set of political commitments that the member states are trying to implement. It makes use of the so-called Open Method of Coordination, where member states agree common objectives and a review process for their national policies. With open coordination the European Commission has developed a role of trying to lead and stimulate social policy reflection in the different countries, proposing common directions, bringing together information for exchanges of good practice, etc. The Commission cannot take decisions in those policy areas that are binding on member states, but it can attempt to orientate the member states in particular directions and the results can be of some significance. On policy towards older people in particular, the Commission has for a number of years tried through various policy statements and other initiatives to develop an EU approach, which is now being applied to specific issues.

Although the European Union and European Commission have some characteristics similar to a national state, such as containing different bodies and policy processes representing different issues and interests, economic and finance issues are much more strongly anchored than social objectives in the Treaties. This reflects the nature of the founding principles of the (then) European Community which was essentially an economic formulation (see Hantrais 2000, ch. 1). The Treaties give the EU its competences for action, and allows them to enjoy higher political priority, especially on the part of national governments.

The Lisbon Strategy and the Open Method of Coordination provide a means of at least putting social issues on the policy 'map' at EU level, giving a forum in which the member states take on board social objectives on, at least in principle, an equal footing with economic objectives. Normally proposals are prepared jointly by different parts of the EU apparatus. For example, the Social Protection Committee and the Economic Policy Committee, representing Social Affairs and Economic/Finance ministries respectively, develop the work on pensions. In reality there often appears to be a fairly unequal competition between the EU's social and economic/financial institutions. Although NGOs may disagree with the Commission departments in charge of social affairs on particular issues, both aim to strengthen the social side of the argument.

Pensions and Social Policy in the EU

Among the first countries in the world to have social security for older people were
Germany and the UK. Throughout the second half of the twentieth century
European, especially western European, countries, built up fairly comprehensive
systems of old-age pensions, health services, unemployment benefit and other
social provisions. By the 1990s a large proportion of older and retired people in the
region as a whole enjoyed a broadly adequate material standard of living. Absolute
deprivation in old age, previously very common, had become rare. At the same
time there were notable improvements in the health and quality of life of very
many older people and at greater ages, although of course there is great variation in
how much of the extra life expectancy is spent in good health. Old-age pensions
contributed to a higher quality of life by allowing more active lives and social
participation, as well as by securing material necessities.

The pension systems established in Western Europe vary greatly.[2] Common to
all is a state-guaranteed first pillar covering either the whole resident population, or
(more commonly) all those who have contributed via the labour market. It is
normally financed by employer and employee contributions, though in Denmark it
is financed from general taxation. The financing is almost entirely on a 'pay-as-
you-go' (PAYG) basis, with the contributions from current workers being used to
pay for the pensions of current pensioners. The pension benefit is related to
earnings in the majority of countries, though in some (for example the UK,
Denmark and the Netherlands) it is flat-rate and paid to an upper limit. In most, but
not all, countries (again, the UK and to some extent the Netherlands, Ireland and
Denmark are exceptions) the first pillar provides the great majority of pension
income and is expected to go on doing so. Where additional cover is missing, then
a social 'safety net' means-tested benefit has been available.

Occupational pensions linked to a particular employer or sector of
employment, and individual private pensions are present to very different extents
in different countries. Most often these are financed by pension funds that invest on
the stock market, though in some countries there are occupational pension funds
working on a PAYG basis. Countries with flat-rate state pensions rely on
occupational and private pensions to a large and increasing extent, and obviously
in these circumstances it is important to establish whether most people really have
access to these pensions.

Despite the major progress made in ensuring decent incomes and living
conditions for older people in Europe, a serious level of poverty and social
exclusion remains. Older people in some countries and some regions are at
particular risk of poverty. It is difficult to quantify how many older people are poor
in the EU, but the EU statistical office (Eurostat) publishes figures for the 'risk of
poverty' of different age groups (defined in relative terms as having an income of
less than 60 per cent of the median income). Its last available annual social review
(*The Social Situation in the European Union 2002*) gave the figures shown in table
3.2.[3]

Table 3.2 At risk of poverty rate (60 per cent of median equivalized income), by age (1998)

	EU15	*B*	DK	D	EL	E	F	IRL	I	L	NL	A	P	FIN	S	UK
Below 16	24	18	3	26	21	25	22	23	28	17	17	16	27	6	11	26
16–24	23	2	15	23	21	24	28	16	25	18	24	12	16	17	25	22
25–49	*14*	11	5	11	16	17	13	14	18	9	10	10	15	7	10	14
50–64	*14*	16	4	13	22	17	15	12	17	10	6	10	17	6	4	13
65+	20	20	27	13	36	14	18	24	16	9	6	21	34	8	7	40

This high level of poverty risk among older people at a time when the population is ageing gives reason for concern and demands a policy response at EU and national level. There are admittedly counter-arguments along the lines that in some countries, future income levels may improve as future older people may have built up more entitlement to occupational pensions.

Poverty among older people is largely, though not entirely, caused by inadequate pension income. Reasons for low pensions are many, including:

- People with an incomplete employment record, for example because of unemployment or because they took time off to care for family members, lose pension entitlements in systems that are dependent on contributions paid through employment.
- Part-time workers or those earning less than a minimum amount may also not be eligible for pensions or unable to contribute to occupational pensions: so low pay and precarious employment conditions affect people throughout their lives.
- Some pensions are in any case set at what could be described as a poverty-line level (for example, the flat-rate state pension in the UK is set at a level *below* the threshold for the 'minimum income guarantee').

However, the most serious determinant for lower income in later life is gender, and in particular motherhood (Ginn 2003). There is a clear gap between men and women in the pensions they receive and a clear majority of older people living in poverty are women. Women's work and life patterns differ considerably from those of men and existing pension systems do not accommodate the life patterns of many women. As Maltby (2001) and others have indicated, retirement pensions have traditionally been designed for men by men and by a patriarchal state. Many pension schemes in the EU member states are still based upon a traditional nuclear-family model of a male 'breadwinner' and a non-employed wife, despite the increased incorporation of women into the workforce. This leaves many women with only 'derived rights' based on their husband's employment record.

In no EU member state do women have *de facto* the same opportunities as men to combine an economically active life with having a family. In some countries, the proportion of women who have had paid jobs is still well below that of men, particularly in the generations who have already reached retirement age (Ginn et al. 2001). Women of all generations still carry the main responsibility for family care. In the majority of member states, 'career breaks' to bring up children or provide care for other family members do not receive pension entitlement. In addition, many women work part-time, which in turn decreases the level of pension received (Ginn et al. 2001).

Future Concerns

In recent years there has been concern expressed by policy-makers and politicians about the financial sustainability and affordability of pension systems in the future. Yet historically, such fears have been a recurring theme from the early twentieth century to the present day, where they have been expressed as a 'time-bomb' and 'a pensions burden'. The public, the media and politicians have become more and more aware that the population of Europe is getting older, as people live longer and birth rates decline, and this has contributed to the panic. It has resulted in the closure of large numbers of (so-called) final-salary (or defined-benefit) schemes being run by companies and to increased concerns over income security for many people in retirement. Yet it should be recognized that the ageing of populations has more to do with the successful implementation of a variety of social policies that have extended life expectancy and quality of life rather than the more general perception as policy failure. How the state responds (or has responded) is the subject of the debate within this text.

The sustainability of pension systems based on PAYG, the predominant model, is under question even from the simplest logical position that there are projected to be relatively more pensioners drawing benefits and relatively fewer workers paying into the system. As these systems are state-financed rather than privately financed, quite alarming predictions are made from time to time about the impact of ageing on public finances as deficits in the pension systems will be covered from the general budget. Alternatively, workers' and employers' contributions towards pensions would have to rise to unsustainable levels. For example, the European Union's Economic Policy Committee produced a projection that

> notwithstanding reforms during the 1990s, ageing populations could lead to increased expenditure on public pensions of between 3 and 5 percentage points of GDP in most member states in the coming decades up to 2050. For the EU as a whole, public pension spending is projected to peak in 2040 at 13.6 per cent of GDP up from 10.4 per cent in 2000. (EPC 2001: 30)

This is the so-called 'pension time bomb'. The increased cost of health care and long-term care for older people is projected to be at least as great, although there are major uncertainties about how much extra need for health care will arise at what stage. As the reader will see, such issues are being, and have been, grappled with in countries like Japan and South Korea.

As a result the idea became widespread that the solution was to replace redistributive state pensions by capital-funded occupational and private pensions. This view has gained credence with the media and is still often heard, no doubt partly because of arguments by financial services industry groups who would see such a shift as an opportunity to sell pension products on a large scale. It has also had some influence on public policy in some countries. The favoured approach to date is for versions of the 'multi-pillar' approach favoured by the World Bank, whereby the state regulates private forms of provision (Bonoli 2001; see also

Hughes and Stewart 2000). Yet questions remain about the ability of such privatized forms to match the adequacy, inclusiveness and security offered by existing social insurance schemes. Indeed, an interim research report from the prominent British think-tank, the Institute for Public Policy Research (Brooks et al. 2001) suggests the British government's new pensions strategy (which adopts a multi-pillar approach) needs to be carefully reappraised (2001: 4). It raises serious concerns around these three issues and in particular the sustainability of the current settlement. There is also the important question of a particular policy's redistributional effects (see also Maltby 2001).

However, the recent slump on the stock markets and financial scandals, some of them affecting pension funds, have, to say the least, dented confidence in capital-funded pensions as a panacea. It is increasingly recognized that funded pensions also depend on transferring current output into pensions. If the economy or the stock market does not perform, the necessary resources are not there. The trend now is to argue that the only sure way to avoid poverty in old age is to work much longer (see DWP 2002). For example, in the UK, a widely quoted October 2002 report by the National Association of Pension Funds (representing pension fund managers) argued that the state pension age would have to rise to 70 (see http://www.napf.co.uk/). It is this simplistic econometric position that is often trumpeted by the media and politicians and is one that treats older people purely as a financial cost, mouths to feed and bodies to care for, rather than contributors to and stakeholders in society (Walker and Maltby 1997; Maltby 2001).

An alternative view and one promoted by AGE and some other NGOs, would be that larger numbers of active, healthy, experienced older people are a major asset and resource for society. Older people provide a large proportion of care for children, other older people and others who need care, and do a considerable amount of socially useful voluntary work. All this work, like the unpaid domestic work done by women of all ages, has a considerable economic value although it is not counted in national economic statistics. If it all had to be paid for from the public budget or by business, the economic impact would be considerable. There is presumably scope for this contribution to increase in step with the proportion of older people in society.

The EU states are working for sustainable solutions to the pensions 'crisis' and we are increasingly seeing greater coordination on policy between member states. This has occurred not only at national governmental levels but through consultation with the European Social Partners such as the relevant consortia of older people's NGOs and via the recently formed AGE platform. An example of this is the ongoing debate over pension provision. Arising out of the Gothenburg Summit, the European Commission has adopted a Communication on supporting national strategies for 'safe and sustainable pensions' (European Commission 2001). The central theme of this Communication is the adoption of what is referred to as 'open coordination', defined as the 'setting of common objectives, the translation of these into national strategies for pensions and the periodic monitoring of commonly agreed and defined indicators' (www.europa.eu.int/comm/employment_social/soc-prot/social/).

Indeed, at the Gothenburg Summit and arranged under ten broad objectives, three principles for pension reform were agreed. These are:

- adequacy of pensions;
- financial sustainability of public and private pension schemes;
- modernization of pension systems in the light of the changing needs of society and individuals.

The proposal was that member states should draw up national strategies on pensions by 2002 for further discussion by the Commission and the Council of Ministers. Out of this consultation, a report was prepared and made available to the spring summit in 2003.[4] Nevertheless, although pensions systems are clearly the primary focus of consultation, debate and policy formulation, the EU and the Commission are also formulating new policy on the care of older people. Indeed, the European Council has called for the Commission to prepare a report. The EU Summit meeting on 21 March 2003 decided that the process should continue up to a review in 2006. In the meantime the Commission and governments need to do more work on the adequacy, financial sustainability and modernization of pension systems and there are expected to be studies on common pension challenges.[5]

As a result and despite the objectives the EU member states have agreed, the real debate tends to be about how we will pay for pensions in future, rather than about how we will provide an adequate income for all older people in future. It tends to be assumed in most European countries (though not in the UK, for example) that pensions are broadly adequate, leaving out of the account the many older people in Europe who are still in poverty.

Most of the EU member state government submissions to the EU process are broadly confident on the future adequacy of pensions, but the Commission (European Commission 2003: 35) points out in its synthesis report:

> It is not possible to assess whether the confidence expressed in the national strategy reports is justified, as future pension levels are very difficult to project in view of the further reform measures that are required and the uncertainty about the performance of financial markets.

Projections have been developed for the future financial cost of pensions, but not yet for their future social adequacy.

In most European countries, social debate and consultation on pension policy is highly inadequate. Most often there is some consultation with trade unions and employers, very rarely with older people's organizations or other civil society groups. For example, in only a few EU member states have older people's organizations been able to have any meaningful discussion with the government on the National Strategy Report to the EU.

Yet older people's organizations are increasingly networking to influence policies at national and European level. As an example, AGE has recently adopted key priorities that they would like to see followed up at European level and has made a comparison with the picture presented by the EU national strategy reports as summarized by the Commission. AGE's key priorities are:

1   Ensure that older people who have reached statutory pension age have the right to a *decent level of pension*, giving them a fair share of society's economic well-being, not just preventing outright poverty. Their pension income level must allow them to participate actively in public, social and cultural life, to be active consumers, and to cover the costs of (risks of) health problems, etc. To ensure this, a country needs a secure, universal, fully adequate first-pillar pension, whether or not second- and third-pillar systems are further developed. In some countries the need for pensioners to claim means-tested benefits in order to achieve a subsistence income indicates that state pensions are inadequate and urgently need to be raised. Furthermore, any trend to weaken general provisions and replace them with means-tested arrangements must be strongly resisted.

2   Guarantee that first-pillar pensions are *indexed so as to ensure that pensioners keep up with progress in society's prosperity. The best method is indexation to average earnings*. Price indexation is not enough, as it will leave pensioners lagging behind society's economic well-being over time.

3   Ensure that individuals are able to obtain a *high income replacement rate* at retirement. This implies ensuring access to pension and saving schemes that do not place all the risk on the individual. It requires an environment in which pensions are secure and pension schemes are transparent and subject to effective governance and regulation. The regulatory framework must allow workers to transfer their occupational and private pension entitlements between member states as well as within them, avoiding problems such as double taxation.

4   *Give equal pension rights to women*, eliminate gender discrimination in pension systems and in the labour market, and ensure that time spent caring for children, the elderly, etc., gives pension entitlements under the first-pillar system, and that pensions rights are individualized.

5   *Allow and encourage older people to continue working for longer*, outlaw age discrimination, promote lifelong learning, training, etc., and allow for gradual retirement. AGE welcomes the target enshrined in the Lisbon Strategy of increasing the EU-wide employment rate for older workers (55–64) to 50 per cent, and calls for a wide range of enabling measures to make this a reality.

All the above are clearly eminently desirable aims, but to some may seem unachievable in the present economic climate. Nevertheless, they are stated as a desirable aim: as something worth campaigning for and working towards. This is particularly so because the current direction of social policy on pensions for older people tends to be resorting to private sector-directed solutions (Maltby 2001; Bonoli 2001) which have differential impacts and which tend to reflect and reproduce existing inequalities into old age. In the case of pensions, the 'multi-pillar approach' has often been adopted and national governments have argued that this structure provides financial sustainability; yet this flies in the face of the evidence. As Walker and Maltby (1997) reported, there is a strong indication of a very powerful inter-generational solidarity and full support across the European Union for the 'social contract'; that is, the payment of contributions or taxes to fund pensions. Furthermore, when questioned about where the responsibility for pensions should lie – with the state, employers or individuals – the majority of respondents in all European Union countries sampled indicated that pensions should be provided by public authorities and funded from contributions or taxes. What is also evident is that although there is some resentment on the part of Europe's senior citizens about the low level of pensions in some countries, there is widespread agreement among them about the importance of their families and widespread expression of favourable attitudes towards young people (Walker and Maltby 1997; Walker 1999). Locating this dialogue within the Asian experience, and determining how far the latter chimes with the experience of countries within the European Union, is part of this APPLE project.

Yet fear about the future can undermine solidarity in society: if people of working age have no confidence that they will receive an adequate old age pension through a redistributive social mechanism, they have no incentive to support this mechanism for present-day pensioners. One way out of this position is to take refuge in individual solutions that may or may not work. Another is to treat adapting to an ageing population as a social challenge that can be faced by making active social and political choices. The official point of view of virtually all governments, as well as the view of actors such as older people's organizations, trade unions and a good deal of the relevant research findings, is that adequate pensions are sustainable, given the right economic and social choices.[6] Although governments shrink from putting it in these terms, it becomes a question of how to distribute income and work equitably.

An Integrated Agenda: Employment and Discrimination

It is increasingly recognized that ensuring adequate and sustainable pensions is not only a matter of 'pension reform' but requires an overall mix of economic and social policy. EU governments see full employment as the key to safeguarding pensions, the more people are employed, the more are paying contributions to support pension systems. The policy focus has more recently been upon increasing the employment rate of 'older workers' (generally those aged between 50 and 60/64 years) and for women. The employment rate for workers aged over 50 or 55 has fallen considerably in Europe since the late 1970s, and is very low in some countries. Table 3.3 provides data for each EU country drawn from Eurostat.

Calculations by the Employment Committee of the European Commission demonstrate that the effective retirement age for the EU as a whole is 59.9 years (for men 60.7 and for women 58.9) with a range from a high for Sweden of an average age of 63.3 to a low for Belgium of 57.5 years. So clearly, in the majority of EU countries the state pension age (generally 65) is not being reached by men (especially) and women before they retire from employment.

Table 3.3 Employment rate of older workers as a share of total population in 2000

Employment rate of OW*	EU15	B	DK	D	EL	E	F	IRL	I	L	NL	A	P	FIN	S	UK
Total %	37.5	25.0	54.6	37.4	39.0	36.6	29.3	45.1	27.3	27.2	37.9	29.2	51.7	41.2	64.3	50.5
Men	47.6	35.1	61.9	46.2	55.3	54.8	32.8	63.0	40.3	37.9	49.9	41.4	62.5	41.8	67.0	59.8
Women	27.7	15.4	46.2	28.7	24.4	19.9	26.0	27.1	15.2	16.8	25.8	17.8	42.3	40.7	61.7	41.4
Total number (thousand)	16,530	247	322	4,515	496	1,672	1,644	149	2,044	17	627	291	552	216	663	3,076

Source: Eurostat.

From about 1980 until recently, early retirement was used as a way of reducing high unemployment figures, principally by giving younger people priority for the existing jobs (see Maltby et al. 2004, for a detailed analysis). In the literature this has been termed 'exit pathways'. Having started out as something compulsory via the retirement pensions route, early retirement came to be seen as desirable or even a social entitlement, particularly in continental Europe with 'exit' to retirement via redundancy, disability, enhanced pension arrangements and a myriad of other schemes and mechanisms. Indeed, many people who had built up sufficient pension entitlements preferred to retire earlier and have more years of leisure while still in good health.

More recently a variety of new policy initiatives can be observed in many European countries, supported by a variety of European Commission-led policy statements. After years of excluding older workers from the labour market, there is an observable trend in many countries to 're-integrate' them, through a variety of policy mechanisms.

The combination of these two trends – an ageing society and the massive early exit from the labour market – of past decades has also resulted in redefinitions of the social meaning of ageing, older workers, the transition from work to retirement and, on a more general level, the meaning of social citizenship.

There remains pervasive age discrimination in European labour markets (as well as sex discrimination, racial discrimination, discrimination against the disabled and so on). In line with ageist prejudices rooted in society as a whole, older workers are often seen as inefficient, non-adaptable, uncreative, and more liable to be off work through ill health than their younger peers. Research has found that older workers are far less likely to receive training, contributing to the outdated quality of their skills. Many employers regard it as a waste of time to provide training for workers due to retire in a few years – not taking into account that younger workers may well move to another company. Employers may also prefer younger workers because, where pay systems are based on seniority, they can pay them lower wages. So older workers are often targeted for redundancy and it is recognized to be much harder for older workers who lose their job to find another one.

Nevertheless, the projected reintegration of older workers into the mainstream labour force has to some extent become a double-edged sword. There is one agenda about fighting discrimination and enabling individuals to continue in paid work for as long as they wish and feel they need to. This includes adapting working conditions and introducing management practices friendly to age diversity, and adapting pension systems to allow for gradual, flexible retirement and provide positive rewards for working longer. Naturally, this agenda is supported by older people's organizations, including AGE. But another agenda says that the right to retire with an adequate pension, and to enjoy a number of years of retirement in reasonable health, is a key social advance that must not be compromised. It is one thing to make a free choice to work longer, quite another thing to be forced to do so by (fear of) poverty. Many feel great concern when debate goes in the direction of raising the age of entitlement to pensions (as has been the general trend across Europe) rather than enabling people to really work up to the existing pension age, which, as we have seen, most do not at present.

Equally alarming to many NGOs as well as to trade unions, is the impression that governments want to raise employment by cutting social protection for people of all ages in order to force them into low-paid and poor-quality jobs. We have already referred to women's generally shorter and interrupted employment careers leading to lower pensions. The converse is that women are often seen as another key labour reserve to make up for the effects of population ageing while improving their own pension entitlements. However, in turn the increased employment of women and older people could reduce the number of people available to provide family care, aggravating a different set of problems. Hence a key element in enabling women, and older people, to take on paid employment is to make adequate care facilities for children and other dependent people available and affordable for all who need them – in order to avoid what has been termed 'the care sandwich' where care might have to be provided (usually by women) to both children and frail parents, at the same time as holding down a job (Jönsson 2003). In short, the policy dilemma for many within EU countries is similar to that posed for their equivalents in East Asia: who is to care?

As Jönsson (2003) demonstrates, women across Europe are delaying childbirth and their children are spending longer periods in full-time education, making them dependent upon their parents for longer. Additionally, the increased incidence of divorce not only has a direct impact upon interpersonal relationships between family members but also has longer-term implications for the care of both children and frail family members. Across Europe, care for dependent children and adults remains in effect the responsibility of female kin (Fagan and Burchell 2002). Yet there are regional differences in the importance of family for the delivery of care. These can, in broad, general terms, be divided into three: southern European, Scandinavian and northern European approaches (Walker and Maltby 1997). In the southern European states (Greece, Italy, Portugal and Spain) the family plays a central role. Indeed, in Greece, Italy and Spain (as in most parts of Asia-Pacific) there is a constitutional obligation for children to support their parents. Older people are less likely to be living alone and more likely to live in multigenerational households. In the Scandinavian countries, by contrast, the state has the primary role for delivery of care. In the remaining countries there is a mixture of these two approaches. In France and Germany for example, although the family is seen as key, the provision of care is seen as an important aspect of 'community' relationships supported by the state, either directly or 'at arms length' via intermediaries. A similar position applies in the UK and Ireland, where an individualistic, case-by-case approach to care is adopted. The family is seen as just one of the central supportive mechanisms, with the care of children and frail kin being also purchased through a market-oriented set of policies, as well as accessed via a base of statutory social provision. However, as the comparative data in the Statistical Appendix demonstrate, the centrality of family as a focus for welfare support can be discerned and approximated by average household size statistics. These particular data demonstrate the broad similarity between the East Asian countries discussed here and the southern European Union states. In Spain,

Portugal, Greece and Italy, and all the East Asian countries, similar average household sizes (approximately 3) are noted. The exception to this trend is Ireland, but here, like the southern European states, religion (and in particular Catholicism) is an important component to family size. All represent strong male breadwinner regime types, and most (and in particular Greece and Italy) share a high age profile, similar life expectancies and birth rates.

European Employment Strategy

We move on now to present and review the policy in the related area of employment. The European Commission's approach to the formulation and implementation of the employment policy process has been given the title of the European Employment Strategy (EES). It started in 1997 and pioneered the use of the Open Method of Coordination. It has been developed since then in an annual review process that has paralleled the overall objectives adopted by the EU as part of the Lisbon Strategy. At successive Spring Summits (the key annual discussion on the economic and social objectives), the EU governments adopted targets of a 70 per cent overall employment rate by 2010, 60 per cent employment for women, and 50 per cent for older workers (55–64). There are also interim targets to be reached by 2005. In 2002 the Spring Summit adopted an ambitious target of raising the average effective retirement age across the EU by five years by 2010.

The EES itself is based on a set of Employment Guidelines that member states agree with the Commission as recommendations for their national policies. National plans are then developed within this framework. Currently the EES is being reviewed to bring it more in line with the overall Lisbon objectives and an evaluation as part of this review concluded that it is difficult to quantify an impact of the EES on employment figures but that it has definitely influenced national policy objectives. Increasing employment for older workers has become an increasingly visible objective. However, real-world progress in this area has been comparatively slow.

As part of the drive of the overall employment policy of the EU, an anti-discrimination programme was proposed. Under a Treaty article (Article 13)[7] allowing EU action against discrimination on a number of grounds including age, in 2000 the EU adopted two anti-discrimination Directives (or laws). One covers racial and ethnic discrimination, the other discrimination in employment and occupation on all the listed grounds. The latter has the most obvious application for older people.

It is a framework Directive, which has to be transposed into national law and implemented in each member state (including those joining the EU in 2004). Potentially this Directive could have considerable impact on improving the position of older people in eliminating or at least reducing the perverse discrimination in employment policy that currently exists. However, from the point of view of age equality in society as a whole, the present EU framework shows a number of important limitations including:

- by its nature it covers only the area of employment and occupation;
- a number of exceptions are made in the Employment Directive, with some quite broad exclusions relating to age discrimination on grounds including legitimate employment policy objectives, which could potentially be used as an escape clause;[8]
- age can in principle be argued to be a genuine occupational requirement for a job;
- the timetable for transposition allows member states to take three years longer to legislate on age and disability discrimination than on other grounds of discrimination;
- the Directive does not require the creation of bodies to pro-actively promote age equality and to ensure compliance.

These issues aside, the Directive has provided a spur for the elimination of discrimination in employment across EU countries, for all that the policy response by national governments has been mixed.

Conclusions

This chapter has attempted to provide an overview of the central issues in EU policy-making with regard to older people, focusing on two key areas currently in the spotlight: pensions and employment. We have demonstrated that these should be seen as inter-related with the first, employment – or rather a longer working life – increasingly becoming the saviour of the second, pensions policy. Linked to these areas, we have briefly discussed the differences of approach towards family policy and the subsequent differences in social policy within and between the countries of the EU.

Within these debates, the central issue remains: how can a social and political consensus be built to ensure that the challenges of an ageing society are met equitably? An ageing population may mean increased expenditure on health and pensions, for example. Yet the policy focus has often been constructed within an ageist framework and older people tend to become pathologized. Many Europeans are likely to work to a more advanced age in future than in the immediate past and out of choice. The key questions for policy are whether the majority of people in their fifties and sixties have genuine access to employment or will a large proportion of those wanting to continue paid work be excluded from it, as at present? A parallel question can be posed about access to retirement pensions.

It is time, therefore, to focus upon the positive contributions that older people can and do make to society and to a reconstitution of the meaning of old age. One such vision lies within the concept of 'active ageing'. As Walker (2002) describes, its genesis can be traced back to the 1960s and to the Disengagement theses (cf. Cumming and Henry 1961) and the promotion of 'successful ageing': the denial of the onset of old age (Havinghurst 1954). A key mover to the newer structural interpretation of this and to the formulation of 'active ageing' has come from the work of the World Health Organization (WHO). It was they who summarized the meaning of 'active ageing' within the slogan 'Years have been added to life; now we must add life to years'. This, as Walker (2002:124) suggests, means that 'active ageing' is

> a general life-style strategy for the preservation of physical and mental health as people age, rather than just trying to make them work longer.

It thus links quality of life with meaningful and productive employment, with mental and physical well-being. It could result in the maximization of the full potential and the enhancement of the quality of life of all society. It has the potential to remove the policy focus away from pathologizing older people as a distinct group, towards recognizing that we are all ageing, constantly. As Walker (2002) again suggests, 'active ageing' can provide a meaningful focus for policy development and has enormous social and economic potential for society at large.

Notes

1   AGE, the European Older People's Platform, as an international NGO aims to voice and promote the interests of older people in the European Union and to raise awareness of the issues that concern them most. It was set up in January 2001 following a process of discussion on how to improve and strengthen cooperation between older people's organizations at EU level. Membership of AGE is open to European, national and regional non-profit-making organizations, and to both organizations of older people and organizations for older people. Organizations of older people will have the majority of votes in AGE's decision-making bodies. AGE is co-financed by its members and by the European Commission. For more detail, see http://www.age-platform.org/EN/.
2   The European Commission's website:
    (MISSOC: http://europa.eu.int/comm/employment_social/missoc/index_en.html)
    provides detailed information on social protection systems in the EU member states, the European Economic Area countries and Central and Eastern European candidate countries for EU membership.
3   Following a number of statistical problems, the 2003 edition may be expected to give a somewhat lower figure for risk of poverty among older people in the EU overall, and substantially different figures for some member states. In particular, the UK is likely to show a substantially lower figure while some other countries appear higher. See figures in the Commission/Council Joint Report on Pensions referred to below. Eurostat's website:
    http://europa.eu.int/comm/eurostat/Public/datashop/print-catalogue/EN?catalogue=Eurostat.
4   An overview of national situations and reforms can be found in the National Strategy Reports prepared by all 15 member states in 2002 and the synthesis report prepared by the European Commission at http://europa.eu.int/comm/employment_social/soc-prot/pensions/index_en.htm.
5   Conclusions of the 21 March summit meeting (Spring European Council) can be found at: http://ue.eu.int/newsroom/GR2003/index.asp?lang=EN.

6   AGE's 2001 statement 'Adequate Pensions for All in 21st-Century Europe' goes over some of the arguments from an NGO viewpoint. See: www.age-platform.org.
7   Article 13 of the Treaty establishing the European Community as modified by the 1997 Amsterdam Treaty provides that, within the limits of its powers, 'the Council, acting unanimously on a proposal from the Commission and after consulting the European Parliament, may take appropriate action to combat discrimination based on sex, racial or ethnic origin, religion or belief, disability, age or sexual orientation'.
8   Article 6 of the Directive includes: 'differences of treatment on grounds of age shall not constitute discrimination, if, within the context of national law, they are objectively and reasonably justified by a legitimate aim, including legitimate employment policy, labour market and vocational training objectives, and if the means of achieving that aim are appropriate and necessary'.

References

Bonoli, G. (2001). The politics of pension reform in Western Europe, *Benefits*, 31 (May/June): 1–4.
Brooks, R., Regan, S. and Robinson, P. (eds) (2002). *A New Contract for Retirement: Modelling Policy Options to 2050*. London: IPPR.
Cumming, E. and Henry, W. (1961). *Growing Old: The Process of Disengagement*. New York: Basic Books.
Department for Work and Pensions (DWP) (2002). *Simplicity, Security and Choice: Working and Saving for Retirement*, Green Paper, Cm 5677. London: Stationery Office.
Economic Policy Committee (EPC) (2001). *Budgetary Challenges Posed by Ageing Populations: the Impact on Public Spending on Pensions, Health and Long-term Care for the Elderly and Possible Indicators of the Long-term Sustainability of Public Finances*. Brussels, 24 October, EPC/ECFIN/655/01-EN final.
European Commission (2001). *Communication from the Commission to the Council, the European Parliament and Economic and Social Committee. Supporting national strategies for safe and sustainable pensions through an integrated approach*. Brussels, 3 July, COM (2001) 362 final.
European Commission (2003). *Joint Report by the Commission and the Council on Adequate and Sustainable Pensions*. Brussels 3 March, 6527/2/03 REV-ECOFIN 51-SOC 72.
Fagan, C. and Burchell, B. (2002). *Gender, Jobs and Working Conditions in the European Community*. Dublin: European Foundation for the Improvement of Living and Working Conditions.
Ginn, J. (2003). *Gender, Pensions and the Lifecourse*. Bristol: Policy Press.
Ginn, J., Street, D. and Arber, S. (eds) (2001). *Women, Work and Pensions: International Issues and Prospects*. Buckingham: Open University Press.
Hantrais, L. (2000). *Social Policy in the European Union*. London: Macmillan.
Havinghurst, R. (1954). Flexibility and the social roles of the retired. *American Journal of Sociology*, 59, 2.
Hughes, G. and Stewart, J. (2000). *Pensions in the European Union: Adapting to Economic and Social Change*. Amsterdam: Kluwer.
Jönsson, I. (2003). *Policy perspectives on changing intergenerational relations*. Social Policy and Society, 2, 3: 241–8.
Kay, T. (2003). The work–life balance in social practice. *Social Policy and Society*, 2, 3: 231–9.

Maltby, T. (2001). Thinking the unthinkable? Pensions policy prospects in Britain. In C. Jones Finer (ed.), *Comparing the Social Policy Experience of Britain and Taiwan*. Aldershot: Ashgate.

Maltby, T., DeVroom, B., Mirabile, M.-L. and Overbye, E. (eds) (2004). *Ageing and the Transition to Retirement: A Comparative Analysis of European Welfare States*. Aldershot: Ashgate.

Maltby, T. and Walker, A. (2004). *Ageing and Social Policy in Europe*. Bristol: Policy Press.

Walker, A. (1999). *Attitudes to Population Ageing in Europe: A Comparison of the 1992 and the 1999 Eurobarometer Surveys*. Available at URL: http://www.shef.ac.uk/socst/staff/a_walker.htm#publications (accessed August 2003).

Walker, A. (2002). A strategy for active ageing. *International Social Security Review*, 55, 1: 121–39.

Walker, A. and Maltby, T. (1997). *Ageing Europe*. Buckingham: Open University Press.

PART II
THE CASE STUDIES

Chapter 4

Malaysia: Supporting Families

Roziah Omar

Introduction

The population of Malaysia is ageing and is doing so against a background of several decades of rapid economic growth and social development. As a result, Malaysia today is experiencing a new scenario, where economically it is one of the most vibrant countries in Southeast Asia, while increasing numbers of its people are living longer. This increase in the proportion and the actual number of the elderly places demands on strategic planning for policies to overcome pertinent issues and challenges in terms of their needs. Ultimately there will be major implications for the country's resources.

The Malaysian situation is by no means unique. As elsewhere, older people have come to constitute what Phillips has described as an 'interim generation':

> Many of today's older persons in the region are in effect an interim generation. They have grown old but are often without substantial personal resources as they had been part of emerging rather than mature economies, so they may well suffer if state and family resources are not available. (Phillips 2000: 13)

More specifically, the situation is that many older people are caught between three long-term developments. Firstly, like other East Asian economies, in terms of welfare Malaysia has been a low-spending, low-providing state. The state has not sought to be a major provider of social services but has rather placed emphasis on national economic growth, individual progress through work, and family and community support. In this model the needs of older people were supposed to be met by a combination of their own endeavours in the workplace and the support of the kinship network (Doling and Omar 2003). However, the second development is that the family and inter-generational relationships are breaking down. Thus, although with some variations across ethnic groups, fertility rates are falling, more women are working outside the home and therefore have less time for traditional caring roles, and the extended family is giving way to the nuclear family system. Thirdly, many older people's situations have been exacerbated because the urban areas to which they and their families have migrated in response to macro-economic developments often do not present environments that facilitate the well-being of older people. For example, journeys to shops and to social facilities may be difficult in an urban setting where distances are large and personal resources enabling easy travel are small.

Since the 1990s the significance of these developments has become more apparent in Malaysia. Moreover, as life expectancies have continued to increase elderly people have become a major focus in development policy. The state has paid more attention to developing strategic plans and programmes for the elderly. This chapter will present a general overview of some of the significant issues and challenges related to the elderly in Malaysia by focusing on the implications for health care and other services related to older people's well-being, as well as on the implications for the financial resources available to them.

Demographic Trends

Malaysia's particular ethnic diversity – just over half the population being Malay, with Chinese forming the largest and Indians the second largest minority groups – is central to all aspects of life. Together these groups constitute the total population of Malaysia, which was recorded in the census of 2000 to be 23.2 million persons. In fact, this represented a large increase – some 5 million extra inhabitants – over the course of the previous decade. This growth could be attributed to a combination of

- growing numbers of young people, reflecting high fertility rates, particularly among the Muslim Malay sections of the population;
- immigration, particularly from the surrounding countries such as Indonesia and Thailand;
- increased life expectancies.

The latter had in fact been rising continuously throughout the post-independence period, with, as table 4.1 indicates, the differentials between the sexes and between the ethnic groups being maintained. Thus, women have a life expectancy averaging about five years longer than men, with the Chinese continuing to have significantly higher life expectancies than other ethnic groups.

The overall impact of the ageing of the population, described by the percentage of the population aged over 60, is indicated in table 4.2. This shows some important trends and changes. Over the course of the last decade there has been a shift in the balance between older people in urban and in rural areas. Although large proportions of the people living in rural areas have continued to be in the over-60 age groups (reflecting the general tendency for younger people – especially Malays and Chinese – to migrate to the cities, leaving their parents behind), there have increasingly been larger absolute numbers of older people in the cities. Malaysia's industrial cities are now home to major concentrations of older people.

Table 4.1 Life expectancy by ethnicity and sex: Peninsular Malaysia

Ethnic	1957		1988		1990		1992	
group	M	F	M	F	M	F	M	F
Malays	50.0	58.2	66.5	68.9	68.9	72.4	69.2	72.6
Chinese	59.4	66.3	68.0	74.0	70.5	76.3	70.6	76.5
Indians	57.2	54.2	62.1	67.0	64.2	70.4	64.3	70.9

Source: Statistics Department 1992, Malaysia.

Table 4.2 Percentage of persons aged over 60 by ethnic group and area of residence

Ethnic group	1991			2000			2020
	Urban	Rural	Total	Urban	Rural	Total	Total
Malaysian citizens							
Malay	3.5	6.6	5.4	3.7	7.7	5.6	7.9
Chinese	7.4	8.0	7.6	8.4	11.3	8.8	14.8
Indian	5.8	4.3	5.4	5.6	5.5	5.6	10.6
Others	4.5	8.0	6.9	3.8	6.1	4.6	8.3
Total	5.4	6.7	6.0	5.6	7.9	6.4	9.5
Non-Malaysian	3.7	1.9	2.7	3.6	1.9	2.9	9.5
Total	5.3	6.3	5.9	5.4	7.5	4.2	9.5
Number (000)	471	562	1032	785	666	1452	3210

Source: Ong Fon Sim (2002).

In addition, the anticipated rise in the older population as a proportion of the total is going to be a steep one, particularly within the Chinese and Indian communities. In absolute terms, between 2000 and 2020 the numbers are expected to more than double. In fact, this reflects a general tendency among the later-developing countries for their older populations to increase at a faster rate than has happened in the older developed nations. Compared with the UK and Sweden, for example, the rate of increase in Malaysia is some 7 or 8 times higher (WHO 1998).

While the proportion of the total population designated as older persons (that is over 60 years old) is still expected, even by 2020, to be somewhat lower than in many more developed countries in Asia and the West, account has nevertheless to be taken of the generally lower retirement age in Malaysia. The official retirement age for both men and women is 55 years (see the Statistical Appendix to this volume) and, although some individuals may extend their working lives for one or more years, their levels of remuneration are often much reduced (Chang and Tho 2000). As a result the scale of the challenges thrown up by ageing populations is understated in table 4.2.

Also important in the case of Malaysia are the significant changes taking place in family structures and relationships. Here, most significant are the tendencies whereby 'smaller family size and a preference for nuclear families are replacing the extended family structure and larger families' (Ong Fon Sim 2002: 115). The shift towards smaller families is partly a function of lower fertility rates, with more women choosing to have none or few children than had hitherto been the norm. This trend is particularly pronounced in the Chinese sections of the population, considerably less so in the Malay. Nevertheless, overall it looks set to continue. The average family size in Malaysia has declined from 4.70 persons in 1995 to 4.53 in 2000, with an expected further drop to 4.3 by 2005 (Malaysia 2001). To be sure, these shifts are also partly a function of choices made by one generation or another to live separately. Even by 1991 about 60 per cent of households were living as nuclear families with only 25 per cent living as extended families (Ong Fon Sim 2002). In many cases this decision has been tied to migration decisions, particularly those linked to the search for the rewards of industrial jobs. As J. T. Arokiasamy presents it:

> The drive towards industrialisation has attracted many young people to work in industries, which are located mainly in urban areas and usually away from their family homes. Rural–urban migration becomes inevitable causing a break up of the extended family structure. (Arokiasamy 2002)

The National Policy Context

The country's ethnic balance has had a formative influence on all aspects of Malaysian politics (Doling and Omar 2003). Particularly important has been the drive to bring the economic status of the Malay majority up to the level of the Chinese minority, which can be seen as the use of political power, vested with one group, to take a more equal share of the economic power, vested with another. One interpretation of policy issues and solutions related to older people is that they particularly reflect the trends and needs identified within the Malay section of the population.

Formal and systematic statements of national policy formulation in Malaysia are contained in its five-year national plans. Covering all the main areas of responsibility of the federal government, each one looks back over the latest plan period to review progress; it then identifies current issues and concerns and presents budgetary and other plans for the coming period. Consequently, the plans provide a chronology of what the federal government decides to commit to the public domain about its thinking and intentions with respect to the range of policy areas.

Up to and including the Sixth Malaysia Plan (Malaysia 1991), covering the period 1991 to 1995, the plans made little mention of the older age groups. Thus in its consideration of the country's population the Sixth Plan concentrated on the working-age population, mainly from the perspective of the labour force needs of the economy, and on the need to ensure that the youth of Malaysia acquired appropriate values, followed healthy lifestyles and were adequately protected from child abuse. The sole consideration given to older groups in the population was contained in a reference to expenditure in the previous plan period of 7.5 million ringits (less than 2 million euro) on the renovation and construction of 'old folk's homes'.

By the time of the Seventh Malaysia Plan (Malaysia 1996), however, there was clear recognition that there were issues associated with the ageing population to which the government needed to respond. The review of the previous plan period noted that a family development programme had been initiated in 1991. Whereas much of the emphasis of this programme had been on aspects of family health, parenting and training in work-related skills, there was also recognition of the needs of older family members. Specifically, that

> in view of the increasing number of nuclear families and longer life expectancies, steps were taken to ensure that family ties were maintained and caring for the elderly continued to be the responsibility of the family. (Malaysia 1996: 571)

Indeed, a year before the publication of the Seventh Malaysia Plan a major development in thinking with regard to the government's role in respect of older people had been formulated. The National Policy for the Elderly aimed to create a society in which older people were contented and could achieve a high degree of self-worth and dignity. They were to be integral to society at large, local communities and families. With the Ministry of National Unity and Social Development having overall responsibility for the implementation of this policy, however, it has concentrated on social issues, largely ignoring the employment and income needs of the older population (Ong Fon Sim 2002).

The Eighth Malaysia Plan (Malaysia 2001) also emphasized the care and social dimensions in its reinforcement of the need for family support:

> With improvements in life expectancy and the increasing trend towards nuclear families, steps were taken to ensure that caring for older persons remained with the family. (Malaysia 2001: 517)

Having established the broad context in terms of demographic developments and national policy responses, this chapter turns to consider a number of specific problems and policy solutions. The first considers health and health care: later sections consider social care and income.

Meeting the Health Needs of Older People

The State of Health of the Elderly

An increase in health problems is an inescapable fact of old age. Some 80 per cent of people over 65 have long-term disorders, and 5 per cent have a disability that requires continuous medical supervision (Kane 1985). In general, the elderly have poorer health than younger age groups; they are more vulnerable to chronic conditions such as cardiovascular disease, osteoporosis, diabetes, cataracts, arthritis and glaucoma. Moreover, numerous local and national-level health surveys are beginning to indicate that, despite low levels of awareness, older people in developing countries already have a high level of disability. This is due in part to the long-term effects of diseases experienced in childhood and early adult life – such as poliomyelitis, leprosy, tuberculosis, schistosomiasis and infections which were not properly treated in their early stages. In addition, common problems that can be successfully dealt with through secondary prevention have often led to complications and permanent incapacity in poorer countries: examples are hypertension and stroke, diabetes and peripheral vascular disease, trachoma and blindness (Kalache and Sen 1999). A survey of the health profiles of 200 elderly women in Malaysia showed that nearly 61 per cent reported some form of reproductive health-related illness; more than 60 per cent had back problems; 45 per cent suffered from cardiovascular problems and 18 per cent had problems with their stomach (Omar 1994).

Economic development, however, brings change. These changes can have two-pronged effects, one positive and the other negative. Progress in the field of medical sciences together with economic and social development improves the status of health. But with development come environments and lifestyles that are unsafe, unhealthy, and have negative effects on health. As Malaysia becomes a more industrialized country, its health profile has begun to resemble that of a country in transition from developing to developed economic status (Chan 1997; Chee 1990; Omar 2000). Health problems typical of both situations are evident, i.e. infectious disease, vector-borne diseases and malnutrition commonly seen in developing countries are found, alongside chronic diseases associated with lifestyle changes – such as diabetes, cardiovascular disease and cancer – more common in developed economies. Consequently, there has been a shift in the major causes of death.

Health Care Provision

One of the greatest legacies left by the British in Malaysia was the Ministry of Health (MOH). From its creation, the ministry became the government's arm for developing the health-care system. At first, the services were mainly intended to eradicate communicable and poverty-related illnesses among the population of Malaya, who were then largely located in rural areas. Today, the MOH through its network of hospitals and clinics has incorporated services to provide health services across the nation for all groups in the population, including the elderly. In addition to the public sector, there is NGO and private sector involvement in health care, with the latter in particular expanding its activities in recent years.

In general, the elderly in Malaysia use the health-care facilities that are commonly used by other age groups, so that, at the present moment, health services for the elderly are largely provided in a non-specialized and non-structured manner. One of the limitations of this is that the systems are mainly geared towards short-term care and hospitalization, whereas the elderly often require long-term care, including rehabilitation from acute illness (Mafauzy 2000). However, there has been a gradual shift in policy towards the special needs of the elderly by increasing the supply of more specialized services. A central aim has been to maintain outpatient treatment and minimize hospitalization, utilizing nursing and social support services to enable the elderly to be transported or nursed at home (Siti Hasmah 1992).

The ministry has to manage programmes that respond to the new lifestyles. The Health Lifestyle Campaign aims to promote healthier lifestyles across the age span, and thereby to control diseases of lifestyle. Special clinics for diabetics and heart patients have been set up at district hospitals to provide services such as blood pressure check-ups and urine tests. Recently, the ministry has set up geriatric clinics in selected major hospitals. However, specialist geriatric clinics in Malaysia are still at a very formative stage. The government is training more doctors to specialize in geriatrics so as, eventually, to serve in the government hospitals throughout the country.

Nursing homes are also crucial when it comes to providing supportive health services for the aged, especially those who are chronically ill and bedridden. There has been an increasing number of private sector nursing homes being built, mostly in urban centres. However, they mainly cater to those who can afford to pay, the main motive being profit. Often the aged poor have no access to them. Although there are also some nursing homes run by NGOs to cater for the needs of lower-income groups, they are as yet relatively few in number.

Financing Issues

Despite its high levels of economic achievement, Malaysia faces problems in meeting demands for expenditure on health. The yearly budget for health care in Malaysia has not increased very much over the last 20 years and remains at a level that, as a proportion of GDP, is low relative to other countries (Mafauzy 2000). But the rising number of elderly patients in Malaysian hospitals puts even more demands on government expenditure. So what happens if the government does not continue to bear these costs? In general, expenditure on health is seen as a liability and the government has avoided allocating additional public funds by pursuing a policy focused on efficiency and saving, which has actually encouraged the private sector to provide health services for the nation (Kalache and Sen 1999). This has not in fact gone well with the increasing population and the increasing numbers of elderly in the country. One observer has argued that, because the private sector functions on a profit basis, it tends to concentrate on low-risk curative care in urban areas and that accessibility is largely dictated by market forces and the availability of money (Chee 1990: 90). In such a system it is often older people who lose out.

> Older persons ... require more care than the general population. However, as a group, they probably have the least private coverage, least income to pay for health care and lack of medical insurance with inadequate coverage provided for medical conditions common to older persons. Health care costs for older persons and their carers are high as a result of increased demand, more costly procedures, lengthy hospital stay, and financially draining long-term care. (Arokiasamy 2002: 3)

To ameliorate the cost burden on individuals, the government introduced subsidies through the tax system in 1992. These may be claimed by children against medical expenditures incurred in respect of their elderly parents. In addition, under the New Remuneration Scheme, the medical benefits provided for public sector employees were extended to cover their parents (Malaysia 1996). But it is significant that, in order to meet the health needs of older people, the public resources involved are expended in a way that is intended to reinforce the family as the institution through which welfare needs are to be met. So, rather than promoting new solutions, the Malaysian government is rather attempting to sustain the old or traditional solutions, by means of new policy instruments.

Social Care

The Sustainability of Family as Carer

As with health care, in Malaysia the family has traditionally played an important role in the provision of general care for the elderly; especially since geriatric facilities are still not available countrywide, nursing homes are expensive and culturally it is not considered appropriate to place your parent in a nursing home. When difficulty occurs – as a result of ill health (short- or long-term) or other problems – an older person's first reaction has generally been to turn to his or her children. In many respects these practices have been sustained. Communication with elderly parents has been maintained through visits, telephone calls and letters. For those living nearby, daily and weekly visits have been a common practice. The concept of the three-generation family has often provided emotional fulfilment with the elderly playing active roles, often in managing their grandchildren.

However, recent studies have shown that the trends are changing. As outlined earlier in this chapter, the extended-family living arrangement is no longer the norm. For many families there is a large geographical separation between adult children and their parents. One survey of older women found that well over half complained of loneliness (Omar 1994). In addition, with the changing role of women – who were formerly the carers of the elderly, but who are now increasingly active in the labour force – other solutions are being sought. Many families will hire a maid to look after their sick parents or seek solutions involving nursing homes. Nursing homes will often be the last resort, however, to be pursued only after all the other avenues have been explored. So far, studies have shown that Chinese families have proved more willing than Malay families to place their parents in a nursing home (Kling and Omar 1999).

Moreover, in an increasing number of cases (which will grow further if fertility rates continue to fall) there is not always a member of the younger generation able and willing to provide support for older people. Furthermore, many people are not marrying. As Chang and Tho (2000: 290) point out, 'the implications in relation to their care and support, particularly during old age or when ill, will become an important issue as, unlike those who are married, they do not have younger members to fall back on'. Increasingly, then, the government is facing a reality in which, left to itself, the institution of the family may not be able to ensure the health and social care of older people.

Ministry of National Unity and Community Development

The government, through the Ministry of National Unity and Social Development – locally known as *Kementerian Perpaduan Negara dan Pembangunan Masyarkat* – provides various social services for the elderly in the country, focusing specifically on the needs of the poor elderly. The Social Welfare Department manages nine old people's homes throughout the country for 2,550 elders. The *Rumah Seri Kenangan* (Home of Wonderful Memories, the name given to these old folk's homes) have been set up to provide aid and shelter to the poor elderly who do not have any heirs/relatives. The age of eligibility for admission is at least 60 years, and those admitted must be able to take care of themselves and be able to do chores such as cooking, gardening and handicraft.

The *Rumah Seri Kenangan* provide basic facilities. Among the services offered are nursing, occupational rehabilitation, counselling, guidance, devotional facilities, recreational facilities and medical treatment. In addition, residents are encouraged to be involved in the activities of food preparation, cleaning, gardening, and to be involved in handicraft and vocational activities (Johari 1992).

Table 4.3 Number of *Rumah Seri Kenangan* occupants and total expenditure by year

Year	Number of occupants	Total expenditure (ringits)
1987	2,541	5,905,885
1988	2,569	5,122,726
1989	2,525	5,380,168
1990	2,485	5,485,440
1991	2,457	5,971,456

Source: Johari (1992).

The numbers of residents in old folk's homes in Malaysia is still relatively very small compared to the numbers of the elderly in Malaysia (see table 4.3). The government has no plans to build more and, in promoting the values of family and a caring society, the ministry often stresses the need for the elderly to remain in their own homes and communities. The Ministry of Welfare provides incentives to instil the Caring Society concept among Malaysians supporting the elderly living in their own homes, through forms of financial support. For instance, the government through incentives to the community encourages the setting up of 'Malay huts' (locally known as *pondoks*) to provide housing for the elderly in villages – especially in some Islamic states in Kedah, Kelantan and Trengganu. These programmes are community-based with major involvement coming from the community itself. Thus, the *Ketua Kampung* (village head) will initiate the plan and forward it to the ministry for approval. The community will be responsible for building the hut, with the government helping to bear some of the costs through the social welfare budget.

Day-care centres are also increasing in numbers in Malaysia, especially in big cities such as Kuala Lumpur, Penang, Johor Baharu and Ipoh. Among the day-care centres available in the country are those set up by NGOs such as PERKIM (Islamic Missionary Organization) and NASCOM (National Council of Senior Citizens). Yet, despite the tremendous campaign by certain sectors to promote day-care centres for all sectors of the older population, those that attend are predominantly of Chinese origin.

Institutions and Services versus the Family

In any case, such services being limited in number and accessibility, the problem, as Ong Fon Sim (2002: 137) points out, lies not so much in the nature of the services and facilities in themselves, but in their 'scale and scope'. There are sufficient old folk's homes, nursing homes and day-care centres to meet only a fraction of the potential need. This could be attributed to the reluctance of the government to meet the public expenditure and taxation consequences, but there is in any case a strong philosophical concern about the provision of social welfare institutions as a solution for meeting the needs of the elderly. Thus, in a speech about policies for older people, one recent Minister of Health argued in terms that 'the issues of ageing must be taken seriously ... so as to overcome the need for institutionalization for the elderly people which should be *the last and the least most wanted outcome in anybody's life*' (Meng 1997: 2; emphasis by present author). The preferred solution, clear from the speech and policy documents such as the national plans, is the reinforcing of the traditional role of the family.

Income in Old Age

Health, old age and poverty are intimately linked. In most societies, a disproportionate number of the poorest are very old (Kalache and Sen 1999). Low-income families, including the elderly, who have no sources of income have fewer opportunities to enjoy good health, while they experience malnutrition and often do not have access to high-quality medical care (Omar 1986; Luft 1978). As the country has progressed economically, and as the traditional means of supporting the income needs of older people, largely through the extended family system, have been eroded, so formal pension arrangements have been extended (Lock 2001). There are two main state-run schemes, one for public servants and one for a number of categories of workers.

Public servants who have at least ten years' service are entitled to a state pension, which is set up on a non-contributory basis and is funded directly from taxation. The amount received is proportional to the length of service, with those who have worked for 25 years or more being eligible for a monthly income during retirement of half their last drawn salary. The normal retirement age for public servants is 55 years. The scheme is also designed to provide financial assistance in cases where, because of illness or injury during the course of performing their duties as a public servant, they are forced to retire early. In addition, where they die in service or after retirement their dependants are eligible for financial support.

The Employees' Provident Fund (EPF), which was introduced in 1951 during the period of British colonial rule, is intended for the majority of workers and their families. The EPF is a defined-contributions scheme whereby employees pay a sum equivalent to 9 per cent of their income, and employers a further 12 per cent, into the individual worker's account. For those working in the formal sector the scheme is mandatory, while increasingly it has been extended to cover self-employed people on a voluntary basis. The account can be drawn upon for a number of specified expenditures including health care and housing. However, the largest single proportion – 60 per cent – is available as a pension, which at different times has been accessible in a variety of ways: as a single lump sum, as periodic lump sums, or as an annuity.

There are a number of limitations to these schemes. Firstly, their coverage is limited. By definition the public servants' pension scheme is restricted to those in public service. Ong Fon Sim (2002: 119) estimates this as covering 'fewer than 1 per cent of the population', while Caraher (2002: 8) indicates a coverage of 'approximately 5–7 per cent of the workforce'. In this respect, the EPF is much larger. Asher (1998) noted that by the end of 1995 the EPF had 7.8 million members, which constituted 49.3 per cent of the workforce, a proportion which still 'implies that one in two workers does not have even the basic provident fund coverage'. Even though the scheme has expanded rapidly in subsequent years to 9.2 million members by 1998 (Lock 2001), a large proportion of workers are still not covered. Coverage is particularly low for female members of the population, partly because of their historically lower labour-force participation rates (Chang and Yatim 1997).

In addition to the problems of coverage, the existing arrangements also fail to provide many of those covered with adequate incomes. The problem has a number of origins related to the nature of the funding of the schemes and the opportunities for early withdrawal of savings:

The fact that the provident fund system is a scheme for compulsory savings means that there is no pooling of risks among the fund's members. In other words, the benefits that each member will get on reaching the specified retirement age will not be based on needs but will depend on the amount of accumulated contributions made by him and for him by his employer over the years plus the earnings on those accumulated savings less any permitted withdrawal made before then. (Lock 2001: 7)

The net effect of the accumulated credits and debits is that the average balance in personal accounts, even for those close to the retirement age, is low. Consequently, retirement income is also low and in the many cases where the account is cleared by a lump-sum payment on retirement the proceeds are not infrequently expended within just a few years (Caraher 2002). Or, in medical terms, 'it may not be enough to cover even one by-pass surgery in a private hospital' (Aljunid 1997: 6).

Finally, both the public servants' pension and the EPF impose costs on public finances and taxation. The EPF scheme attracts fairly generous tax benefits in terms of both payments into the fund and of capital gains. In addition, over time much of the fund has been invested in Malaysia Government Securities that have paid risk-free high rates of interest. Insofar as this constitutes an implicit subsidy, EPF, despite its apparent individualization of pension accumulation, could be viewed as a 'partial PAYG system' (Asher 1998: 12).

As in many other countries, one of the responses to the inadequacies of the existing arrangements for meeting people's income needs in old age, as well as to the specific pressures on the state to meet their stated commitments, has been to consider the raising of the formal retirement age. This issue has become particularly pertinent as the average life expectancy now considerably exceeds 55 years, promising more and more people a prolonged retirement life. There is, however, little unanimity over this issue and, indeed, even within interest groups, there is some ambivalence. Thus, Chang and Tho (2000: 286) comment on perceptions of the short-term and long-term interests of young people:

> The younger population may feel that the retirement age of 55 years should be maintained because they want to be promoted and do not want their social mobility jeopardised by the older folks remaining. But, these persons in their thirties should be the very people who agitate for a rise in the age of retirement as they will be 55 years and over in the year 2020. They are also likely to be the ones burdened by rising medical and other costs of caring for older parents and relatives who may not have their own resources.

Concluding Remarks

Up until the start of the 1990s the arrangements that had been in place for many decades seemed to be meeting older people's needs adequately. In part, this can be explained in terms of scale: fertility rates were high, so the population of the country was expanding rapidly, while life expectancies were still low. Overall, the population pyramid had a wide base and a narrow, pointed tip. In other words, there were relatively small numbers of older people. At the same time, the family, supported by the community, was apparently continuing to fulfil its traditional role whereby older people received financial, emotional and other support.

Although the desirability of setting in place some arrangements, whereby at least some members of the population could provide for their income needs in old age, was recognized early on, it has only been in the last ten years or so that policy-makers in Malaysia have come to see other needs of older people as requiring specific government attention. The ageing of the population has not progressed to levels now common in many European countries; nevertheless, the balance between old and young has shifted markedly. The population pyramid has changed in shape as fertility rates have dropped and average life expectancy has increased. While the size of the older population has increased, in both absolute and relative terms, so the nature and role of the family has substantially shifted. Increasingly, as women have taken roles as wage-earners, their role as mothers has decreased and likewise has their capacity to care for parents. In addition, parents and grandparents are, less frequently than before, living together. As the basic unit into which Malaysian society is divided, the extended family is giving way to the nuclear family. In part, because of rural–urban migration, this has often been accompanied by large geographical distances between generations.

It is important to note, however, that there are significant ethnic differences in these trends. In general, the traditional family structures and roles, including high fertility rates have tended to change less quickly among the Malay people. It is among the Chinese, by contrast, that fertility rates have fallen most markedly, while their urban locations and higher average incomes have facilitated their greater use of private sector services to support their older people's health and care needs.

Nevertheless, there is a new context, in which it is recognized that it can no longer be assumed that the well-being of older people will be dealt with through traditional institutions, and this recognition has led the state to act. At least at the level of rhetoric this is clear. The National Policy for the Elderly, supported by the national plans and other policy statements, indicates a recognition both that current trends, left unchecked, would increasingly result in social problems *and* that it is the responsibility of the state, albeit with other elements in society, to find solutions. Some progress in the required direction is evident in, for example, the development of age-specific provision such as geriatric hospital wards and old folk's homes. The number of people enrolled in the EPF system increased rapidly in the second half of the 1990s. These developments have all contributed towards the improved health and social care of groups of older people.

Yet in a number of ways this progress has been limited. Firstly, the scale of activity involved has been small. The government is reluctant to pursue a policy of the large-scale provision of institutions catering for older people so that, for example, across the country as a whole the available care homes meet the needs of only a minute fraction of the country's older people. Secondly, the emphasis placed on the contribution to be played by the private sector has resulted in provision that in practice is accessible mainly in the larger urban centres and to wealthier sections of the population. Those living in smaller towns and rural areas and those with the least personal resources are not well served.

One of the main policy approaches has been to try to reinforce the traditional role of the family. The introduction of subsidies operating through the tax system provides an increased incentive to children to look after their parents both by sharing the same home and/or by purchasing appropriate facilities and care. While this has undoubtedly had some success, the critical issue will be whether or not it will prove to be anything other than a short-term fix. This will hinge on the extent to which such tax breaks will be sufficient to reverse the socio-economic trends which in Malaysia – and indeed in all other economically advanced countries – have led to the long-term decline of the extended family model. If the trends in fertility rates, the involvement of women in the labour market and the separation of the living arrangements of the generations, continue, even tax breaks may do little to prevent a significant deterioration in the position of many older people.

References

Aljunid, S. M. (1997). The ageing population: developing a coordinated plan of care in the veteran community. Paper at Conference of Financing Health Care in Malaysia, Kuala Lumpur.

Arokiasamy, J. T. (2002). *Malaysia's Ageing Population.* Available at: Malaysian Medical Association (www.mma.org.my/info/1_ageing_99.htm).

Asher, M. (1998). The future of retirement protection in Southeast Asia. *International Social Security Review*, 51, 1: 3–30.

Caraher, K. (2002). *Malaysia: Securing an Income in Old Age?* Paper to Social Policy Association Conference, University of Teesside, UK.

Chan, K. E. (1997). Ageing and health in Malaysia: a policy perspective. *Malaysian Journal of Arts and Social Sciences*, 14: 1–11.

Chang, T. P. and Yatim, Masita Mohd (1997). Old age financial security for women in Malaysia. In Kalyani, Mehta (ed.), *Untapped Resources: Women in Ageing Societies across Asia.* Singapore: Times Academic Press.

Chang, Tan Poo and Tho, Ng Sor (2000). Ageing in Malaysia: issues and policies. In D. R. Phillips (ed.), *Ageing in the Asia-Pacific Region: Issues, Policies and Future Trends.* London: Routledge.

Chee, Heng Leng (1990). *Health and Health Care in Malaysia: Present Trends and Implications for the Future.* Kuala Lumpur: Institute of Advanced Studies, University of Malaya.

Doling, J. and Omar, R. (2003). The welfare state system in Malaysia. In C. Aspalter (ed.), *The Welfare State in Emerging Market Economies.* Taichung City, Taiwan: Casa Verde Publishing.

Johari Mat (1992). Towards the formulation of national policies on the elderly. In *Proceedings of the National Seminar on Challenges of Senior Citizens Towards Vision 2020.* Kuala Lumpur: Ministry of National Unity and Community Development, Social Obgyn and University of Malaya and Cumberland Foundation.

Kalache, A. and Sen, Kasturi (1999). Ageing and health. In *The Ageing and Development Report: Poverty Independence and the World's Older People.* London: Help the Aged International.

Kane, W. M. (1985). *Healthy Living: An Active Approach to Wellness.* Indianapolis: Bobbs-Merrill Educative Publications.

Kling, Zainal and Omar, Roziah (1999). Family and care of the aged in Malaysia. *Man and Society*, Journal of the Department Anthropology and Sociology, University of Malaya, 11: 1–10.

Lock, Lee Hock (2001). *Financial Security in Old Age: Whither the Employees Provident Fund of Malaysia?* Subang Jaya, Malaysia: Pelanduck Publications.

Luft, H. S. (1978). *Poverty and Health: Economic Consequences of Health Problems.* Cambridge: Cambridge University Press.

Mafauzy, M. (2000). The problems and challenges of the ageing population in Malaysia. *Malaysian Journal of Medical Sciences*, 7, 1: 1–3.

Malaysia (1991). *Sixth Malaysia Plan 1991–1995.* Kuala Lumpur: Government Printer.

Malaysia (1992). *Social Statistics Bulletin.* Kuala Lumpur: Department of Statistics.

Malaysia (1996). *Seventh Malaysia Plan 1996–2000.* Kuala Lumpur: Government Printer.

Malaysia (2001). *Eighth Malaysia Plan 2001–2005.* Kuala Lumpur: Government Printer.

Meng, Dato' Chua Jui (1997). Speech on the occasion of the celebration of people's day (Senior Citizen's Night). Thean Hou Temple, Kuala Lumpur, Malaysia.

Omar, Roziah (1986). Health and health care services to the poor in Malaysia. *Ilmu Masyarakat*, Malaysian Social Science Association Publication (April–September), 11: 46–55.

Omar, Roziah (1994). *The Malay Woman in the Body: Between Biology and Culture.* Kuala Lumpur: Fajar Bakti.

Omar, Roziah (2000). *Health: Bridging the Gaps.* Kuala Lumpur: University of Malaya Press.

Ong Fon Sim (2002). Ageing in Malaysia: a review of national policies and programmes. In D. R. Phillips and A. C. M. Chan (eds), *Ageing and Long Term Care: National Policies in the Asia-Pacific.* Institute of Southeast Asian Studies: Singapore.

Phillips, D. R. (2000). Ageing in the Asia-Pacific region: issues, policies and contents. In D. R. Phillips (ed.), *Ageing in the Asia-Pacific Region: Issues, Policies and Future Trends.* London: Routledge.

Siti Hasmah Ali (1992). Women and ageing. In *Proceedings of the National Seminar on Challenges of Senior Citizens Towards Vision 2020.* Kuala Lumpur: Ministry of National Unity and Community Development, Social Obgyn and University of Malaya and Cumberland Foundation.

WHO (1998). *Population Ageing – A Public Health Challenge*, Fact Sheet 135. Geneva: World Health Organization.

Chapter 5

Population Ageing in Singapore: The Challenge of Using the Central Provident Fund for Retirement Needs

Tee Liang Ngiam

Singapore may be a first-world country in economic terms, but it is not, as a matter of deliberate government policy, a welfare state. Yet the republic has one of the fastest-ageing populations in Asia. So how does it – and how may it be able to – provide a high standard of living for its citizens and ensure the existence of an adequate social safety net in the country, including provisions for older persons in the areas of social care and housing? Singapore offers an interesting example of social development in a country where people are its only natural resources, where its main livelihood stems from competing in the global economy, and which is facing a greying population. It presents an alternative model of how social security and social services might be rendered available to the public without the need for large direct fiscal provision from the state. This chapter will examine how this is done in Singapore, and the challenges arising from it.

Background

Singapore gained independence on 9 August 1965 after separating from Malaysia, and became a republic on 22 December 1965. It has a parliamentary system of government with a unicameral parliament. Members of parliament are democratically elected at general elections held every five years or earlier. The president of the Republic of Singapore[1] is the head of state and is elected separately by Singapore citizens for a six-year term. The administration of the government rests with the Cabinet, headed by the prime minister. Both the prime minister and the Cabinet are appointed by the president from among the members of parliament of the majority political party in office (Ministry of Information and the Arts 1997b: 14, 16; Ministry of Information and the Arts 1998). However, it was as early as 1959 that the British granted Singapore limited internal self-government, and that a Legislative Assembly was established. The People's Action Party (PAP) won the majority of seats in this Legislative Assembly and has been the ruling party in government ever since.

Singapore is a small country and has one of the highest population densities in the world (United Nations Development Programme 1998: 55). It has no natural resources such as oil, gas, minerals, forestry and so on, other than its human resource. Even water has to be imported for now, to supplement what it has naturally. Yet, the country is well planned in its use of land, only 49.7 per cent being used for residential, commercial and industrial purposes, with the rest reserved for marsh, forests and water catchment areas (Ministry of Information and the Arts 1997a: 1).

Historically, Singapore was an immigrant society. Prior to the arrival of the British in 1819, there were a few hundred Malays living in fishing villages (Church 1997: 113). The British turned Singapore colony into a trading post and a free port. It was able to attract the Chinese, Malays, Indians and other minority communities to seek their fortunes and settle down in Singapore. By the time Singapore became fully independent in 1965, it was possessed of a multi-ethnic, multilinguistic and multireligious population, which made multiracial and religious harmony vitally important for the nation's stability. By now, the majority of the resident population in Singapore is local-born.

Despite its small size and limited non-human natural resources, Singapore has a per capita income second only to Japan in Asia (Church 1995: 113). Consequently, in 1996 the Organization for Economic Cooperation and Development (OECD) accorded Singapore the status of a 'more advanced developing country' (*Straits Times*, 17 January 1996: 1). Yet the question remains as to how a small and culturally heterogeneous country can continue to provide for the welfare needs of its citizens. As the people cannot live off its land, and its open economy has to compete competitively in the global market, this question strikes at the core of its existence. In addition, the republic is finding the prospect of maintaining steady economic growth in the years to come a big challenge. Indeed, Singapore is already experiencing low GDP growth, following the recent Asian financial and economic crisis and the aftermath of the terrorist attacks in the USA on 11 September 2001; this in addition to the multifaceted processes and unintended consequences of globalization, rapid modernization and social change.

Social Problems

In contemporary Singapore, economic and social modernization has transformed the country into what it is today. At the same time, there are concerns about some of the impact of modernization and rapid social change.

> In spite of increasing economic prosperity and a decline in the incidence of poverty in Singapore, there will remain segments of the population who will require assistance because of age or mental or physical disability. In such a highly urbanised and rapidly changing environment, families are also more likely to undergo pressures leading to divorce, single parent families and delinquency unless these problems are recognised and dealt with. (Yap 1991: vii)

Fortunately, the family institution is still relatively stable, when compared to some Western nations in terms of divorce rates and family dysfunction (*Straits Times*, 20 July 1994: 3), although certain trends have emerged that may threaten its stability.

Nuclear-family households now constitute the norm in Singapore, forming 82 per cent of all households in 2000 (Leow 2001b: ix). Without the benefit of extended family living, caring for children by dual-working parents poses a problem for quite a number of families. Similarly, caring for dependent older adults, particularly the oldest-old and those with ill health, can be difficult. While families who can afford to hire carers of young children and older adults employ foreign domestic maids, there are long-term implications for the nation of this reliance on a pool of foreign nationals, themselves driven to seek employment overseas due to the weak economic conditions in their own countries.

Since 1977, the total fertility rate (TFR) has fallen below the replacement level of 2.0. For instance, it dropped as low as 1.43 in 1986 – among the lowest levels in the world. It was probably the first developing country to have a prolonged below-replacement fertility level (Department of Statistics 1995: 22). Thanks to the introduction of a new population policy started in 1987, offering incentives to married couples to encourage higher fertility, the trend of falling TFR reversed slightly. It rose to 1.86 in 1990 and was 1.78 in 1993 (Cheung 1994: 34). However, it has been dropping again since 1993 and the TFR was 1.70 in 1996 (Department of Statistics 1996: 22). As cited by the then acting minister for Community Development and Sports, Associate Professor Yaacob Ihrahim, the rate has continued to fall, from 1.6 in 2000 to 1.41 in 2001, to a record low of 1.37 in 2002 (Singapore Parliament Reports 2003: 1848). The decline occurred despite the availability in 2000 of new pro-fertility measures such as the Baby Bonus given by the government. The serious implications of a below-replacement TFR on the future human resource requirements of the country cannot be taken lightly. Not least, it speeds up the ageing of the population and reduces family size, which can affect the availability of family support for older people.

Singapore has one of the fastest-ageing populations in Asia (*Straits Times*, 3 August 1996: 1; Inter-ministerial Committee on Ageing Report 1999). In the coming years, it will have an increasing proportion of retirees and older adults in the population. In 2000, the elderly aged 65 years and above constituted 10 per cent of the population (Leow 2001a: viii). By 2030, the population aged 60 years and above is estimated to increase to 26 per cent (Chen and Cheung 1988: 4).

The average life expectancy at birth in 2002 was 76.4 years for males and 80.4 years for females (Ministry of Information, Communications and the Arts 2002). It was 60.3 years and 65.2 years respectively, as late as 1957 (Shantakumar 1994: 9). Then again, in 1990, the old dependency ratio was 7.4 working adults (15–59 years) to one older person aged 60 years and above. This is expected to decrease to 2.2 working adults to one older person by the year 2030 (Ministry of Community Development 1989: 3).

Nevertheless, one of the main social concerns of the government over recent years has been the supposed erosion of traditional moral and family values among Singaporeans, as the country becomes a more consumer-oriented society preoccupied with the acquisition of wealth. Some of the negative effects of this 'erosion' are to be seen in recent marriage and divorce rates. Their impact in the end could lead to society slowly losing its dynamism over the next generation (*Straits Times*, 18 January 1994: 21). Certainly there is concern that notions of filial responsibility, on the part of adult children towards their elderly family members, will be adversely affected – and inter-generational support thus diminished – if traditional, positive Asian values are not actively transmitted through the generations.

Welfare Philosophy and Approach

These and other social issues and problems pose ideological and philosophical challenges to Singapore, requiring value and policy responses that are adapted to Singapore's conditions and rising expectations of its people. What emerges is a unique system of social security and services based on the following state philosophy and approach towards the notion of welfare. Thus Singapore is not a welfare state in the conventional sense of the term as used in the West, although the government argues that it is nevertheless a 'compassionate society' (*Straits Times*, 12 September 1993: 1).

The Western welfare state has long been seen as failing to live up to its expectations (George and Wilding 1976: 106–17). The PAP government believes that Singapore lacks the deep, recurrent financial capability to sustain a welfare state system, especially for unemployment and other direct cash allowances and benefits. Moreover, such a system is deemed neither politically nor socially desirable. It is presumed unwise to increase the public burden of taxation in order to provide for comprehensive state welfare services and income supplements. Accelerated economic development to ensure Singapore's viability as an independent nation is seen as a much more urgent priority, especially after the separation from Malaysia. More cogently, the government is seriously afraid that one consequence of state welfarism could be a loss of work ethic among the population (Goh 1972: 35), affecting Singapore's competitiveness in the global economy.

This was very clearly stated by the government, early on. In an article entitled 'The philosophy of government', the Prime Minister's Office explains (Ministry of Culture 1977: 8):

> The programmes and policies which the Government will pursue in the fields of finance and economics, social and medical services, education and defence are all based on the inexorable premise, that rewards must be correlated to work, and must correspond to the contributions one makes to the total national well-being. We believe one truth to be self-evident: that more and more pay for less and less work must lead to greater and greater borrowing and eventual bankruptcy.

Nevertheless, the same article clarified that this did not mean a complete anti-welfare posture on the part of government (Ministry of Culture 1977: 8):

But the government is committed to help the most needy. They should never be allowed to become a permanent burden on the rest of the community. They should be helped through better education and health because then they can better themselves.

In other words, helping citizens is acceptable as long as it does not conflict with the incentives to work and make a living. Better education and health are plus factors for labour productivity, whereas generous financial aid is not.

Consequently, the PAP government's initial welfare approach was to concentrate on three basic social services – education, housing and health. These were considered priority areas for human capital formation and nation-building (L. Y. C. Lim 1989: 172). Remedial welfare was left largely to the non-government sector – primarily the voluntary welfare and religious organizations – although it did offer modest public assistance to the indigent and rehabilitation for such as juvenile offenders (Ngiam and Vasoo 1998: 3). The basic financial assistance approach of the personal social services continues to be governed by the principle that 'assistance to the less fortunate [is] to help them achieve self-reliance, economic independence and productive living' (Ministry of Community Development and Sports 2003). In other words, the various financial aid schemes provided by the government are not meant to be handouts creative of welfare dependency among those otherwise able to work.

Some of the government schemes applicable to older adults *not* deemed capable of work are:

- *Public Assistance (PA)*: This scheme is provided for Singapore citizens who, due to old age, illness, disability or unfavourable family circumstances, are unable to work and have no other means of subsistence and no one to depend on. Modest monthly grants are given to eligible distressed senior citizens aged 60 years and above for their basic living expenses.
- *Special Grant (SG)*: Singapore permanent residents can apply for the Special Grant, which uses the same eligibility criteria and rates of payments as the Public Assistance Scheme.

Depending on the needs of the recipients, additional financial support from other philanthropic sources and community-based grassroots organizations – such as the Community Development Councils (CDCs) – usually supplement the monetary amounts given out from these government schemes.

Therefore, instead of being a 'welfare state' that unintentionally creates welfare dependency amongst its citizens, the Singapore government adopts an alternative welfare approach. The present prime minister, Mr Goh Chok Tong, spelled this out as a four-pronged strategy (Chua 1993: 1; Ngiam and Vasoo 1998: 3):

1   Tackle the root cause of a problem, and not just the symptoms. For example, find out the underlying factors causing families to be in rent arrears, instead of just helping them with financial assistance.

2   Focus on preventive and developmental services. For the elderly, this means keeping them alert mentally and physically so that fewer of them would be frail and sick.

3   Help the disadvantaged become more independent by training them for jobs. This is to 'teach them how to fish so that they would live a lifetime' instead of just 'giving them a fish so that they could live for a day'.

4   Motivate the underclass to get out of the poverty trap through incentive programmes such as the Small Families Improvement Scheme, which will help poor families keep their family size small, provide grants for their children's education and improve their asset enhancement of home ownership.

Prime Minister Goh explains that such a welfare strategy is a compassionate approach that will not erode Singapore's economic competitiveness, will maintain the individual's responsibility to look after himself or herself, and not produce a 'crutch mentality' implying that the state owes him or her a living (Chua 1993: 1). The government emphasizes the importance of 'individual responsibility', and thus the ordinary Singaporean is not expected to think that he or she has a 'right' to welfare. Instead, the social policy ideology of the state stresses four dimensions of action to help individuals (Ngiam 1997a).

- First: self-care
- Next: family, and community care
- Last: state care

Reinforcing the above message is the concept of providing help and care that should involve 'many helping hands', meaning that human service provisions should involve the participation of all sectors of society – family, community, non-government, non-profit, for-profit and the government (Government of Singapore 1991: 117–29). This concept sees the various sectors as partners in the social services industry.

In this regard, the government is prepared to contribute budgetary resources and surpluses to improve Singapore's human capital. Hence, the human development strategy is focused on education, training and retraining, skills upgrading and promoting a training culture among the people. The new emphasis for future economic growth in the country is on developing a 'knowledge-based economy' (Baharudin 2002: 5, 11). At the same time, the Singapore government is aware that there must also be social development and community bonding, to strike a balance between the harsh competition of the market place and the provision of a supportive and cohesive living environment for the population.

The CPF Safety Net

By not providing direct cash benefits to the people, how then does the country provide a social safety net for them? When Singapore was a British colony, the colonial administrators adopted a laissez faire attitude to welfare, providing some basic services and leaving the rest largely to the various voluntary welfare organizations and ethnic communities to complement and supplement with other social services for themselves. Interestingly, while Britain was setting up its own welfare state, it decided not to transplant the idea to Singapore, as the colonial government did not want to be saddled with the financial responsibility of making old-age provision for its colonies (Low and Aw 1997: 15). Instead, it chose (as it did for its colonies elsewhere in South Asia, with the exception of high-risk Hong Kong) to create, in 1955, a fully funded and self-financed provident scheme called the Central Provident Fund (CPF), even though four committees and studies between 1951 and 1956 had unanimously recommended either a pension or social insurance plan instead (Low and Aw 1997: 14–21). Yet, while the CPF may have been intended as a purely 'stopgap measure' by the British, it has evolved over the years of the People's Action Party's (PAP) rule into an institution lauded for being the 'correct formula at the right time' (1997: viii).

The original scope of the CPF was modest, being intended only as a compulsory old-age savings scheme. Consequently, there was, and still is, no social security scheme such as social insurance or national health insurance for the populace. Rather, the PAP government continues with the Fund to this day, with modifications and additional schemes added over the years. Therefore, while Singapore does not have a comprehensive social security system, the CPF approaches it in scope (United Nations 1996: 142). In short, the CPF Scheme has transformed itself, over the years, from being a 'simple savings-withdrawal or save-as-you-earn (SAYE) plan' (Low and Aw 1997: viii) into an ambitious 'instrument for achieving wide-ranging socio-political macroeconomic objectives' (1997: viii). Manifestly, it has gone beyond old-age and social security provisions.

The CPF covers all employees who are Singapore citizens or Singapore permanent residents. Those who are self-employed and earning a net trade income of more than S$2,400 a year can voluntarily opt into the Scheme, except for Medisave,[2] one of its health-financing schemes, which is mandatory. It also allows homemakers and retirees with no earned income who wish to benefit from the government's top-up schemes[3] to open or maintain a CPF account, provided they are 21 years of age or above, and are citizens or permanent residents of Singapore.

Both employers and employees contribute to the Fund, which is guaranteed by the Singapore government and managed by a statutory Central Provident Fund Board. Contribution rates vary according to the employee's age, a younger worker having higher rates than an older worker (see table 5.1). The rate differential takes into account the heavier financial outlays facing workers starting out in life, or with young families, relative to those facing older workers who have fewer financial commitments, whose children have already grown up. Regardless of the age of the employee, the monthly maximum contribution from the employer and employee is capped at S$1,200 each, based on a salary ceiling of S$6,000 per month. In other words, the total monthly maximum contribution that can go into an employee's CPF account is S$2,4005.[4]

Table 5.1 CPF contribution rates

Worker's age (years)	Employer's rate (%)	Employee's rate (%)	Total (%)
55 and below	20.0	20.0	40
56–59	7.5	12.5	20
60–65	7.5	7.5	15
Over 65	5.0	5.0	10

Source: Central Provident Fund Board (1995: 9).

Each working CPF member is given three accounts with the Fund, namely the

- *Ordinary Account*: Savings can be used for housing, approved investments, insurance, education and transfers to top up parents' Retirement Accounts.
- *Medisave Account*: Savings are for meeting hospitalization and medical expenses such as hepatitis-B vaccinations. It can also be used to buy approved medical insurance (MediShield, MediShield Plus and IncomeShield[5]).
- *Special Account*: Savings in the Special Account are reserved for old-age and contingency purposes.

Each account is dedicated to specific purposes and the monthly contribution of each member is distributed into each of the three accounts according to the respective percentage points shown in table 5.2. The various accounts and schemes under CPF were introduced at different times, and the contribution rates were adjusted, according to prevailing circumstances, and changing specific policy objectives.

Table 5.2 Distribution of CPF contribution rates

CPF account	Age of CPF member (years)					
	<35	35–44	45–55	55–60	60–64	>65
Ordinary	30.0	29.0	28.0	12.0	7.0	2.0
MediSave	6.0	7.0	8.0	8.0	8.0	8.0
Special	4.0	4.0	4.0	—	—	—
Total (%)	40.0	40.0	40.0	20.0	15.0	10.0

Source: Low and Aw (1997: 35).

The government has fixed the long-term employee–employer CPF contribution rate for each CPF member below the withdrawal age to be 40 per cent. This is considered sufficient to cover CPF schemes for housing and medical needs, in addition to generating 'a retirement annuity equivalent to between 20 per cent and 40 per cent of the individual's last take-home pay' (Low and Aw 1997: 26).

Members can use the three types of accounts in the CPF for various purposes under a number of schemes which reflect the wider policy goals of the PAP government to provide an individual social safety net for every adult Singaporean that can also cover his or her dependent family members.

Retirement

Under the present CPF legislation, members are allowed to withdraw their savings from the Ordinary and Special Accounts on reaching 55 years of age, subject to CPF withholding a minimum sum, which will be deposited into a new account created for them called the Retirement Account. When it was first started, the minimum sum to be put aside was a maximum of S$30,000 for an individual and S$45,000 for a married couple. The amounts are adjusted upwards according to a schedule and are targeted to be S$80,000 in 2003. This is to ensure that the minimum sum, adjusted for inflation, 'could guarantee an income for life' (Low and Aw 1997: 24). Note that it is meant to be a minimum sum required for very basic daily living. Additional financial means from other sources would be required if someone wishes to have a higher standard of living. The minimum sum scheme allows the CPF members' property to be pledged up to a predetermined limit in lieu of cash in the Retirement Account, the reasoning being that the property can be sold off to make up for the shortfall in cash if necessary.

The minimum sum scheme provides three options for its usage. It can be left with the CPF Board with interest earned and a monthly payment given to the individual member or married couple from age 60 years onwards, until the sum is exhausted. However, at any time the CPF member can top up the amount to the maximum allowed either using his own cash or from the contribution of his own children, using either cash or savings from their CPF Ordinary Account.

Another possibility is to leave the minimum sum with an approved bank, again earning interest and getting a monthly payment until the savings are exhausted. This option is given to offer CPF members a choice to decide on the rate of returns their savings could obtain from the banks in comparison with the CPF Board, plus other personal considerations.

A surer way to ensure sufficiency in the Retirement Account is to use the minimum sum to buy a life annuity from an approved insurance company. This guarantees a lifetime income from age 60 years onwards and is the preferred mode that the CPF Board would like to encourage CPF members to adopt (Low and Aw 1997: 26).

Housing

As explained earlier, housing was one of three basic social services the PAP government was committed to in the early 1960s. The government has remained faithful to this commitment to this day. The existence of the CPF allowed the government to borrow its funds to finance its massive and ambitious public housing programme for its people. It was 'more a socio-political decision than an economic one which brought housing into the social security arena' (Low and Aw 1997: 39).

When Singapore attained self-government in 1959, it had squalid and overcrowded housing conditions, characteristic of urban centres in many third world countries at that time. The Housing and Development Board (HDB) was established in 1960 to take over the functions of the former Singapore Improvement Trust (SIT) as the public housing authority in the state. The remit of HDB was to build new towns in various parts of Singapore for people to live in, in improved physical and social environments. High-rise public housing flats for both rental and home ownership catering to households from low-income to lower middle-income groups were built in these new towns. At present, about 85 per cent of the population live in HDB apartments (Ministry of Information, Communications and the Arts 2002: 193).

The Ordinary CPF Accounts of eligible individuals can be used for house purchase and mortgage payments under the Home Ownership Scheme, for both HDB and private properties. By 2002, 94 per cent of residential properties in Singapore were under home ownership (Department of Statistics 2003). For HDB purchases, first-time buyers are entitled to purchase the flats at varying rates of subsidy given by the government, depending on the size of flats bought. HDB apartment owners are allowed to sell off their flats five years after purchase in the open market, and any profit accruing after returning the housing loans and interest to their own CPF Accounts is at the disposal of the flat-owners. Many have chosen to upgrade their property status by selling off the existing HDB flat and buying a more expensive residential property, which is either another HDB unit or a private property.

In this way, Singaporeans can enhance their assets by treating their properties as investment opportunities. Policy-makers saw this as one way for Singaporeans to accumulate wealth for themselves, as the property can be sold off when they retire, when they can downgrade to a smaller unit. This is seen as another avenue for individuals to enhance their old-age security.

However, the implication of using housing as both shelter and wealth-generation for older adults meant that for many of them, they are 'asset rich but cash poor'. This is because they will have used the bulk of their CPF Ordinary Account funds to purchase property, resulting in very little available CPF savings left for their retirement needs. There was also the assumption that property prices which saw such spectacular profit gains in the 1970s and 1980s would continue unabated. Unfortunately, the property 'bubble' burst just at the time when Singapore was going through economic difficulties in recent years. Hence, there is no guarantee that using a high proportion of CPF savings for property purchases is going to help to increase older persons' nest eggs.

In recognition of this situation, the HDB has started building studio apartments for older persons (Ministry of Information, Communications and the Arts 2002: 193–4), so that they can sell off their HDB flats and purchase the smaller units at lower cost, to enable them to have more disposable income during their retirement years. In May 2001 the eligibility of older persons for the scheme was extended to those owning private property as well as non-property owners.

Healthcare

Medisave The principal vehicle in the CPF that its members can use to finance medical care is the Medisave scheme. For those without employment medical benefits or private personal health insurance, the Medisave Account provides the means for CPF members to pay for approved hospitalization and certain other medical expenses. Members can also use it to complement other employee medical benefits and health insurance policies that they might have. While the government continues to subsidize health care in the hospitals and health centres under its auspices, it is mindful of the heavy financial burden of providing free medical benefits, particularly in the face of a looming ageing population. At the same time, it is also aware of the pitfalls of having a comprehensive national health insurance scheme for the whole population, as seen in some other countries. Hence, it initiated the Medisave Scheme.

Under the scheme, CPF members are required to put aside part of their monthly income into their Medisave Account to meet their own hospitalization expenses or those of their immediate family members. The contribution rates are given in table 5.2. The scheme is especially targeted for members' hospitalization needs after retirement, hence the progressive increase in the proportion of CPF savings channelled into the Medisave Account for older persons. There are daily limits and other conditions to prevent the overuse and misuse of the Medisave Account by patients who might be uninformed about the potentially high costs of medical care for certain types of illnesses and operations. Besides, the Medisave Account is a person's own savings and he or she ought therefore to be prudent in its use.

As mentioned earlier, the Medisave Scheme also covers the self-employed earning more than S$2,400 a year. When the scheme to include them was first started, they had to contribute 5 per cent of their yearly 'net trade income', with the amount increasing every year by 1 per cent until the rate reached the same as that for employees.

For older Singaporeans who retired before or soon after the Medisave Scheme started, the government introduced a Pre-Medisave Top-up Scheme in July 1995 so that they, too, could have some Medisave savings.[6] The top-ups range from S$100 to S$350 depending on age. To be eligible for the government's Pre-Medisave Top-up Scheme, they first have to contribute a token sum, currently S$20, into the elderly person's Medisave Account. In addition, to encourage family responsibility in providing for health care needs of such as parents and grandparents, they are allowed to contribute a token sum on behalf of their older family members. For that matter, anyone can also help any single older Singaporean qualifying under the Pre-Medisave Top-up Scheme in the same way. The scheme is funded from the government's budget surpluses, and is intended as a gesture to acknowledge older Singaporeans' past contributions to the nation. It is also to enable them to benefit additionally from the dividends the government pays out to its citizens for the nation's good economic performance over the previous year. By definition, therefore, it is not a guaranteed scheme, but, for example, when the Singapore economy did very well in 1995, the government contributed S$200 each into the Medisave Account of every adult Singaporean, during the following year.

MediShield As discussed earlier, the PAP government is not in favour of a general national health insurance programme for Singapore, thus avoiding the attendant problems of moral hazard and adverse selection (Low and Aw 1997: 80). Nevertheless, it recognizes that for most Singaporeans the Medisave savings they have might not be sufficient if they were to be struck down with catastrophic illnesses involving prolonged, high-cost medical treatment. Therefore, to supplement the Medisave Account, the government introduced a low-cost national medical insurance scheme called MediShield. Later, MediShield Plus with higher premium rates was added to cater for those who wanted a higher class of hospital stay. A non-government insurance cooperative[7] is also offering a similar plan called IncomeShield. The CPF Board allows its members to deduct the premiums for all three medical insurance schemes from their Medisave Accounts. CPF members are automatically covered under MediShield and can opt out if they wish. They can also opt to join MediShield Plus or IncomeShield, but not both. Additionally, they can also enrol their immediate family members, including grandparents, into these schemes.

When the scheme first started, coverage was only for those under 65 years of age. At present, it covers MediShield members up to 80 years of age. For IncomeShield members, coverage is for a lifetime. There are claim limits set for hospitalization and medical expenses, and for yearly and lifetime charges. There are also deductibles.

For those without a Medisave, MediShield (including MediShield Plus) and IncomeShield Account, or any other private medical insurance scheme, who has insufficient balance in these schemes, or who has insufficient savings, or who has no immediate family member to pay for them from his or her own pocket or Medisave Account, the government has created the Medical Endowment Fund (Medifund). It is to help needy citizens pay for their hospitalization expenses in the more heavily government-subsidized wards of non-private or restructured hospitals. This is in keeping with the PAP government's promise that no Singaporean will be denied basic hospital care even if he or she cannot afford it. Medifund is not part of the CPF schemes. Neither is it a health insurance scheme. Rather, funds for it again come out of government budgetary surpluses and it is therefore dependent on the economy's performance. Only income from the Medical Endowment Fund will be used to reimburse approved hospitals and medical institutions for valid Medifund claims. The government established this Fund with an initial capital of S$200 million, with the capital set to increase by S$100 million per year, until there is a sufficient amount in it (Ministry of Health 2003).

Notwithstanding the availability of these three 'Ms' (Medisave, MediShield and Medifund), it has become clear over time that these schemes were not providing adequate cover for the health care costs for older adults with certain medical and health conditions. Hence, in 2002, the government introduced the ElderShield scheme as an affordable, severe disability insurance plan for older Singaporeans requiring long-term care.

All Singapore citizens and permanent residents between 40 and 69 years of age with Medisave accounts have to pay small monthly premiums into the pooled insurance fund, unless they opt out. The scheme is scheduled to provide basic financial protection and help defray out-of-pocket expenses, in the event that the claimant is medically certified as being unable to perform three or more out of the six ADLs (Activities of Daily Living).

As an interim measure, those who were 70 years and above or who were already suffering from three or more ADL conditions at the inception of ElderShield – and hence not eligible to join the scheme – were automatically covered by another new scheme called the Interim Disability Assistance Programme for the Elderly (IDAPE) Scheme. Under this scheme, the government bears the cost of the programme (Ministry of Health 2003).

Overall Policy Impact and Implication

The popularity and success of the CPF Fund can be gauged in the following statement (Loh and Aw 1997: 29):

> After 40 years, the CPF has some 2.7 million members – 1.2 million of whom are active – with balances of $66.0 billion[8] ($94.6 billion if amounts withdrawn for various schemes are included) by the end of 1995. The total CPF membership in 1995 comprised 89.8 per cent of the resident population while the active members constituted 70.6 per cent of the labour force.

Overall, considering the policy objectives of the CPF Scheme, the impact of CPF is felt extensively by the bulk of the population, directly or indirectly. Many of its schemes reinforce the 'trustee model' of the PAP government (Low and Aw 1997: ix–xi). This is where the state manages the citizens' savings and at the same time gives them a range of choices to decide how to use their savings within bounded conditions. People then have some measure of self-determination without the state worrying too much about their ability to save enough for old age.

> Also, through individualized CPF accounts, members are conditioned not to equate good government with cradle-to-grave provision. Instead, the principle of looking after oneself and one's family as the emerging social pillar is reinforced. The trustee element further permeates the CPF through the government's regular topping up. (Low and Aw 1997: x)

In this way, the welfare dependency syndrome is avoided. At the same time, the social psychological effect so created enhances the 'stakeholder principle' of citizenship for Singaporeans. Being a relatively young nation and with many of its people having migrant backgrounds, the government had to find ways and means to get Singaporeans to sink their roots and make Singapore their home. By design and by accident, the CPF is used to advantage to bring this about.

However, the continued benefits of the CPF Scheme presuppose continuing economic growth for the country and no massive unemployment for the people. In this respect, the government's policies on education, economic investment, employment and skills upgrading are geared to minimizing such an eventuality. In any case, Singapore has enough foreign reserves to tide the country over any economic rough patches if need be, thus safeguarding the viability of its non-welfare state ideology.

Conclusion

Singapore's present social security system evolved from a historical serendipity that so far has been working in its favour. By adopting the Central Provident Fund scheme originally developed by the British, and then adapting it over the years, Singapore has been able to provide a welfare system which avoids the pitfalls of a conventional pay-as-you-go (PAYG) welfare state. Such a welfare state system is untenable when the macro-economic conditions necessary to sustain it are not there. In addition, experience from some developed countries has shown that welfare statism can create disincentives to work through generous cash benefits and the increased burden on its taxpayers.

Nevertheless, the CPF system is still serving a relatively young population. In the future, the proportion of older (60+) Singaporeans will increase dramatically, with one out of four Singaporeans being aged 60 years and above by the year 2030. At present, the proportion in that age group is about 11 per cent (Leow 2001a: 35). For the senior citizens of the future, their expectations and demands for social security and the good life will have to be qualitatively and quantitatively different from those of the present older generation. How far the CPF-led system will be able to accommodate the issues of a rapidly ageing population for twenty-first-century Singapore is another landmark challenge for its leaders and people to meet with creativity and practical wisdom.

So far, with the CPF as a major safety net available for the population, the government has been able to hold taxation at a reasonable level and to generate budget revenue surpluses that can be channelled to help the non-profit sector provide better social services to their service users. The Singapore government helps non-profit human service organizations to develop and improve their programmes and service delivery capabilities through subsidies and grants for capital and recurrent expenditure (Ministry of Community Development 1996). In addition, the National Council of Social Service has a fund-raising arm, the Community Chest of Singapore, that also provides per capita and programme funding to its affiliates for approved programmes managed by them (National Council of Social Service 1998).

In addition, in line with its overall welfare objectives, the government continues to commit budgetary resources and surpluses to improve Singapore's human capital. This is especially so in its human development strategy, which focuses on areas such as education and workers' skills, housing and health. To compete in the global economy successfully, the government is also aware that it has to look after the social well-being of its people. There has to be 'community-bonding' for Singaporeans, to strike a balance between the harsh competition of the market place and the provision of a supportive and compassionate living environment for its citizens (Chua 1993: 1).

The issues and challenges of globalization and the need for Singapore to remain competitive in the world economy and yet remain a compassionate society continue to set the stage for social work and human service intervention into the new millennium. The pull and push to become a developed country will subject its present brand of social welfare philosophy to increasing scrutiny by its people regarding its ability to deliver the welfare goods, without succumbing to the temptations and costs of state welfarism. The government is not against welfare *per se*. Rather, it is worried about adopting the sorts of welfare policies capable of undermining the very economic policies which have rendered Singapore so efficient and successful.

Singapore's alternative has been to adopt the partnership approach of having 'many helping hands' to do the job. It remains open to question whether such an approach to providing the necessary social safety nets for different groups of Singaporeans will remain a viable alternative. If it works – either in its present form or modified and fine-tuned over time – the Singapore case will be a useful model for other countries to adopt and adapt. It will also mean the availability of more policy options for countries to strike a healthy balance between economic growth and human well-being. If it does not work, then the government of the day will have to face the seemingly inevitable: that you cannot have welfarism without being a welfare state of some sort. For the near future, the indications are that Singapore does not need to go down that path, just yet.

Appendix: Background Information on Singapore

(*Source*: Ministry of Information, Communications and the Arts 2002: 37; 45–50)

Land size (main and small islands)	682.7 sq km
Total Population (June 2001):	4,131,200
Citizens and permanent residents (resident population)	3,319,100
Foreigners residing 1 year or more	812,100
Population density (per sq. km)	6,055

Resident Population

Table 5.A1 Population profile (mostly descendants of immigrants from Malay Peninsula, China and Indian subcontinent)

Ethnic group	Proportion (mid-2001, percentage)
Malays	13.9
Chinese	76.6
Indians	7.9
Other races	1.5

Life expectancy at birth	Females: 80.4 years
	Males: 76.4 years
Infant mortality rate (per 1,000 live births)	2.2
Median age	34.6 years
Population growth rate	1.7
Sex ratio (males per 1,000 females)	996

Table 5.A2 Population estimates by sex and age group (end June 2001)

Sex	Total	Age group (years)							
		0–9	10–19	20–29	30–39	40–49	50–59	60–69	70+
Females (N) (thousand)	1,663.2	223.4	221.6	243.5	309.7	293.9	174.9	108.2	88.1
Males (N) (thousand)	1,656.0	238.4	236.6	234.7	301.5	299.9	175.6	101.5	67.9
Females (per cent)	100.0*	13.4	13.3	14.6	18.6	17.7	10.5	6.5	5.3
Males (per cent)	100.0	14.4	14.3	14.2	18.2	18.1	10.6	6.1	4.1

*Rounding effect.

General literacy rate (per 100 residents aged 15 years and over): 93.2 per cent
  Females 96.8 per cent
  Males 89.7 per cent
Labour force as percentage of population aged 15 years and over 65.4
Per capita GNP (S$) 37,433
Percentage of population living in public housing 85.0
No. of doctors per 10,000 people 14
No. of home telephone lines per 10,000 people 3,483

Table 5.A3 Religious affiliation (those aged 15 years and above) (Census 2000 data)

Total	Buddhism	Islam	Christianity	Taoism	Hinduism	Other religions	No religion
2,494,630	1,060,662	371,660	364,087	212,344	99,904	15,879	370,094
100.0%	42.5	14.9	14.6	8.5	4.0	0.6	14.8

Notes

Parts of the paper are extracted from another paper on 'Globalization, Competitiveness and a Greying Population: The Challenge for Social Security in Singapore', presented at the Second Asia Regional Conference on Social Security, 24–26 January 2000, Hong Kong.

1   At present, HE The President is Mr S. R. Nathan, one of the graduates in the pioneering class of students of the Department of Social Work and Psychology in 1952 (then known as the Department of Applied Social Studies).
2   More details about Medisave are given below.
3   Details about the top-up schemes are given below.
4   Information about the CPF Scheme and contribution rates were taken from its homepage at: http://www.cpf.gov.sg. Very recently, during the annual Budget Debate in Parliament in March 2003, revisions to some of the contribution rates and their maximum amounts were announced, with details to be provided to the public later.
5   The MediShield, MediShield Plus and IncomeShield schemes are discussed below.
6   Additional top-ups were given periodically over time to eligible CPF contributors, depending on the availability of budget surpluses. Other types of top-ups were also given to Singapore citizens such the New Singapore Shares and the Economic Restructuring Shares, with older adults receiving a higher quantum of these shares.
7   Known as NTUC Income, it is an insurance cooperative society of the Singapore National Trades Union Congress.
8   This and other sums mentioned in the quotation are in Singapore dollars.

References

ASEAN Secretariat (1997). *Asean at 30.* Jakarta: The Secretariat.
Asher, M. G. (1996). Financing old age in Southeast Asia: an overview. In D. Singh and T. K. Liak (eds), *Southeast Asian Affairs.* Singapore: Institute of Southeast Asian Studies, pp. 72–98.
Baharudin, Z. (2002). Singapore 2002: The Remaking of Singapore. In *Singapore 2002.* Singapore: Ministry of Information, Communications and the Arts, pp. 2–12.
Chen, A. J. and Cheung, P. P. L. (1998). *The Elderly in Singapore: Singapore Country Report,* Phase III Asean Population Project, Socio-Economic Consequences of the Ageing of the Population. Singapore: Population Coordinating Unit.
Cheung, P. (1994). *Yearbook of Statistics, Singapore 1993.* Singapore: Department of Statistics.
Chew, E. C. T. (1991). The foundation of a British settlement. In E. C. T. Chew and E. Lee (eds), *A History of Singapore.* Singapore: Oxford University Press, pp. 36–40.
Chua, M. H. (1993). PM spells out welfare policy, S'pore-style. *Sunday Times (Singapore)* (12 September): 1.
Church, P. (ed.) (1995). *Focus on Southeast Asia.* St Leonards, NSW, Australia: Allen and Unwin.
Department of Statistics (1993). *Singapore Census of Population 1990: Literacy, Languages Spoken and Education,* Statistical Release 3. Singapore: The Department.
Department of Statistics (1995). *Yearbook of Statistics Singapore, 1995.* Singapore: The Department.
Department of Statistics (1996). *Yearbook of Statistics, 1996.* Singapore: The Department.

George, V. and Wilding, P. (1976). *Ideology and Social Welfare*. London: Routledge and Kegan Paul.

Goh, K. S. (1972). Some delusions of the decade of development. In *The Economics of Modernization and Other Essays*. Singapore: Asia Pacific Press.

Government of Singapore (1991). *Singapore: The Next Lap*. Singapore: Times Editions.

Inter-ministerial Committee on Ageing Report (1999). Singapore: Ministry of Community Development.

Kim, J.-J. A. (1991). Geographical setting. In E. C. T. Chew and E. Lee (eds), *A History of Singapore*. Singapore: Oxford University Press, pp. 3–14.

Lau, K. E. (1992). *Singapore Census of Population 1990: Demographic Characteristics*, Statistical Release 1. Singapore: Department of Statistics.

Lee Kuan Yew (2000). *From Third World to First: The Singapore Story: 1965–2000*. Singapore: Times Editions.

Leow, B. G. (2001a). *Census of Population 2000: Demographic Characteristics*. Singapore: Department of Statistics.

Leow, B. G. (2001b). *Census of Population 2000: Households and Housing*. Singapore: Department of Statistics.

Lim, B. H. (1994). Family values. Speech at the opening of the NTUC Seminar on Family Values, 19 November, at NTUC Pasir Ris Resort. (Mimeo.)

Lim, L. Y. C. (1989). Social welfare. In K. S. Sandhu and P. Wheatley (eds), *The Management of Success: The Molding of Modern Singapore*. Singapore: Institute of Southeast Asian Studies.

Low, L. and Aw, T. C. (1997). *Housing a Healthy, Educated and Wealthy Nation through the CPF*. Singapore: Times Academic Press for the Institute of Policy Studies.

Ministry of Community Development (1989). *Report of the Advisory Council on the Aged*. Singapore: The Ministry.

Ministry of Community Development (1997). *Annual Report 96/97*. Singapore: The Ministry.

Ministry of Community Development and Sports (2003). Homepage: www.mcds.gov.sg.

Ministry of Culture (1977). Philosophy of government. *The Mirror: A Weekly Almanac of Current Affairs*, 13, 9 (28 February).

Ministry of Health (2003). Homepage: www.moh.gov.sg.

Ministry of Information and the Arts (1997a). *Singapore Facts and Pictures 1997*. Singapore: The Ministry.

Ministry of Information and the Arts (1997b) *Singapore 1997: A Review of 1996*. Singapore: The Ministry.

Ministry of Information and the Arts (1998). *Singapore 1998: A Review of 1997*. Singapore: The Ministry.

Ministry of Information, Communication and the Arts (2002). *Singapore 2002*. Singapore: The Ministry.

National Council of Social Service (1998). *Annual Report 1997*. Singapore: The Council.

Ngiam, T. L. (1997a). The elderly in Singapore in the context of economic and social development. In *Ageing and the Elderly in Asia*. Tokyo: Social Work Research Institute, Japan College of Social Work, pp. 121–40.

Ngiam, T. L. (1997b). The family in Singapore: issues, challenges and responses. Paper presented at the International Seminar on the Family in the Context of Social and Economic Development, organized by the Social Work Research Institute, at the Japan College of Social Work, Tokyo, 4–7 November.

Ngiam, T. L. and Vasoo, S. (1998). Reviewing social and policy impacts of Singapore's Central Provident Fund. Paper presented at the International Conference on New Prospects for Social Welfare System in East Asia: Health Care, Pension and

Employment Services, at the Department of Social Policy and Social Work, National Chi Nan University, Taiwan, 10–12 April.

Shantakumar, G. (1994). *The Aged Population of Singapore*. Singapore: Census of Population, 1990, Monograph No. 1.

Sherraden, M., et al. (1995). Social policy based on assets: the impact of Singapore's Central Provident Fund. *Asian Journal of Political Science*, 3, 2 (December): 112–133.

Singapore Department of Statistics (2003). *Singapore in Brief 2003*. Singapore: Ministry of Trade and Industry.

Singapore Parliament Reports (2003). Vol. 76, No. 12. Singapore: Parliament of Singapore, 21 March.

United Nations (1998). Economic and Social Commission for Asia and the Pacific, *Lifelong Preparation for Old Age in Asia and the Pacific*. New York: United Nations.

United Nations Development Programme (1998). *Human Development Report 1998*. New York: Oxford University Press for UNDP.

Wee, A. (1986). Early social work resource literature in Singapore. In B. K. Kapur (ed.), *Singapore Studies: Critical Surveys of the Humanities and Social Sciences*. Singapore: Singapore University Press for the Centre for Advanced Studies, Faculty of Arts and Social Sciences, National University of Singapore.

Yap, M. T. (1991). *Social Services: The Next Lap*. Singapore: Times Academic Press for the Institute of Policy Studies.

Chapter 6

Ageing Issues and Policy in Hong Kong: Lessons for Other Countries

Joe C. B. Leung

Introduction

Historically, Hong Kong has been known for its reliance on the family rather than on publicly financed social welfare programmes to provide social protection against contingencies. The Hong Kong government has always refused to develop a comprehensive social security system similar to the welfare states in the West covering contingencies such as old age, unemployment and sickness, even though it evidently has had the economic capacity to do so. Ironically, even though Hong Kong is not a 'welfare state', its quality of life measured in terms of the Human Development Index was ranked twenty-sixth in the world in 2003, down from twenty-third in 2002. In particular, life expectancy at birth was ranked third in the world after Japan and Sweden (United Nations Development Programme 2003: 237). With a per capita GDP of US$24,850 in terms of Purchasing Power Parity in 2001, Hong Kong was ranked fifteenth in the world. Its income level is even higher than some of the European countries, such as Germany, the United Kingdom, Sweden, Italy and France (United Nations Development Programme 2003: 237). Nevertheless, the Hong Kong government has only maintained a residual means-tested public assistance programme to offer a safety net for those whose income falls below the prescribed level.

With Hong Kong facing a rapidly ageing society, a privately operated Mandatory Provident Fund (MPF) scheme has just been introduced, but it will take another 30–40 years for the scheme to provide sufficient income protection to the younger workforce. Over the years, the government has developed an integrated network of long-term care (LTC). This chapter describes the background and provides an analysis of these programmes in the context of economic recession and demographic transition. The operation of the MPF is basically dependent on the private sector, while the government acts as a regulator. Being financed fully by public funds, the public assistance scheme and the LTC system have to face the issue of mounting demands and expenditures. Finally, this chapter, based on the Hong Kong experience, discerns key lessons for other countries.

Traditions of Social Policy and Family Care for the Elderly

Under the cherished philosophy of 'minimum intervention', government intervention in social welfare has been limited. As Hong Kong was a society of migrants from 1949, the colonial government was afraid that any improvement in social services and social protection would entice more people from mainland China to come to Hong Kong. Therefore, it was mainly the responsibility of the voluntary sector – churches and traditional charity groups – to provide limited social welfare support and relief to those people living in hardship. The government was partially responsible for relief in kind (food rations). However, with Hong Kong's expanding population and thriving economy, and with the need to maintain social stability, the government, in 1971, reluctantly took over the responsibility of providing public assistance in the form of cash payments. The basic rate included food, fuel and light, clothing, transport and durable goods. Over the years, the government has continually improved the public assistance scheme. The Review Report on the Comprehensive Social Security Assistance (CSSA) scheme published in 1998 claimed (Social Welfare Department 1998: 2):

> Over the years, apart from inflation adjustments, many improvement measures have been introduced. These included real increases in payment rates, provision of disregarded earnings, and introduction of special supplements and a wide range of special grants to take account of changes in social expectations and to meet special needs of different categories of recipients. The Scheme has evolved from a scheme providing for basic subsistence to a comprehensive safety net meeting not only the basic but also individual needs of its recipients.

However, thoughts of introducing a more comprehensive social security system, including contributory and publicly financed social insurance schemes for retirement and health care, not to mention unemployment, have been rejected. To be sure, the government introduced the non-contributory and universal Disability and Infirmity Allowance and the Old Age Allowance (OAA) in 1973 (Jones 1990; Brewer and MacPherson 1997). These universal allowances, now called Social Security Allowance, are meant to provide financial assistance to families to relieve the burden of caring for their older and disabled members. In practice, they can often provide meagre financial support to enable these disadvantaged people to avoid relying on the public assistance scheme. For the Old Age Allowance scheme, those elders aged 65–69 may receive a monthly payment of HK$625 (US$1 = HK$7.80) subject to making an income and asset declaration, while those aged 70 or above receive HK$705 a month regardless of means.

As Hong Kong does not aspire to a social security or income protection system based on 'risk-sharing' and 'income redistribution', the possibility of introducing a state-subsidized social insurance retirement scheme based on cross-generational support or adopting a pay-as-you-go approach has been obstinately rejected. Under the Colonial administration, the government did not have a compulsory pension system, and only about 30 per cent of the workforce was covered by privately operated pension funds, with another 5 per cent, constituting the civil service, being entitled to non-contributory government pensions (Tang 1997). Most retirees had to rely mainly on their own savings and family support and, in the last resort, the government-financed CSSA to ensure financial security. Facing the prospect of an ageing society and economic insecurity, the present government reluctantly introduced the MPF scheme (see below), which is financed by both employers and employees. Under this privately operated scheme, the value of individual and employer responsibility is emphasized. The role of the government is merely to regulate and supervise these private pension plans. This development seems to confirm Kwon Huck-ju's claim that East Asian states play an important role in welfare, but only as regulators. Instead of providing services by themselves or using fiscal and spending instruments, they rely on their regulatory power to force the private sector to provide and finance specific types of welfare benefits (Kwon 1998).

In most of its policy papers, the government has reiterated the need to maintain the cultural tradition of relying on the family as the central resource to support the elderly. However, as family size continues to shrink and family solidarity is compromised by the rising divorce rate, the capacity of the family to support its ageing members is rapidly diminishing (Leung 1995). Such social security schemes have been identified as the defining features of welfare states. The resounding opposition from the business sector to turning Hong Kong into a welfare state has been critical to the government's decision. To the government, any commitment moving towards a welfare state would lower its economic competitiveness.

In any case, as a Chinese society, Hong Kong is supposed to espouse the cherished traditional virtue of 'filial piety', which prescribes the responsibility of children to take care of their older parents during their lives as well as after their deaths. To be specific, filial piety consists primarily of economic support, respect, obedience and caring during sickness. According to Confucius, the practice of filial piety includes providing parents with the necessary materials for the satisfaction of their physical needs and comforts, including attending to them when they are ill; paying attention to parents' wishes and obeying their preferences; and behaving in such a way as to make parents happy and to bring them honour and the respect of the community (Chow 2001: 127–8). A survey by Chow indicated that 82.5 per cent of the respondents said that they regularly gave money to their parents, while 43 per cent of them helped their parents with accommodation. To be sure, the authority of the elderly parents in exercising influence over young people is eroding (Chow 2001). Nevertheless, young people in Hong Kong still believe that they have some responsibility to meet the physical needs of their parents, and the value of filial piety is still largely intact.

A survey by the Census and Statistics Department in 1999 on the characteristics of dependent parents indicated that 30.1 per cent of persons aged 15 and over had supported their parents' living expenses in the past 12 months; and that some 57.8 per cent of them lived with their dependent parents. (Dependent parents were defined as those who received monetary support from their children, and were broadly defined to include parents-in-law, step-parents and grandparents as well.) Among the dependent parents, some 53.5 per cent were supported only by children with whom they actually lived; 21.5 per cent by children living apart, and the remaining 25 per cent by both children with whom they lived and by those living apart. In general, the percentage of persons who had supported their parents' living expenses increased with educational attainment. Persons aged between 20 and 39, economically active and with higher incomes, were more likely to be supporting their parents (Census and Statistics Department 2002). The median annual expenditure for supporting the dependent parents with whom they lived was HK$25,000, while for those dependent parents living apart it was HK$30,000. Some 23.3 per cent of these last dependent parents were themselves economically active. Another 45.9 per cent were retired persons and 29 per cent were homemakers.

The Census and Statistics Department carried out a survey of the financial disposition of the current and the next generation of older persons in 2000 (Census and Statistics Department 2001). The findings showed that the family was still the main provider, with 58 per cent of the older persons receiving contributions from adult children, averaging HK$2,300 a month. Only 12 per cent of the older persons had a formal source of income (a working income). In fact, according to the 2001 Census, the proportion of older people belonging to the labour force has declined steadily from 14.1 per cent in 1991 to 7.29 in 2001 (Census and Statistics Department 2002). In a sense, a lesser proportion of older people has had to rely on income from work to support their livelihood. In addition, some 58 per cent of them were receiving Old Age Allowance, and 89 per cent were receiving income in the form of interest from savings and dividends from stocks. Only 4.5 per cent had pensions.

Not surprisingly, therefore, the General Household Survey in 2000 had revealed that 74 per cent of households in the lowest income bracket included elderly family members, and most of these households consisted of single elderly persons or elderly couples. Some 38 per cent of older people, or 280,000 of the 750,000 elderly population, had an income of less than HK$2,000 a month (the assistance level of the CSSA), and so could be considered to be living in poverty. Of particular note is the fact that 43 per cent of them had never applied for CSSA (*Mingpao*, 2 November 2002: 11). According to the 2001 Census, some 56.8 per cent of older people still lived with their children (57.3 per cent in 1991). About 18.4 per cent of them lived with spouses only and 11.3 per cent lived alone.

The same survey, targeting the next generation of older persons, revealed that some 30 per cent of them will have retirement benefits provided voluntarily by their employers. Even though they will be financially better off than the current generation – having more investments, assets, bank deposits and income from retirement schemes – around 67 per cent of them had not made any specific arrangements for meeting their financial needs. Some 58 per cent of them still indicated that they would rely on financial support from their children after retirement. However, the fact is that, as families are getting smaller, the numbers of potential carers and supporters are going to be smaller. The survey carried out by the Census and Statistics Department in 2002 revealed that only about 38 per cent of people aged over 18 had participated in private life insurance schemes (these being more popular among educated and high-income groups). The primary reasons for participating in life insurance schemes are to protect income and to save (*Apple Daily*, 13 November 2002: 4).

The government has been criticized for paying lip service to the ideals of family care. Yet there is a tax allowance for people providing financial assistance to their parents and, in making an application for public housing, an applicant will have priority if he/she includes his/her elderly parents in the list of people to be housed. Most importantly, however, the government's commitment to the provision of heavily subsidized medical care, public housing, education and social care has been phenomenal. About half of the Hong Kong population lives in public housing, and tenants only pay a maximum of 10 per cent of their average household incomes in rent. Primary and secondary school education is free, and university students pay on average only for 17.5 per cent of the total cost of their higher education (*Mingpao*, 12 January 2003: 7). Some 96 per cent of Hong Kong residents use public hospitals, paying fees that only account for 4 per cent of the total expenses (*Mingpao*, 18 November 2002: 15.). In fact, less than 20 per cent of Hong Kong residents have any type of medical and health insurance (Harvard Report 1999). Government funding accounts for more than 80 per cent of the social welfare expenditure on social care.

All of these commitments have been able to be supported by a continuously thriving economy, government budget surpluses and a substantial amount of government reserves – before 1997. Hence, social service expenditures still only constitute a small proportion of the government budget and total GDP (see table 6.1). For developed countries, government expenditures on health care and education can amount to 5–6 per cent and 5 per cent of GDP respectively (United Nations Development Programme 2003: 254, 266). Noteworthy is the fact that all these social programmes have been financed by a low-tax system in which corporate taxation and maximum personal income tax rates have been 16 per cent and 15 per cent respectively.

Table 6.1   Social service expenditures as a proportion of government budget and total GDP in 2002

	Expenditure (HK$)	Proportion of government budget (%)	Proportion of total GDP (%)
Education	49.3 billion	24.1	3.9
Health care	32.4 billion	15.8	2.5
Social welfare	32.1 billion	15.7	2.5

Source: Radio Television Hong Kong (2003).

In summary, Hong Kong has been an economically prosperous place: perhaps the only top rich place in the world not governed by a popularly elected government and which is not a 'welfare state' by Western standards. The Hong Kong experience runs counter to the 'modernization theory' that democracy and welfare states are inevitable outcomes of economic growth (Rieger and Leibfried 2003). It has maintained low social expenditures, yet its quality of life remains high. As it was a 'borrowed place', the colonial government neither had a long-term commitment to develop a comprehensive social security system, nor was it under popular pressure to do so. Social welfare issues have not been a popularly contested topic on the government agenda. Even though there is growing awareness of citizenship rights, welfare provisions have never been rights-based (Tam and Yeung 1994). All along, from the colonial government to the government of the Special Administrative Region, the dominant governing philosophy has been to keep a balanced budget, maintain a low and simple taxation system, uphold the work ethic, minimize labour costs, and ensure that the role of the government remains residualistic, leaving individuals and families to bear the major responsibility for protecting themselves against social risks and contingencies.

The Ageing Population and Economic Recession

According to the 2001 Population Census, the population of Hong Kong stands at 6,708,389. In recent years, population growth has mainly been a result of the increase in migration rather than of natural growth. The natural growth rate was only 2.7 per 1,000 population, declining from 4.9 per 1,000 population in 1996. The natural increase in population in 1999 was only 19,800 persons, accounting for only 13 per cent of the total growth, compared with 23 per cent in 1996. Between 2002 and 2031, natural increase is likely to account for only 7 per cent of total population increase (Health and Welfare Bureau/Social Welfare Department 2002). The existing policy of allowing a quota of 150 migrants to move into Hong Kong from mainland China each day will remain the major cause of population increase.

Due to low fertility and mortality rates, the population is ageing fast. In 2001, life expectancy at birth was 78.2 years for men and 84.1 years for women, as compared with 75.2 and 80.7 years respectively in 1991. By 2031, it will be 82.3 years for men and 87.8 years for women. The median age rose from 31 in 1991 to 36 in 2001. The proportion of the population aged 65 and over rose from 8.7 to 11.1 per cent over the same period. In 2001, the number of elderly reached 0.75 million. By 2031, it is estimated that the proportion of the population who are elderly will have reached 24.3 per cent, or 2.1 million people (see table 6.2).

Concomitantly, the elderly dependency ratio (the number of persons aged 65 or over per 1,000 persons aged between 15 and 64) will increase from 155 in 2001 to 380 in 2031, and the proportion of the 'old-old' (aged 85 or over) from 0.9 per cent to 2.4 per cent over the same period (see table 6.3).

The postwar baby boomers, now middle-aged, will enter their old age in the coming decades. Many of them, such as those who are low-skilled, poorly educated, or who have been engaged in manufacturing jobs, will be affected by the rapidly developing knowledge-based economy. The 2001 Census showed that the educational standard of some 45.5 per cent of people aged 50–59 was below primary school level (Census and Statistics Department 2002). Some of them will become unemployed or under-employed, and others will be forced to retire early. Many of them will have to turn to the public assistance scheme for help.

Table 6.2 The ageing population over the years

Year	Population aged over 65 (%)		Population aged over 85 (%)	
1981	344,300	(6.6)	16,400	(0.3)
1991	502,400	(8.7)	29,700	(0.5)
2001	753,600	(11.1)	62,600	(0.9)
2011	919,700	(12.2)	116,300	(1.5)
2021	1,414,000	(17.2)	186,000	(2.3)
2031	2,120,000	(24.3)	209,000	(2.4)

Source: Census and Statistics Department (2003).

Table 6.3 Total population and elderly population growth rates

Year	Annual growth rate (%)	
	Total population	Older persons
1997	0.8	2.7
1998	0.8	2.8
1999	1.0	2.8
2000	0.9	3.3
2001	0.9	3.3
Projected		
2006	1.2	2.4
2011	1.1	1.7
2016	0.9	4.3
2021	0.8	4.5
2026	0.6	4.7
2031	0.5	3.6

Source: Census and Statistics Department (2003).

After decades of continuous economic growth, Hong Kong experienced unprecedented negative GDP growth of –5.1 per cent in 1998. The growth rate in 2001 was only 0.6 per cent. Inflation rates have also recorded negative growth. From 1998 to 2002, the consumer price index declined by 11.5 per cent and wages stayed roughly the same, with the median household income at around HK$18,000 a month (*South China Morning Post*, 11 November 2002: 3). Meanwhile, the Official Receiver's Office revealed that a record of 25,300 people declared bankruptcy in 2002, compared to a total of only 9,151 personal bankruptcies in 2001 (*South China Morning Post*, 18 January 2003: 3). As a consequence of economic setback, along with the continued expansion of the supply of labour, and more extensive corporate downsizing and layoffs, the unemployment rate rose dramatically from 2.2 per cent in 1997 to 5.1 per cent in 2001, and further to 7.8 per cent by July 2002, equivalent to 275,000 unemployed persons (Hong Kong Special Administrative Government 2003). The government budget revealed a substantial deficit of HK$65.5 billion (equivalent to 5.2 per cent of GDP) in 2000/1, and a projected deficit of HK$45.2 billion (revised estimate of HK$80 billion) for 2002/3. The government has pledged to reduce public spending, and control its own spending by decreasing it from 24 per cent of GDP in 2002/3 to 20 per cent by 2006/7 (Hong Kong Trade Development Council 2003a). In fact, the proportion of the economy constituting public expenditure increased from around 16 per cent in the mid-1980s to about 17 per cent in the mid-1990s and then to 22 per cent in 2001–2.

According to data from the 2001 Census, the median monthly household income in 2001 was HK$18,705, compared to HK$9,964 in 1991. The monthly median wage increased from HK$5,170 to HK$10,000 over the same period. As an increasingly unequal society, the Gini coefficient of Hong Kong, at 0.434, was ranked the fifth highest, after the South American countries, in the world in 2003 (United Nations Development Programme 2003). If half the median wage is used as the poverty line, the proportion of the population living in poverty reached 16.1 per cent in 2000, compared to only 11.7 per cent in 1991 (Hong Kong Council of Social Services 2001). Based on this measurement, 22.2 per cent of children aged under 15 live in poverty. The poverty rate for older persons is 31.7 per cent.

The Mandatory Provident Fund

Regarding the development of pension schemes, heated public debate raged in 1985–6 over the proposed government-operated central provident fund for retirement benefits. Eventually, it became evident that the government preferred to work towards facilitating and regulating the development of private pensions. In 1993, the Occupational Retirement Schemes Ordinance came into effect. Under this ordinance, all employers had to register their retirement schemes with the government. The main requirements were professional certification from the legal, actuarial and accountancy professions, and, after initially registering all schemes, annual registration (Watson Wyatt Data Services 2000: 82).

In 1995, the government enacted the MPF Scheme Ordinance, which required all employers to provide retirement arrangements for all their employees. The long-awaited pension scheme in the form of 'compulsory savings' was finally introduced in 2000. Under this scheme, contributions from employers and employees are put into individual accounts. Benefits received after retirement as a lump sum are dependent on contributions and investment return. One of the main differences of the MPF scheme from previous provident fund designs is that the employer contributions are fixed. The earlier schemes required a percentage of salary/wage contribution that increased with an employee's length of service.

The MPF is a mandatory savings programme. Unlike other social insurance programmes, all accounts are individualized. It does not involve risk-pooling and interpersonal redistribution. Exemptions are granted to domestic employees, self-employed hawkers, non-residents temporarily working in Hong Kong, civil servants, and members of occupational retirement schemes that have obtained MPF exemption. The MPF requires joint contributions by the employer and employee, each contributing 5 per cent of the employee's income (which includes salary, leave pay, fees, commission, bonuses, gratuities and allowances) to a registered trust scheme managed by approved trustees. The accrued benefits are fully vested in the scheme members and can be transferred from scheme to scheme when employees change or cease employment. A self-employed person will have to contribute 5 per cent of his or her income. There are minimum and maximum levels of relevant income. Those employees whose monthly income is below HK$5,000 (raised from HK$4,000 in 2002) are not required to contribute (though their employers are still required to do so). No mandatory contributions are required beyond the income level of HK$20,000 per month. Employers, employees, and self-employed persons may choose to make additional contributions to the schemes (Hong Kong Trade Development Council 2003b).

Contributions from employers and self-employed persons are regarded as operating expenses and are therefore tax-deductible. MPF benefits, constituting the total employer and employee contributions plus investment earnings, will be preserved and become payable when the member attains the retirement age of 65, or attains the age of 60 and retires early, permanently departs from Hong Kong, becomes totally incapacitated, or dies. Benefits are also to be portable from one MPF scheme to another on change or cessation of employment. After a massive publicity and educational campaign, MPF products became available on the market in February 2000 and contributions to the schemes began in December 2000. Employers, employees and self-employed persons had a variety of choices of service providers. Meanwhile, existing retirement schemes could seek exemption from the new mandatory schemes.

The whole system was to be supervised by a newly established MPF Schemes Authority. This Authority was established to regulate the operation of the MPF system and to ensure that the trustees comply with the legislative requirements. Trustees are required to submit returns, financial statements and an auditor's report to the MPF Schemes Authority on a regular basis (Hong Kong Trade Development Council 2003b). In addition, the Authority operates a Compensation Fund to provide compensation for losses of MPF scheme assets attributable to fraud or misfeasance. In essence, the funds are entirely private, as accounts are wholly contributed by employers and employees, and managed by the private sector. The role of the government is as a regulator and an enforcer of participation.

All MPF schemes can charge their members operational expenses, and they have to comply with MPF regulations on investment guidelines. These regulations include a requirement of a minimum exposure to Hong Kong dollars of 30 per cent, and the compulsory inclusion of a Capital Preservation Product designed to achieve a return similar to, or better than, bank deposits. MPF schemes also have to provide investment choice to their members (Watson Wyatt Data Services 2000).

According to the Census and Statistics Department, the employed population is 3.22 million people, comprising 2.82 million employees and 0.38 million self-employed persons. The MPF Schemes Authority reported that 62 per cent of the employed population should be covered under the MPF schemes, leaving 23 per cent covered under other retirement schemes, such as the Civil Service Pension Scheme and MPF Exempted Occupational Retirement Schemes Ordinance Schemes. Some 11 per cent of the employed population, including domestic employees and employees who are aged above 65 or below 18, are not required to join any local retirement schemes. By 30 June 2002, the MPF system involved 212,000 employers, 1,702,000 employees, and 297,000 self-employed persons. The population sizes relevant to the MPF system were 228,000 for employers, 1,786,000 for employees, and 360,000 for self-employed persons. The compliance rates were 92.9 per cent, 95.3 per cent, and 82.7 per cent, respectively. Since the establishment of the schemes, the overall enrolment rate has increased. However, while the compliance rates for employers and employees are gradually increasing, the rates for self-employed persons have declined from 91 per cent in December 2001 to 82.7 per cent in June 2002. This is largely due to the increase in the number of self-employed persons (Mandatory Provident Fund Schemes Authority 2002). To enforce compliance, cases have been brought to court involving failure to enrol in a scheme or remit contributions.

There has been some opposition to the system because of the declining economy and rising unemployment. The contributions constitute further costs for both employers and employees. Furthermore, it will take 30 to 40 years for the MPF to mature and even then it will hardly offer adequate income protection for low-income people. According to the Financial Services Bureau, the actuarial projects for the design of the MPF system were based on a median income of HK$10,000, a net annual investment of 1 per cent, and a contribution period of 47 years (18–64 years of age). The target income replacement rate was 40 per cent (Financial Services Bureau 2003).

As of June 2002, the MPF Authority had registered a total of 20 trustees, 311 constituent funds, 220 approved pooled investment funds, and 28,591 MPF intermediaries, comprising 473 corporations and 28,118 individuals. By 30 June 2002, the net asset values of all MPF schemes amounted to HK$47 billion. Based on a defined contribution model, the viability and return of the schemes is largely dependent on the financial performance of the funds. Because of the global economic recession, among the 252 approved pooled investment funds of the MPF, 176 (70 per cent), were reported to be in the red in October 2002 (Mandatory Provident Fund Schemes Authority 2002).

To sum up, Hong Kong has finally set up its own retirement programme, based on a fully funded system. Looking into the future, this system should generate a large capital, reaching HK$1,000 billion in 30 years, given annual contributions of about HK$60 billion. The whole system is largely privately operated, with the government acting as regulator and supervisor. The schemes currently cover 85 per cent of the workforce, including the self-employed, and compliance rates so far have been satisfactory. Yet in the face of an economic recession, both the profits of employers and the wages of employees are declining. Most small business operators and low-skilled employees have found the MPF contributions to be costly. More importantly, most participants have found the return on investments less than promising, and the vital issue of whether the schemes can ensure basic living standards after retirement remains uncertain. To be sure, with only a two-year history, it is too early to comment on the long-term viability of the system. What is certain is that it cannot provide adequate retirement protection to the *present* generation of older persons and those who are going to retire within the next 20 or 30 years.

Comprehensive Social Security Assistance

Social assistance is non-contributory, financed mainly by taxation and government revenue. It is a means-tested benefit. The CSSA Scheme in Hong Kong provides cash allowances to all categories of people, including the aged, the disabled, and the sick, who suffer from financial difficulties for various reasons such as illness, unemployment and inadequate income. Subjected to a financial test, recipients have to show that their household income is insufficient to meet recognized needs, and the total value of their capital assets must not exceed the prescribed limits. In addition, able-bodied adults aged 15–59 in normal health are expected to be either working or seeking work, including participating in the Support for Self-reliance Scheme (Social Welfare Department 2003).

Elderly and severely disabled recipients can receive a relatively high rate of assistance level, while a family comprising more than three able-bodied adults or children will receive a relatively low rate per person. In addition to the standard rate, special grants can cover expenses for rent, water, burials, childcare, schooling and medical care. A long-term supplement is provided to those who are medically certified to be in ill health and those who have been receiving assistance continuously for 12 months in order to meet the extra costs of replacing household goods. Single parents are also eligible for a single-parent supplement.

Over the years, CSSA expenditure and the recipient population have continued to escalate. From 1993 to 2002, the number of CSSA cases increased 2.8 times, while expenditure increased 6.6 times (table 6.4).

In 1993, CSSA expenditure constituted only 2.6 per cent of the government budget, or 24 per cent of the total welfare expenditure. By 2002, these figures had burgeoned to 7.8 per cent and 50 per cent, respectively. By September 2002, there was a total of 262,987 cases receiving CSSA, comprising 444,453 persons, or 6.5 per cent of the total population. Regarding the age distribution of recipients, 22.9 per cent were children under 15, while 37.6 per cent were persons aged 60 or over. According to the classification of the nature of the cases, older persons constituted over half of all CSSA cases – or 16.7 per cent of all older persons aged over 60 in Hong Kong. Nevertheless, there has been a proportionate – though not an absolute – drop in such cases (table 6.5).

Table 6.4 Number of CSSA cases and expenditure over the years

Year	Cases	Expenditure (million HK$)
1990	66,675	960
1991	72,969	1,136
1992	81,975	1,409
1993	95,104	2,443
1994	109,461	3,417
1995	136,201	4,831
1996	166,720	7,128
1997	195,645	9,441
1998	218,400	13,029
1999	228,015	13,623
2000	228,263	13,560
2001	235,556	14,405
2002	262,987	16,000

Source: Social Welfare Department (various years).

Table 6.5 Composition of CSSA cases in 1993 and 2002

	1993	(%)	2002*	(%)
Old age	53,397	(65.1)	141,897	(54.0)
Permanent disability	8,051	(9.8)	14,398	(5.5)
Temporary disability/ill health	8,889	(10.9)	20,842	(7.9)
Single-parent family	4,597	(6.0)	32,262	(12.3)
Low earnings	1,007	(1.2)	10,234	(3.9)
unemployment	2,957	(3.6)	39,375	(15.0)
Others	2,777	(3.4)	3,979	(1.5)
N	81,675		262,987	

* as at July 2002.

Source: Social Welfare Department (2003).

In the 1980s and early 1990s, elderly recipients constituted on average 65 per cent of the total caseloads. Recently, however, other types of categories, such as 'unemployed' and 'single-parent families', have emerged which have resulted in many people receiving CSSA. As such, the profile of the CSSA recipients has become more heterogeneous.

One worrying trend is the rise in the proportion of CSSA recipients who are able-bodied (the unemployed, low-earners, and single parents) from only 10.8 per cent in 1993 to 30.4 per cent in September 2002. Among unemployed people receiving CSSA, those aged between 50 and 59 constituted 32 per cent of the total (*Mingpao*, 28 November 2002: 2). There is a high probability that this group of older unemployed people will remain dependent on CSSA for the rest of their lives. How these recipients might be brought back into the labour market has become a primary concern of the government. Aside from the moral issue of creating 'welfare dependency', the high rate of increase may make the CSSA scheme too costly to be sustainable.

Introduced in 1997, the Portable Comprehensive Social Security Assistance Scheme is intended to enable elderly CSSA recipients to continue to receive CSSA assistance if they choose to retire permanently to Guangdong province in mainland China. According to the 2001 Census, some 79 per cent of current older people were born in mainland China. Many of them would still have a close relationship with family members and relatives inside China. Therefore, the scheme would provide a choice for the elderly CSSA recipients to move back to China because of the availability of family care and the lower cost of living there. However, the high cost of medical care in China remains one of the major concerns of CSSA recipients. Hence, so far, there have been only 2,709 participants in this scheme, out of a total of 140,000 elderly CSSA recipients (Leung 2004).

According to the findings of the 1999–2000 Household Expenditure Survey and the 2000 Study of CSSA recipients, the estimated average monthly CSSA payments for families without any income are higher than or close to the average monthly expenditure of those non-CSSA households in the lowest 25 per cent expenditure group. Based on these findings, the government considers CSSA payments to be adequate to cover the daily necessities of the recipients (Social Welfare Department 2001). The current CSSA standard rates were derived from a household expenditure survey conducted back in 1995, and adjustments have been made in line with inflation rates. But since 1998, Hong Kong has experienced deflation. With the CSSA standard rates remaining unchanged, recipients should be 12.4 per cent better off in terms of purchasing power (*Mingpao*, 4 October 2002: 2). In fact, the proportion of benefits being spent on food decreased significantly to about 56 per cent in 1999/2000 from 69 per cent in 1994/5. On the other hand, transportation expenses for CSSA recipients doubled over the same period (*Mingpao*, 24 October 2002: 4).

With mounting CSSA expenditure, reaching HK$16.1 billion in 2002/3 and HK$18.5 billion in 2003/4, the government is actively seeking ways of controlling the level of increase. The government has warned that a reduction in benefits is inevitable (*Mingpao*, 22 October 2002: 4). Drastic measures may also include limiting the period of assistance to three years, requiring new arrivals to have been resident in Hong Kong for more than one year, increasing the amount of community work for the unemployed, and denying benefits to those unemployed who do not actively seek work. By April 2003, the beginning of the financial year, the government reduced benefit levels in line with deflation, by 11 per cent. For elderly recipients, the cut is to be carried out in two phases, in October 2003 and January 2004.

In line with the trend in population ageing, the numbers of CSSA old-age cases and recipients, as well as OAA recipients, have shown a steady increase in recent years (table 6.6).

Table 6.6 Elderly recipients and expenditures on CSSA and OAA (1996/7 to 2002/3)

	CSSA Old-age cases	CSSA Recipients	CSSA Expenditure (million $)	OAA Recipients	OAA Expenditure (million $)
1996/7	98,765	112,367	3,592	437,827	3,005
1997/8	112,067	134,232	4,570	440,814	3,238
1998/9	124,304	150,511	6,124	445,001	3,416
1999/2000	133,070	151,914	7,030	445,835	3,464
2000/1	135,409	154,291	7,211	453,734	3,563
2001/2	139,288	161,365	7,538	458,041	3,581
2002/3	141,897	167,028	7,800	457,157	3,976

Source: Health, Welfare and Food Bureau (2002).

Taken together, expenditure on the two schemes amounted to HK$11.8 billion in 2002/3, as compared with HK$6.6 billion in 1996/7. But as a proportion of the overall public expenditure and GDP, the increases have been modest, from 4.2 per cent and 0.6 per cent to 5.4 per cent and 0.9 per cent, respectively (Health, Welfare and Food Bureau 2002). By international standards, the expenditures can still be regarded as low, and the Hong Kong government can still afford to support the schemes financially, as a substitute for a publicly funded pension system.

Long-term Care

As in most other developed countries, older patients account for about half of the bed occupancy in hospitals in Hong Kong. Nevertheless, a study on the care needs of elders in Hong Kong concluded that their overall health conditions are good. About 72 per cent of the population aged 60 or above do not have any physical or cognitive impairment, and have good self-care ability. Only 3 per cent of older people have severe cognitive or physical impairment (Deloitte and Touche Consulting Group 1997). According to the experiences of developed countries, it is expected that about 5–10 per cent of the older population in Hong Kong will seek some form of assistance in long-term care. At present about 39,000 to 78,000 elders aged 65 or over are in need of some form of assistance with regard to long-term care services (Health, Welfare and Food Bureau 2003). One of the objectives of the LTC system is to relieve the financial pressure on the health-care system by moving LTC patients from hospitals to less expensive care settings, i.e. other forms of residential care and community-based care.

Building on the policy of 'ageing in place', the Hong Kong government has tried to develop a mix of integrated community and home care services to help frail elders to live at home for as long as possible. They include home-based care, day care, respite, carer support and education. For those elders who can no longer be supported at home, a continuum of residential services has been provided. They include self-care hostels and homes for the aged with a low level of care needs, and care and attention homes and nursing homes for those with a high level of needs. As such, elders do not need to leave their familiar environment when their health conditions deteriorate (Elderly Commission 2001).

The total number of places in government-subsidized residential care homes for the elderly has increased from 11,600 in 1992 to 26,200 at the end of 2002. Over the same period, the number of privately operated (for-profit) homes rose from 377 to 563, providing a total of 43,800 places (Social Welfare Department 2003). Taken together, the institutionalization rate is about 7 per cent. Among these 70,000 residential places, some 37.4 per cent are subsidized directly by the government. So, at first glance, the LTC market is dominated by the private sector. However, among those places provided by the privately operated homes, some 5,800 places are also subsidized places under the government Bought Place Scheme. In addition, there are 21,600 CSSA recipients living in private homes, with their fees being paid by the government (plus another 26,300 such CSSA recipients in subsidized homes). Altogether, therefore, the government is subsidizing a total of 53,600 places, or 76.6 per cent of the total (Health, Welfare and Food Bureau 2003). In 2002, there were 27,414 applicants on the centrally administered waiting lists for these residential places. There is an estimated waiting time of two to two and a half years for admission to subsidized places, and half a year for purchased places from the private sector (Social Welfare Department 2003).

Because of the wide range of differences involved in the different forms of subsidies, the government is intending to introduce a 'voucher' or 'money following the user' system, in which the government will subsidize directly eligible elders who have care and financial needs, to enable them to receive residential care services at homes of their own choice. All elders with care and financial needs, possibly taking into account the income and assets of the elders' children, will be means-tested to determine eligibility. In short, the key message of reform is that subsidized welfare services should be targeted towards those in need and people should be asked to shoulder a greater responsibility for their own health and care costs (Health, Welfare and Food Bureau 2003).

In terms of community-based provisions, home help and home care services now cover about 16,200 elders, and day-care centres are taking care of 1,400 frail elders. In addition, the newly introduced enhanced and integrated home and community care services support over 1,450 frail elders, so that they can continue to live at home (Social Welfare Department 2003). Introduced in 1999, the enhanced home-care programme is designed to support older persons with moderate impairments to continue to live at home through home helps, personal care, nursing, and health and carer support services. Still, for some families, the employment of domestic helpers, particularly from Southeast Asian countries is the only way to support frail elders at home.

An international standardized care need assessment mechanism (MDS-HC) has been introduced to ensure the provision of appropriate services and effective care planning. The assessment tool, introduced in 2000, assesses the care needs of older persons applying for LTC services, taking into account the physical, functional, psychological, cognitive, social and health factors of elders. Trained assessors include nurses, occupational therapists, physiotherapists working in clinics and hospitals, medical social workers, and family-care workers. Recent developments include a quality assurance mechanism, strengthening support and training for family carers, better inferfacing between health and long-term care system, re-engineering of community and home-care services to expand coverage and support, and increasing the financial contribution from the elders and their families (Elderly Commission 2001).

The expenditure on direct welfare services for elders increased from HK$0.6 billion in 1993/4 to HK$1.7 billion in 1997/8, and further to HK$3.6 billion in 2003/4 (Health, Welfare and Food Bureau 2003). Facing the escalating cost of residential care, the government has tried to strengthen community care as an alternative. Through re-engineering and upgrading existing home- and community-based services, such as the social centres for the elderly, multi-centres for the elderly, and home-help teams, the social care function of these services has been strengthened to target more vulnerable older persons. The provision of recreational and leisure activities by these services has been reduced, with the emphasis increasingly being placed on satisfying the physical and psychosocial needs of older persons. Since 2001, the government has introduced competitive bidding to invite tenders from both NGOs and the for-profit sector, to operate new care and attention home facilities. As a consequence, the operational costs have been significantly reduced.

To enhance service quality, all residential homes have to fulfil the minimum licensing requirements prescribed by the legislation. The government has also made preparations to establish an accreditation system for all the residential homes.

Finally, the government is committed to promote active and healthy ageing aimed at building up a positive image of ageing, promoting more opportunities for elders to pursue lifelong learning, and encouraging senior volunteerism, to enable older persons to remain active and to participate in both family and community.

Lessons for Other Countries

With its cherished principle of minimum intervention, Hong Kong was rated as the world's freest economy for the ninth consecutive year by the Heritage Foundation in 2002. According to the World Economic Forum, however, the economic competitiveness of Hong Kong in 2002 dropped to seventeenth among 80 countries, down from thirteenth in 2001 (*South China Morning Post*, 13 November 2002: 3). Facing negative economic growth coupled with expected budget deficits until 2006/7, the Hong Kong government has pledged to cut government spending and reduce the budget deficit (*South China Morning Post*, 15 November 2002: 7). According to the Basic Law, the mini-constitution of Hong Kong, the government should avoid budget deficits, maintain a low-tax policy, and formulate social welfare policies in the light of economic conditions and social needs.

Against this background, the government has striven to keep labour costs and regulations, as well as government expenditure, to a minimum. Influenced by the New Public Management paradigm advocated by the World Bank and the OECD, the Hong Kong government, like many European and East Asian countries, has adopted widespread pubic service reforms. Under the paradigm of the 'plural state' and 'community governance', the government is expected to increase privatization through the contracting-out and marketization of public services, complemented by its key role in developing and negotiating partnerships with the voluntary, community and private sectors (McLaughlin et al. 2002). To revitalize the private housing market, the government has ceased building public housing under the Home Ownership Scheme. In the field of medical care, the government has raised hospital fees, and now only those with financial difficulties can have these fees reduced or waived. The principle of cost-sharing implies that patients should share the cost of services, especially those who can afford to pay more (Health, Welfare and Food Bureau 2002). In the field of social welfare, the government has changed the subvention mode to delimit financial commitment, introduced competitive bidding for new projects, and included the private sector as potential providers of government-subsidized services for older persons. It has also been proposed that a means test for elderly applicants for government-subsidized homes will be introduced (*South China Morning Post*, 18 November 2002: 2). In short, the top priority of the government is to reduce costs, enhance productivity, and empower the private market to provide services (Leung 2002).

In this climate, the Hong Kong government is not convinced of the need for, or the feasibility of, a social security system based on social insurance and the redistribution of risk. So it will not introduce any publicly funded social insurance system for unemployment, medical care or retirement. Likewise, it will avoid any social security scheme that would place an additional burden on the private sector. With the benefit of hindsight, having no defined-benefits social insurance system, financed by pay-as-you-go contributions and supported by high rates of personal income and social security taxes, Hong Kong has no need to face the uncertainties and the intractable issues being experienced by many OECD countries trying to re-engineer their pension systems. Overall, the strength of the Hong Kong system, amidst all its shortcomings, is the persistent reliance on individual and family responsibility (Health, Welfare and Food Bureau 2002). Without a strong government commitment, individuals have to look to other means of protection for their old age, such as family support and personal savings – or working for longer.

In this context, the CSSA and the OAA will continue to be overloaded, having to cope with rising numbers of older persons devoid of pensions. A public opinion survey has revealed that more people regard the use of public services as their right (Hong Kong Federation of Youth Groups 2002). Thus the stigma associated with seeking help from public assistance should become less of a deterrent. There remains a small group of older persons, lacking family support or retirement benefits, who will prefer to live at subsistence level supported mainly by the OAA. But the size of this group of people should shrink in the future.

The MPF will remain the major retirement scheme for people in Hong Kong, and it is expected that there will be only a few minor adjustments to the system in the coming years. But since it will be another 40 years before the MPF can effectively provide financial support to retirees, more and more older persons are going to have to rely on CSSA for financial protection in the meantime. As such, CSSA expenditure will continue to increase – since it would be dangerous, politically, if the government's commitment to provide CSSA support to the elderly were to be reduced.

On the whole, the development of the social security system in Hong Kong has lagged behind that of other East Asian countries where there are already established social insurance-based programmes for retirement and health care. The Hong Kong government is steadfastly committed to its traditional role as a regulator and facilitator of retirement protection, and as a provider of a basic means-tested public assistance. Overall, the government claimed that Hong Kong has in place the recommended three-pillar approach of the World Bank for old-age financial protection (Health and Welfare Bureau 2001b):

1   First pillar of a compulsory public plan for poverty alleviation and prevention – the CSSA and the Social Security Allowance Scheme.
2   Second pillar of a privately managed compulsory pension plan for income maintenance – the MPF Scheme launched in 2000.
3   Third pillar of a voluntary savings-annuity plan to supplement the first two pillars to provide supplementary sources of retirement income – the high saving rates of Hong Kong residents.

At first glance, Hong Kong's social policy addressing the needs of older persons has more shortcomings than strengths – and so can hardly provide a clear learning model for other countries. Nevertheless, there are Hong Kong experiences which can stimulate policy discussion.

The traditional value of filial piety has been eroded. Yet the commitment to provide care for elderly parents is still strong. The majority of older persons are still dependent on the care and support provided by family members. Unlike Singapore and mainland China, Hong Kong has rejected the idea of using legislation to enforce the obligation of grown-up children to provide financial support for their elderly needy parents. Nevertheless, in taxation and public housing policy, there are incentives to encourage the exercise of filial obligations. To be sure, many older persons, living at subsistence level, remain influenced by the traditional virtues of self-reliance, and would regard it as a shame to be dependent on welfare. The issue of how these virtues are to be sustained and encouraged by the government will remain high on the policy agenda.

Under its multi-pronged approach, the government of Hong Kong is confident that the multiple needs of older people can be met satisfactorily (Health, Welfare and Food Bureau 2002). So, in a sense, Hong Kong might be considered a 'welfare state', even though it does not have a publicly financed pension system. The essential question is whether the social assistance scheme, together with the OAA, can be financially viable and sustainable in the long term. Yet, given the low-tax environment, there remains room for a moderate increase in taxes to support welfare programmes. Indeed, the use of social assistance and social allowances, supplemented with LTC services, may be a viable alternative to developing a costly social-insurance type of pension system, which cannot, in any case, fully guarantee financial security for all the vulnerable elders.

References

Brewer, B. and S. MacPherson (1997). Poverty and social security. In P. Wilding, A. S. Huque, and J. Tao (eds), *Social Policy in Hong Kong*. Aldershot: E. Elgar.

Census and Statistics Department (2001), *Thematic Household Survey, Report No. 11*. Website: www.info.gov.hk/censtatd.

Census and Statistics Department (2002). *2001 Population Census, Thematic Report – Older Persons*. Website: www.info.gov.hk/censtatd.

Census and Statistics Department (2003). *Hong Kong Population Projections 2002-2031*. Website: www.info.gov.hk/censtatd.

Chow, N. (1998). The making of social policy in Hong Kong: social welfare development in the 1980s and 1990s. In R. Goodman, G. White and H. J. Kwon (eds), *The East Asian Welfare Model: Welfare Orientalism and the State*. London: Routledge.

Chow, N. (2001). The practice of filial piety among the Chinese in Hong Kong. In I. Chi, N. Chappell and J. Lubben (eds). *Elderly Chinese in Pacific Rim Countries – Social Support and Integration*. Hong Kong: The University of Hong Kong Press.

Deloitte & Touche Consulting Group (1997). *Study of the Needs of Elderly People in Hong Kong for Residential Care and Community Support Services* (November). Hong Kong: Social Welfare Department.

Elderly Commission (2001). *Long Term Care for the Frail Elders*, Discussion Paper (20 September). Hong Kong: Elderly Commission.

Financial Services Bureau (2003). *1997 Policy Programme*. Website: www.info.gov.hk/pa97/english/pfsb.htm.

Harvard Report (1999). *Improving Hong Kong's Health Care System: Why and for Whom?* Hong Kong: Government Printing Office.

Health and Welfare Bureau (2001a). *2001 Policy Address – Care for Elders*. Hong Kong: Government Printer.

Health and Welfare Bureau (2001b). Financial Support for Older Persons, *Legislative Council Panel on Welfare* Services (9 July). Hong Kong: Health and Welfare Bureau.

Health and Welfare Bureau/Social Welfare Department (2002). *Implications of 2001 Population Census on the Provision of Social Welfare Services*, Social Welfare Advisory Committee Paper No. 12/02 (March).

Health, Welfare and Food Bureau (2002). *Financial Assistance for Older Persons*. LegCo Panel On Welfare Services, Paper No. CB(2)294/02-03(15) (11 November).

Health, Welfare and Food Bureau (2003). *Subsidy Arrangements for Residential Care Services for Frail Elders*, Legislative Council Panel on Welfare Services, Paper No. CB(2)2015/02-03(03) (12 May).

Hong Kong Council of Social Services (2001). *Views on Poverty Alleviation Procedures Submitted to the Welfare Panel of the Legislative Council* (November). Hong Kong: Hong Kong Council of Social Services.

Hong Kong Federation of Youth Groups (2002). *A Study on Social Capital with Regard to Citizenship* (October). Hong Kong: Hong Kong Federation of Youth Groups.

Hong Kong Special Administrative Government (2003). *The Hong Kong Economy.* Website: www.info.gov.hk/hkecon/labour/content/htm.

Hong Kong Trade Development Council (2003a). *Economic and Trade Information on Hong Kong.* Website: www.tdctrade.com/main/200010s5.htm

Hong Kong Trade Development Council (2003b). *Guide to Mandatory Provident Fund.* Website: www.tdctrade.com/sme/gmpf.htm.

Jones, C. (1990). *Promoting Prosperity: The Hong Kong Way of Social Policy.* Hong Kong: Chinese University Press.

Kwon, H. J. (1998). Democracy and the politics of social welfare: a comparative analysis of welfare systems in East Asia. In R. Goodman, G. White and H. J. Kwon (eds), *The East Asian Welfare Model: Welfare Orientalism and the State.* London: Routledge.

Leung, J. (1995). Social welfare. In S. Cheung and S. Sze (eds), *The Other Hong Kong Report.* Hong Kong: The Chinese University Press.

Leung, J. (2002). The advent of managerialism in social welfare: the case of Hong Kong, *Hong Kong Journal of Social Welfare*, 36, 1: 61–81.

Leung, J. (2004). A review of the portable comprehensive social security assistance for elderly persons retiring to Guangdong Province. In A. Yeh (ed.), *Socio-economic and Infrastructure Development for a Competitive Pearl River Delta.* Hong Kong: The University of Hong Kong Press.

Mandatory Provident Fund Schemes Authority (2002). *Mandatory Provident Fund Schemes Statistical Digest* (June). Hong Kong: Mandatory Provident Fund Schemes Authority.

McLaughlin, K., S. Osborne and E. Ferlie (eds) (2002). *New Public Management: Current Trends and Future Prospects.* London: Routledge.

Radio Television Hong Kong (2003). Website: www.rthk.org.hk/special/budget2002.

Rieger, E. and S. Leibfried (2003). *Limits to Globalization – Welfare States and the World Economy.* Cambridge: Polity Press.

Tang, K. L. (1997). Noncontributory pensions in Hong Kong: an alternative to social security. In J. Midgley (ed.), *Alternatives to Social Security: An International Inquiry.* Westport, CT: Auburn House.

Social Welfare Department (1998). *Report on Review of CSSA* (December). Hong Kong: Government Publishers.

Social Welfare Department (2001). *The CSSA Safety Net.* Social Welfare Advisory Committee Paper No. 10/01 (November). Hong Kong: Social Welfare Department.

Social Welfare Department (2003). Website: www.info.gov.hk/swd.

Social Welfare Department (various years). *Departmental Report.* Hong Kong: Government Printer.

Tam, T. and S. Yeung (1994). Community perception of social welfare and its relations to familism, political orientation, and individual rights: the case of Hong Kong, *International Social Work*, 37: 47–60.

United Nations Development Programme (2003). *Human Development Report 2003.* New York: Oxford University Press.

Watson Wyatt Data Services (2000). *Benefits Report: Asia/Pacific.* Hong Kong: Watson Wyatt Worldwide.

Chapter 7

Universal Values Versus Political Ideology: The Virtual Reform Experience of Taiwan's National Pension Plan

Hsiao-hung Nancy Chen

Introduction

This chapter seeks to illustrate the underlying significance of the various national pension plans proposed in Taiwan under the governments led by the Kuomintang (KMT) and the Democratic Progressive Party (DPP). Both parties have placed great importance on the planning of a national pension system, but the stark differences in their approaches underscore a deeper ideological rift.

Respecting the values of diligence and thrift in Chinese culture and preoccupied with economic growth, social security during the period of KMT rule was limited to the truly needy, and the roles of the public (government) and the private (individual, family and community) sectors were clearly demarcated. When multiparty politics first emerged in Taiwan in 1987 and the question of a social security system could no longer be delayed, priority was given to planning a social insurance system and not a 'taxation system', reflecting both the KMT government's desire to keep the country on a solid financial footing and nodding to the enduring culture of 'self-help and mutual help' in Taiwan. An individual account system was rejected, in part for fear of the complications that a 'mentality of dishonesty' would present in implementation. However, when the DPP – the self-proclaimed spokesman of the disadvantaged – came into power in 2000, it continued to support the idea of a tax-based national programme providing basic guarantees for retired people. Nevertheless, it later bowed to the need for financial stability by proposing a savings insurance system in the spirit of defined contribution and merging the functions of an insurance and savings plan. This initiative led to a revision of the plan that had been formulated over several years by the KMT. The display of *realpolitik* in the process further exemplified the differences between the two parties on the welfare issue. The DPP (a party claiming to care more about the well-being of the less privileged groups in society) was trying to work out a pension scheme based on taxation policy when it came in to power in May 2000. It was hoped by them that anyone over 65 might receive NT$5,000 and even more per month from the government. However, financial constraints made it impossible to adapt such a system built purely on taxation.

Therefore, the DPP, instead of accepting the scheme charted out by its predecessor the KMT, came up with two major sets of planning ideas, which will be elucidated in a later section of this chapter. Worth emphasizing here, though, is that even if the DPP could not deliver NT$5,000 per month to the elderly, it somehow has managed to provide NT$3,000 in monthly allowances to those over 65 since 2003, not only to fulfil the party's political promise during the last presidential election but demarcating the differences between the two parties' stands on the pension issue.

Coinciding with these events was the spread of globalization. Income redistribution, financial viability, economic efficiency, social equity, and the other driving concepts in the welfare reforms vigorously promoted by advanced Western countries had long become the accepted yardstick and commonly accepted values for planning pension systems. To be sure, such planning had technical as well as structural dimensions. Most countries approached the technical aspects, including premium rates, benefits and fund management, according to 'rational' rules. In Taiwan, the deep-rooted ideal of ensuring 'a secure future for the elderly, jobs for the able-bodied, the means of development for children, and care for widowers, widows, orphans, those without family, and the handicapped' came up against the limits of reality. Globalization, it seemed, offered a chance of restoring reason to the welfare debate, and the hope that the pensions issue would soon be disentangled from purely political considerations.

The Ethos and Background of Social Security Establishments under the KMT

The concept of social security emerged in Chinese society some 2,500 years ago in Confucius's Commonwealth ideal of 'Chapter of Great Harmony'. Yet the systematic promotion of such a system would have to wait until the implementation of the national health insurance programme in 1995! Under the KMT leadership, Taiwan introduced an insurance-based social security system catering to the healthcare needs of the country. Soon after, the government began formulating a national pension system, offering a guaranteed pension for the elderly.

Economy-led Social Security Development

Analysed from an ideological viewpoint, it is easy to identify the 'two fears' that drove the KMT, which had long pursued rapid economic growth and whose expertise was rooted in finance, economics, science and engineering. One was the fear of giving such preference to social security that people were discouraged from working. The other was the fear of dampening the willingness of people to save. These worries contributed to the 'passive' social welfare attitude of the party towards social security. KMT leaders regularly emphasized the importance of the family for steering Taiwan away from repeating the mistakes that led to the financial headaches of Europe and America. In consequence, the DPP derided the social security of the KMT period as 'residual' welfare.

Factors Impinging on the Development of Social Security in Taiwan

Oddly, while the KMT government originally had no intention of actively expanding social security, several subjective and objective factors emerging in the late 1980s compelled the KMT to move in this direction. Specifically, the opposition DPP was whipping up expectations at the city and county level for government subsidies to people aged 65 or older. In the contest for voters, the then ruling KMT government was forced to promote aggressively a series of social security policies and measures. A further, underlying factor was the rapid greying of Taiwan's population. Currently, 9 per cent of the population in Taiwan is over 65 years of age, and this percentage is expected to double in 26 years, far faster than in advanced welfare states, such as France (115 years), Sweden (85 years), and the USA (69 years) (see figure 7.1).

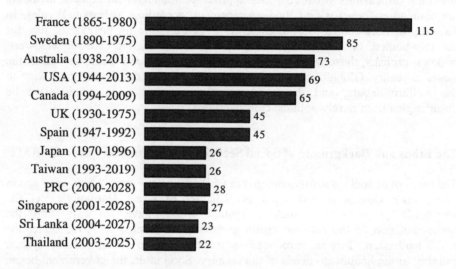

France (1865-1980) — 115
Sweden (1890-1975) — 85
Australia (1938-2011) — 73
USA (1944-2013) — 69
Canada (1994-2009) — 65
UK (1930-1975) — 45
Spain (1947-1992) — 45
Japan (1970-1996) — 26
Taiwan (1993-2019) — 26
PRC (2000-2028) — 28
Singapore (2001-2028) — 27
Sri Lanka (2004-2027) — 23
Thailand (2003-2025) — 22

Figure 7.1 Comparative ageing in Taiwan: number of years required for the ratio of those aged 65+ to the total population to grow from 7 to 14 per cent

Source: CEPD (2002).

Moreover, the rapid ageing of Taiwan has coincided with a decline in the number of households in which parents are living with their adult children. In 1986, the cohabitation rate stood at 70.2 per cent. A decade later the figure had fallen to 64.3 per cent. At the same time, the ratio of economic support contributed to retired people by their children has steadily declined from 65.8 per cent in 1986 to 48.3 per cent in 1996 (see table 7.1). Family structure has also altered considerably. The number of nuclear families has soared, the divorce rate and the percentage of unmarried people has increased, and the number of single-parent/single-person households is rising, creating a major demand for welfare resources to care for the young and elderly. The increased participation of women in the workforce has added to the number of double-income households, but it has also weakened the function of household care and increased the burden on the public welfare system. Moreover, economic adjustment in Taiwan has exacerbated the problem of structural unemployment, while increased public awareness of 'welfare rights' has heightened the public's expectations of the state welfare system, forcing the authorities to respond. Regrettably, these increased demands on government welfare come as Taiwan's economy is slowing and its financial position is weakening. Since 1999, Taiwan's public debt has worsened from 1.3 per cent of gross domestic product (GDP) to 4.8 per cent in 2000, and it remained at 4.3, 4.2 and 4.0 per cent in 2001, 2002 and 2003, respectively. Even with the overall improving economy in 2004, the deficit is expected to remain. Moreover, Taiwan's star economy – once such a source of pride for the country – has faded in recent years to the point where the luxury of double-digit growth has given way to the shame of recession.

Table 7.1   Trends in the number of the aged and their living conditions in Taiwan

Ratio of the aged (65+) to working population (15–64) (%)

Year	1998	2002	2025
65+/15–64	11.9	12.7	25.2

Living arrangements (%)

Year	1986	1996	1998	2001
Living alone	—	—	11.30	10.55
With their children	70.2	64.3	—	—
With spouse only and living alone	24.93	32.9	—	29.05

Source of living expenses (%)

Year	1986	1996
From their children	65.8	48.3

Source: Compiled from *Social Indicators: The Republic of China 2001*, published by Directorate-general of Budget, Accounting and Statistics, Executive Yuan, Republic of China (2002).

Current Income Maintenance Systems

Before moving on to the details of the National Pension Scheme, a brief illustration of the current income maintenance systems geared to the elderly would seem appropriate. From tables 7.2 and 7.3, it can be observed that in Taiwan there are two working systems containing provisions for old-age benefit. One is based on the social insurance scheme targeted at civil servants, teachers, military servicemen, labourers, etc. The other is by nature more of a social assistance scheme. The first system consists of a first and a second tier of benefit/allowance, whereas the second takes the form of either a living/welfare allowance or a social assistance/subsidy. In addition, retirees covered by the social insurance scheme can choose between lump-sum and monthly payment, whereas beneficiaries under the social assistance scheme can only get a monthly means-tested cash payment. In summary, the following are considered the main weaknesses of the existing old-age benefit schemes:

(1) *Limited coverage*: Of the total population of 22.41 million (2001) in Taiwan, about 4.5 million people in the age group 25 to 64 lacked any form of economic safeguard. It is estimated that 32 per cent of those aged between 25 and 64 have never been covered for old-age benefit and 22 per cent of those over 65 is without any forms of old-age benefit (see table 7.2).

Table 7.2 Coverage of social insurance including old-age benefit, 2001

Category	Population (000)	Population (%)
Total population aged 25–64	12,120	100.0
Covered by Social Insurance Scheme	7,570	63.0
Persons have already claimed old-age benefit	710	6.0
Persons never covered by old-age benefit	3,840	32.0
Coverage of Old-age Income Protection		
Total population aged 65+	1,970	100.0
Without any forms of old-age benefits	450	22.8

Source: CEPD (2002).

(2) *Specifically biased coverage*: The existing system covers mainly public sector employees with the possible exception of private school teachers, labourers and elderly farmers – though there are still discrepancies among these in terms of government subsidies, coverage, insurance fee, etc. Since civil servants, military servicemen, schoolteachers and farmers were considered to be the principal supporters of the KMT government, such a system left much room for criticism from the then opposition party, whose own supporters came mainly from relatively less privileged groups. The DPP often cynically labelled the existing social welfare system as 'Civil servants, Military Servicemen and Teachers' welfare'. Hence the reform stance of the DPP government itself, which in recent years has favoured cutting off benefits granted to civil servants, military servicemen and teachers. To be specific, as of 2003, former policy with regard to special premium provision (around NT$500,000 per person) for those who retired at age 55 with 25 working years has been terminated. The 18 per cent interest rate for pensions has also undergone severe reassessment, and is likely to be either cancelled or reduced to a

lower rate soon. The government is also studying the possibility of postponing the current retirement age from 65 to either 67 or even 70. Strict criteria as to when one can start to receive a monthly annuity rather than a lump-sum pension are also being studied seriously. Recently, the government even proposed to put a stop to those veterans' elderly allowances should they move to Mainland China after retirement, mainly for ideological considerations.

Table 7.3 Social insurance: the status quo in Taiwan

Item	Insured population (2002)	Insured item	Insurance fee rate (%)	Government subsidy (billion NT$)
Civil Servant Insurance		Disability, pension, decease, family survivors' decease	6.40	78.9
Teachers and Staffs' Insurance of Private Schools	626,652	Disability, pension, decease, family survivors' decease	4.75	2.6
Govt. Retirees' Insurance	836	Disability, pension, decease, family survivors' decease	8.00	—
Military Servicemen Insurance	420,000 (1999)	Disability, veteran, decease	8.00	56.0
Farmers' Health Insurance	1,748,558	Birth, disability, funeral and burial	2.55	39.5
Labour Insurance	7,857,842	Birth, disease, disability, pension, decease (survivors), unemployment	6.50	245.7
National Health Insurance	21,869,000	Disease, injury, birth	4.25	680.0

Source: Compiled by the author from various sources.

Table 7.4 Income maintenance for the aged population

Category	Old-age benefit/allowance		Average payment (NT$)	
			Lump sum	Monthly payment
(A) Social Insurance Scheme (2002)				
Retired civil servants	2nd Tier	Government Employees, Teachers and Military Servicemen's Retirement and Compensation Fund	186,374	10,652
	1st Tier	Old-age Benefit of Government Employees and Teachers' Insurance	1,380,794	—
Retired private schoolteachers and	2nd Tier	Private Schoolteachers and Staffs' Retirement and Compensation Fund	n/a	11,733
administrative staffs	1st Tier	Old-age Benefit of Government Employees and Teachers' Insurance	668,209	—
Retired labour	2nd Tier	Labour Retirement Fund under Labour Standards Law	1,200,364	—
	1st Tier	Old-age Benefit of Labour Insurance	883,055	—
Retired military servicemen	2nd Tier	Government Employees, Teachers and Military Servicemen's Retirement and Compensation Fund	n/a	n/a
	1st Tier	Retirement Benefit of Military Servicemen's Insurance		
(B) Social Assistance Scheme (2002)				
Veteran	Living allowance		—	13,100
Middle- and low-income	Living Allowance Below 1.5 times official poverty line		—	6,000
senior citizens	1.5–2.5 times official poverty line		—	3,000
	Living Subsidy of Social Assistance		—	6,000–13,288
Aged farmers' allowance	Welfare Allowance		—	3,000

Source: CEPD (2002).

In short, the system as it now stands seems tilted very much in favour of particular groups in society, thus arousing feelings of unfairness among other groups in society. For instance, as indicated above, while about one-quarter of the total population receives no retirement benefits at all, civil servants can enjoy as much as a 95 per cent income replacement rate after retirement (see table 7.5). Furthermore, a proportion of their pension funds is eligible for an 18 per cent bank interest rate (compared to the ordinary interest rate of 1–2 per cent). Figures 7.2 and 7.3 demonstrated the differences of old-age benefits among different groups in both lump-sum and monthly payment terms.

Table 7.5 Income replacement rate of civil servants' pension

Position ranking and wage point	Monthly pension income replacement rate (%)	Lump-sum income replacement rate (%)
800 point	98.61	78.49
535 point	97.71	77.24
370 point	95.28	75.72

Note: The point system can be taken as denoting different ranks in an organization. The higher rank one gets, the higher the point one gets in terms of salary and, consequently, pension as well.

Source: Examination Yuan and Control Yuan (2002).

Moreover, since the minimum working years qualification for retirement is 25 for civil servants and schoolteachers, many of them retire in their early fifties and enter another career, while continuing to receive their monthly pension. In addition, they receive both first- and second-tier old-age benefits/allowances. As of September 2002, supplementary retirement fund attendance grants were claimed by 292,186 (47.39 per cent) of civil servants, 323 (0.05 per cent) of retired high-ranking officials, 201,708 (32.72 per cent) of teachers and 122,269 (19.83 per cent) of military servicemen (Executive Yuan and Control Yuan 2002). The Supplementary Retirement Fund for military servicemen, civil servants and public schoolteachers was established in 1995. Before the end of 2003 the fee was set at around 8 per cent of doubled basic salary, of which 65 per cent is taken care of by the government whereas 35 per cent is shouldered by the employee. The government has to work out the fee through an annual budget while the military servicemen, civil servants and public schoolteachers as employees are levied the fee through their monthly salary. According to the Civil Servants Insurance Law, the fee is set at between 8 and 12 per cent. However, due to the growing ageing trend, less than efficient fund management, as well as government financial constraints, the fee was increased from 8.8 to 9.8 per cent as of January 2004. The law allows the Fund to be used to purchase government bonds, certain stocks, mutual funds, etc., by contracting out to money market-related institutions. In order to maintain a viable stock market, the government nevertheless, since 2000, often utilized the Fund together with the Labourers' Fund, and the Postal Fund to interfere in the stock market, thus arousing some suspicion and mistrust among civil servants, particularly about the future adequacy of the Fund. This perhaps explains why nowadays many civil servants retire early at about 50 or 55.

(3) *Lump-sum vs. monthly payments:* Although 470,000 people over 65 years of age receive social insurance benefits, payments are mostly made in one lump sum, leaving them vulnerable to inflation. There is consequently a need for government policies to address the issue of poverty among the elderly, specifically through the integration of current old-age benefits systems and insurance and subsidies into one cohesive national pension scheme.

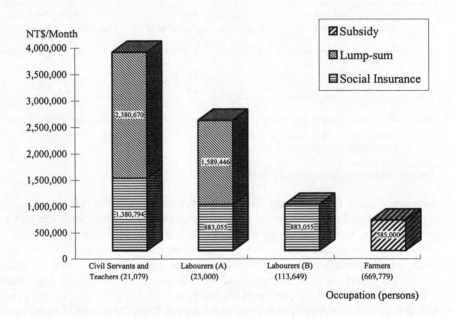

Figure 7.2   Lump-sum old-age economic security: a comparison among civil servants, teachers, labourers and farmers (2002)

Notes:
1. Labour (A) = labourers received a pension according to Labour Standard Law (the lump-sum figure is 'mean').
2. Labour (B) = labourers received old-age benefits through Labour Insurance (the lump-sum figure is 'mean').
3. Aged farmers' subsidies = NT$3,000* 12 (months)* 16.3 years (average lifespan for farmers after 65).

Source: Compiled by the author from various statistics.

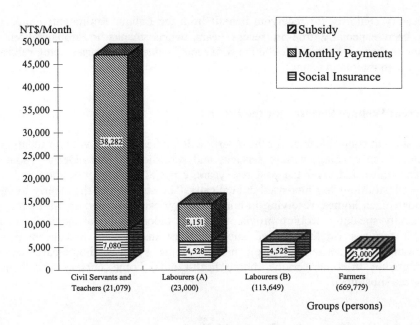

Figure 7.3 Monthly old-age economic security: a comparison among civil servants, teachers, labourers and farmers (2002)

Source: Calculated from figure 7.2.

(4) *Non-portable working experience:* Insured working years among the existing social insurance programmes are normally non-portable, thus hampering labour mobility.

(5) *Imprecise retirement age eligibility:* The age of initial entitlement for old-age benefit is too low, especially among elementary schoolteachers and military servicemen. This not only augments the governmental financial burden, but also constitutes a waste of manpower.

(6) *Unrealistic law/regulations:* Due to the frequency of job-change, linked to the short average lifespan of the small and medium-sized enterprises that make up 95 per cent or more of Taiwan's industry, few of their employees can acquire the

necessary seniority for receiving benefit from the Labour Retirement Fund. This has been especially true in recent years, when, thanks to globalization, the economy has seen lots of deliberate bankruptcies due to industries being relocated (mainly in mainland China).

Current Welfare Services for the Elderly

The story of social security for the elderly will not be complete without mentioning some of the existing welfare services and subsidies for the elderly. Table 7.6 demonstrates that, over the past few years, especially after 1998, the number of caring institutions has increased dramatically. The numbers of the elderly living in senior citizen homes, receiving in-house and day-care services, are all increasing. Generally speaking, welfare provisions for the elderly include: medical care and health services (including free supplementary instruments and hospital care allowances for serious disease); nursing home services; home-care services (comprising in-home service, home health aids, home nursery and housing services/subsidies).

Table 7.6 Welfare services for the elderly

Year	Aged 65+ (no.)	Caring institution			Elderly receiving domiciliary service (no.)	Elderly receiving day-care service (no.)
		Caring inst. (no.)	Caring persons (no.)	Elderly living in senior citizen house (%)		
1994	1,562,356	54	—	—	161,496	119,912
1995	1,631,054	61	—	—	152,541	184,513
1996	1,691,608	64	9,215	0.5	165,297	197,086
1997	1,752,056	70	9,759	0.6	193,221	256,132
1998	1,810,231	83	9,779	0.5	294,645	314,358
1999	1,856,472	237	12,100	0.7	580,870	176,659
2000	1,921,308	524	17,579	0.9	699,724	215,393

Source: Directorate-General of Budget, Accounting and Statistics, Executive Yuan, R.O.C., *Social Indicators of the Republic of China* (2002), pp.154–5.

However, the absence of an integrated national pension system has given rise to a host of different subsidy programmes, including subsidies for elderly people in low- to middle-income households, elderly farmers, and veterans. An estimated 710,000 people currently receive such benefits (see table 7.7) and, as the number of applicants grows, the financial burden on the state also mounts. Because these subsidies are tied to the particular status of the recipient, there has been much debate over the social inequity of this system also, making it a perennial issue for reform at election time.

Table 7.7 Various welfare subsidies for the elderly in Taiwan

Item	Eligibility	Monthly allowances	Recipients
Low-income elderly living allowances	Aged 65+ whose family income is lower than 1.5–2.5 times the set minimum income standard	NT$3,000–6,000	As of December 2001, 205,000 elders have benefited (10% of the total elderly population)
Elderly farmers' welfare subsidies	Aged 65+ joining farmers' insurance or its equivalents for more than six months	NT$3,000	By November 2001, 654,000 farmers have benefited (33% of the elderly population)
Low-income households' disabled living allowances	Disabled whose average family income per person per month is lower than 2.5 times the set minimum living standard	NT$2,000–6,000 per person per month (according to degree of disability).	346,953 persons (53.47% of the total disabled)
Veterans' living allowances	Veterans fit certain conditions and pass means tests (such as in service for more than 10 years or injured or disabled) during the war.	NT$13,100 (2001)	As of December 1999, altogether 120,094 veterans benefiting
The elderly welfare allowances	Per county/city	NT$3,000–5,000 per month per person.	

Source: Compiled by the author from various sources.

As the population ages, long-term care will soon become a priority for elderly welfare services. Table 7.8 shows the forecast long-term home-care demand for the period 1995 to 2035. The data reveal that the number of elders needing both a carer and supplementary instruments (such as wheelchairs, walkers, etc.) will be higher than those needing only a carer. This certainly represents another pressure on government to think about elderly welfare in terms other than income maintenance. The Bureau of Health strongly suggested that long-term care should be made part and parcel of the pension scheme, during the latter's planning process under the KMT. However, cognizant of the likely heavy financial burden, the KMT government declined this proposal and instead endorsed a three-year pilot project on long-term care. A group of scholars, with backgrounds in public health, social work and public finance, have worked on this ever since 2000. This pilot project, geared to 'ageing in place', expects to achieve the following goals:

- the integration of health and social welfare to provide comprehensive long-term care to disabled people;
- the establishment of a community-based service network;
- the establishment of a care management system;
- an estimate of the long-term care costs of supporting family caregiver;
- placing emphasis on the provision of home and community services.

Table 7.8 Forecast demand for long-term domiciliary care in Taiwan, 1995–2035 (000)

Item/category		1995	2000	2010	2020	2030	2035
Three ADLs and above	A	62.9	77.3	106.7	145.9	223.6	265.6
	B	46.7	57.5	80.5	109.7	166.6	199.0
Two ADLs and above	A	83.1	100.9	139.4	192.1	289.0	341.9
	B	60.9	73.9	102.8	141.7	212.3	252.7
Any one ADL	A	113.3	138.7	192.4	262.5	398.1	469.0
	B	76.3	93.2	128.8	175.7	266.3	315.9
Any one ADL or IADL	A	253.6	310.5	439.7	611.2	917.5	1,097.6
	B	244.6	299.7	424.6	590.5	887.1	1,062.3
Any one ADL or cognitive barrier	A	309.9	379.4	535.3	747.3	1,125.1	1,335.0
	B	301.6	369.4	521.2	727.9	1,096.7	1,302.1

Notes:
A = needs both caregiver and supplementary instruments; B = needs caregiver only;
ADLs = activities of daily living; IADLs = instrumental activities of daily living. The former stands for things such as eating, putting on clothing, going to the toilet, taking a shower/bath, and getting on/off the bed. The latter depicts activities such as shopping, washing clothes, cooking, domestic chores, outdoor walking, making phone calls, taking medicine and dealing with money.

Source: Wu et al. (1998: 23).

It is exactly with this in mind that the government started to think seriously about launching a national pension scheme. Originally, the scheme was intended to cover all people above 25 or in the workforce, but it turned out that the scheme was eventually to cover only those not so far participating in the system of old-age benefits/allowances. In itself, this was a comment on the country's worsening financial viability after the DPP stepped into power in 2000.

Planning the First-stage 'National Pension' System: In the Spirit of Social Insurance

The first stage of Taiwan's national pension plan, drafted at the end of the KMT administration (2000), was based on the spirit of social insurance with a particular emphasis on managing the financial burdens of this system. The main planning strategies were as follows:

(1) Under the principle of 'separation of tasks, integration of content', to progressively integrate the various existing old-age economic security systems, the new pension system, together with the existing social insurance systems and social assistance plans into one comprehensive system.

The national pension insurance plan was the most important social security policy to be formulated by this government since the national health insurance plan. Its purpose was to address the shortcomings mentioned above in the system of guarantees available to elderly retirees in Taiwan at that time.

In order to bring about an integrated system, planners thus considered an approach by which new beneficiaries would have to join the new system, whereas existing beneficiaries would be allowed to choose, within a one-year period, to take part in the new or old plan. Additionally, in order to achieve the income redistribution effects of social insurance, the national pension was made into a 'compulsory insurance' plan, with a special 'means-tested floor', below which low-income earners would receive an NT$3,000 subsidy.

(2) Reflecting limited public financing and downward international economic trends, this national pension plan embraced the spirit of the World Bank's 'Three Pillar' system. It began, pragmatically, with the provision of a basic pension, later to be extended to include an occupational (supplementary) pension, at the same time as creating an environment conducive to the introduction of various commercial pension funds.

In other words, to prevent the problem of poverty among the elderly, the government was prepared to adopt a pay-as-you-go (PAYG) plan or at least a partially funded plan, as its first (basic) pillar of living guarantees for retirees. On this foundation, a second (occupational/supplementary) pillar could be offered to military personnel, civil servants, teachers and workers, using compulsory savings methods to encourage their participation in occupation-specific pension plans – or else the 'defined-contribution' method specified for pension systems under the Labour Standards Law of 1984. Moreover, under the principle of voluntary savings, a fully funded system could be adopted to encourage individuals and households to save or buy commercial pension insurance to further solidify their financial safety nets in later life, with the government simply providing tax incentives to this end. The state, employers, families and individuals would therefore assume different roles at the various levels of this pension plan.

(3) Premium-linked benefit – under which the standard of benefits is set according to an even weighting of the consumer price index and the actual rate of wage increase, to achieve 50 per cent of average consumer spending over the long term – was intended to safeguard the financial position of retirees while also reflecting the need for financial viability.

(4) An additional levy of 20 per cent on business tax (effectively raising the business tax by 1 per cent) was imposed to fund the government's national pension system and its social insurance financial obligations, thus amply reflecting the considerations of feasibility and fairness/universality in this planning process.

(5) In order to prevent abuses of the system, careful standards were specified. For instance, pensions for the physically and mentally handicapped were limited to people with major or severe disabilities – a stipulation strongly contested by groups representing handicapped people. Different benefit amounts were also stipulated for survivor annuities, depending on whether the surviving spouse or children were employed or out of work. These stipulations simply proclaimed that this was to be an 'insurance' system, rather than a 'welfare' plan. A pension system should naturally provide special care for the disadvantaged, but without giving rise to an attitude of dependence.

The above key characteristics underlined the perceived key importance of 'economic efficiency' and 'social equity' as the dominant criteria in the planning of a first-stage national pension plan. The plan was set to be implemented at the end of 2000, but it was effectively postponed by the '921' earthquake in 1999 (so called because it occurred on 21 September) and then shelved as a result of the transfer of political power to the DPP in 2000.

New Government, New Version

Since assuming power in 2000, the new (DPP) government has revised the national pension system several times. Although no final decision has been made to date, after three years of exchanges between the various parties under the charge of the minister-without-portfolio, an economist, Dr Hu Sheng-cheng, two versions[1] seem to have emerged calling, respectively, for a 'national pension savings insurance system' and a 'national contribution balanced fund' (see tables 7.9 and 7.10, or figures 7.4 and 7.5). However, after the National Social Welfare Conference in late May 2002, public opinion seemed to favour a 'social insurance system'. It remains to be seen whether new variables will emerge once the plan is submitted to the legislature for deliberation.

Table 7.9 The features of NPI

	Compulsory	Those not covered by any social insurance
Nature		
	Voluntary	• Those who had claimed old-age payment of social insurance • The insurer of Farmers' Insurance
Benefits		*Old-age, disability, survivors and funeral*
Full pension		NT$7,500 (first year), indexed by CPI and wage level (50% of each)
Old-age pension		• Under 5 years: lump-sum payment, 1 year for 1 unit of full pension • 5 years and over: full pension* (insured months/480) • Guaranteed minimum pension: NT$3,000
Disability pension		• Extremely disabled: 40% of full pension • Heavily disabled: 20% of full pension
Survivors' payment		Under 1 insured year: 5 units of full pension 1 insured year and over: 5 units of full pension + 2 insured years for 1 unit
Funeral allowance		5 units of full pension
Contribution		NT$750/month (subsidy NT$150 + individual NT$600), may be adjusted based on financial solvency
Subsidy		
Citizens		20% (NT$150)
The disabled		• Slightly disabled: 40% (NT$300) • Medium disabled: 60% (NT$450) • Extremely disabled: 100% (NT$750)
Low-income citizens		• Medium- and low-income: 40% (NT$300) • The poor: 100% (NT$750/month)
Welfare allowance		Old-age allowance: NT$3,000 (means-tested)

Source: CEPD (2002).

Table 7.10 Comparison of the different versions of Taiwan's National Pension Plan, as compared with existing welfare subsidies for the elderly

Versions	KMT Version	DPP Versions		Welfare subsidies for elderly
		National pension savings insurance system	National contribution balanced fund	
Nature of the system	Social insurance	Savings insurance and social insurance	Taxation	Taxation
Integration with other social insurance	May and/or may not integrate	May and/or may not integrate; possibility of integration is lower than for the KMT version	Feasibility of integration is rather low	No integration
Coverage	Old-age, disability, survivors' pension, funeral allowances	Old-age, disability, survivors' pension, funeral allowances	Old-age, disability, and orphanage pension	Old-age benefit
Allowances: Old-age	• Full pension: NT$8,700/month • Transitional period, NT$3,000 /month is guaranteed	• Defined contribution. • Full pension: NT$7,500/month 3. Transitional period, NT$3,000/month is guaranteed	• NT$3,000/month for the first year after implementation • Payment to be adjusted according to price index and government financial situation	NT$3,000 /month is fixed and will not be adjusted

Disability	• Extremely seriously disabled: 100% full pension • Seriously disabled: 80% full pension	• Extremely seriously disabled: 100% full pension • Seriously disabled: 80% full pension	• NT$3,000/month for the first year after implementation • Will be adjusted according to price index and government financial situation	None
Survivors	• Spouse pension: 40% full pension • Siblings pension: 60–100% full pension • Parents pension: 40% each for full pension; may go as high as 100% • Have to choose one from the aforementioned	• Spouse pension: 40% full pension • Siblings pension: 60–100% full pension • Parents pension: 40% each for full pension; may go as high as 100% • Have to choose one from the aforementioned	• Orphanage pension: NT$2,000 for the first year after implementation • Will be adjusted according to price index and government financial situation	None
Income replacement rate	• Full pension: 23% • Real old-age pension for 2002 is 8%; will reach 23% by 2031	• Full pension: 19% • Real old-age pension for 2002 is 8%; will reach 10% by 2031	8% for 2002; 3% for 2031	8% for 2002; 1% for 2031
Financial burden	Compare to the national pension savings insurance system, the payment level is higher, the insurance fee rate is lower, financial burden is higher	NT$262 billion for 2002; NT$358–404 billion for 2031 (price index 1% or 3%)	NT$282–91 billion for 2002; NT$1.030–1.874 billion for 2031 (price index 1% or 3%)	NT$107 billion for 2002; approx. NT$220 billion for 2031

Source: CEPD (2002).

Table 7.11 Analysis and comparison of pension reforms in major European welfare states, the USA, and Taiwan

	GERMANY	BRITAIN	FRANCE	THE NETHERLANDS	UNITED STATES	TAIWAN
Elderly population	16% in 2001 (65+)	16% in 2001 (65+)	20.5% in 2000 (60+)	14% in 2001 (65+)	13% in 2001 (60+)	9.0% in 2002 (65+)
Retirement age	62 65 (in the future)	60 65 (in the future)	57 60 (in the future)	65	67	65
Labour Participation rate	57.2% (2001)	63% (2001)	—	67.0% (2001)	66.9% (2001)	57.3% (2002); 7.8% (65+)
Men	4.4% (65+)	8.3% (65+)	2.6% (65+)	3.1% (65+)	15.8% (65+)	68.2% (2002)
Women	1.6% (65+)	3.0% (65+)	1.4% (65+)	0.3% (65+)	7.9% (65+)	46.6% (2002)
Unemployment rate	10.4% (2002)	3.3% (2001)	9.0% (Sept. 2002)	2.1% (2001)	4.8% (2001)	5.17% (2002)
'Welfare state' tradition	Strong	Strong	Strong	Strong	Weak	Weak
Power of trade unions and private associations	Strong	Average	Strong	Average	Average	Weak
Soundness of capital markets	Strong	Strong	Average	Average	Strong	Weak
Soundness of financial viability	Average	Strong	Average	Average	Strong	Weak

Pension reform direction	1.From 'defined benefit' 'defined contribution' 2.Developing 'retirement savings funds'	1.From 'defined benefit' 'defined contribution' 2.Encouraging more 'individual retirement' or 'retirement savings' and 'individual account' plans	Developing a hybrid PAYG and 'funded scheme' system	1.Respect for wage modernization 2.Expansion of job opportunities 3.Juxtaposition of basic pension and retirement savings	Developing toward privatization schemes	
Impact of pension reforms on income distribution	Progressively unfavorable	Neutral	Progressively unfavorable	Neutral	Unfavorable	Neutral
Pension payment method	Linked to price index and wages	Linked to price index but not wages	Linked to wages	Linked to wages	Extrapolate social security fund from payroll tax	Linked evenly to price index and wages
Income replacement ratio	Average	Average	High	Average	Low	Military personnel, civil servants, teachers: High; Laborers: Low
Other social welfare benefits	Average	Good	Average	Average	Poor	Poor

Source: Compiled by the author from various sources.

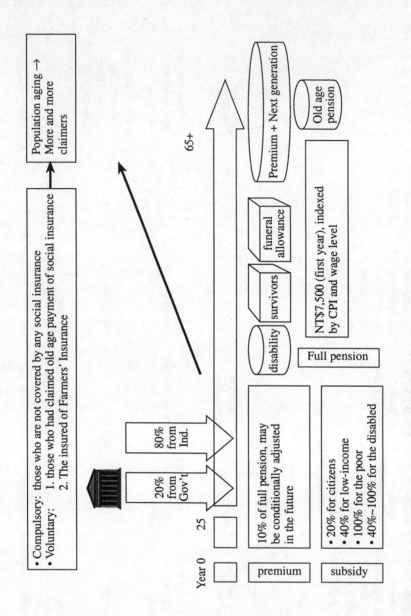

Figure 7.4 Social insurance system – National Pension Insurance

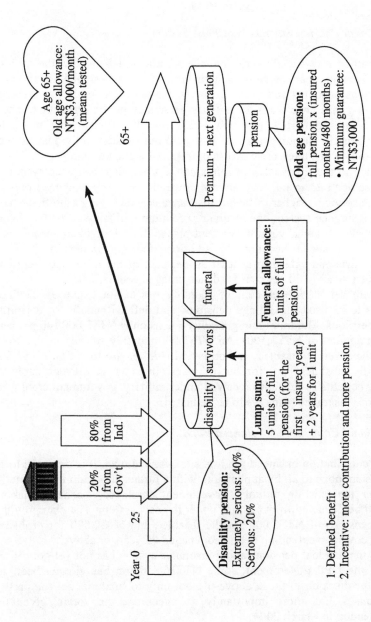

Figure 7.5 National Pension Insurance (continued)

Source: Figures 7.4 and 7.5 are derived from CEPD (2002).

Plan 1: A National Pension Savings Insurance System

As its name implies, a savings-linked insurance scheme brings together the spirit of an individual savings account and social insurance. It is designed to establish individual savings accounts and social accounts for those ineligible for coverage under the existing insurance plans for military personnel, public servants, teachers and labourers. Insured parties who have paid into the system and meet the conditions for benefits disbursement are first paid out of their individual savings accounts and, only when these are exhausted, from the social account.

Perhaps due to the financial constraints of the state, this insurance system is limited to those aged 25 to 64, who are not covered under any existing forms of military, public service, teacher or labour insurance schemes. As in the first-phase (KMT) social insurance system, the insurance premium will amount to 10 per cent of the total pension amount, with 80 per cent placed in an individual account and 20 per cent in a social account. In addition, the government will cover administrative costs and subsidize at least 20 per cent of the insurance premium, rising to between 40 and 100 per cent for disadvantaged people.

Benefits are set at 50 per cent of monthly per capita expenses. Defined contribution is to be used for old-age pensions, and defined benefit for disability and survivor pensions. The minimum guaranteed pension is NT$3,000 (40 per cent of the pension amount of NT$7,500). An NT$3,000 monthly subsidy is also to be provided for the severely disabled, and orphaned children are to get an NT$2,000 allowance, with subsidies paid for out of taxes. In order to prevent duplicate payments, any benefits or subsidies received under military, government employee, teacher or labour insurance plans are to be deducted.

Plan 2: A National Contribution Balanced Fund

The 'national contribution balanced fund' is a tax-funded plan. It is designed to be a universal system open to all by application, with a further stipulation that benefits received under the existing military, government employee, teacher or labour insurance shall be deducted from payouts under the new system. The plan provides for monthly pensions of NT$3,000 for the disabled and NT$2,000 for orphaned children, with coverage extending to all people aged 65 years or above.

Although the national pension saving insurance system has not yet got off the ground under the DPP government, some NT$160 billion has already been set aside (2003) for dispatch to those above 65, not only to 'materialize' the party's electoral promises, but, more importantly, to encourage the voters, given the presidential election in March 2004.

Table 7.10 sets out the differences between the original KMT pensions version, the two revised DPP versions and the existing array of welfare subsidies for the elderly.

Universal Values, Ideological Conflict, and Taiwan's National Pension Plan

No national pension system has been implemented in Taiwan to date, for all that it has been a decade since planning first began in November 1993. During this time, debate over the issue of social security has gradually gained focus. In respect of the pension system alone, there has been a clear domestic response to what are evidently issues of global concern. For example, what should be the obligations and rights of government/state, society, communities, the market and individuals? And how can the system be designed to achieve a balance between economic efficiency and social equity? These are not questions unique to Taiwan.

The ambitious welfare reform efforts taking place in Europe and the USA in the late 1990s have involved, to varying extents, a reorganization 'downwards' of *existing* welfare state systems. In Sweden, one of the world's leading welfare states, individual payment exemptions have been scrapped in the cause of pension reform – owing to lack of funding. Other Western European countries have followed up by extending the retirement age (for instance from 65 to 67) to relieve the financial burden on their pension systems. In several countries, reforms have focused on whether or not retirement benefits should be calculated on the basis of the highest salary earned in the course of one's working career, the average salary across the entire career, the average wages in the final years of work, or should be based on defined contributions rather than defined benefits. There has even been discussion over whether or not old-age retirement benefits should be linked to inflation or should rise in line with average wages. Meanwhile, globalization has given rise to other reform issues, such as whether or not pension safeguards should be granted to immigrants, and whether – and under what conditions – to allow for the international portability of pensions.

Clearly, to *embark* on the introduction of a comprehensive pensions system is not the same thing as (in the West) fine-tuning long-established systems considered overdue for reform – yet with their own built-in resistance to reform.

Pension Reform in Advanced Western Welfare States and its Implications for Taiwan

Since the 1990s, advanced welfare states have been forced to streamline their social security programmes in order to enhance their international competitiveness and respond to financial crises. Pension reform has been an important aspect of these efforts.

As a part of social security policy, pension systems involve broad and complex issues. Generally speaking, the experience of reform suggests the planning of pension systems has at least four repercussions:

- the impact on overall economic development, including the impact on overall savings, investment, inflation and income distribution;
- the impact on various social groups, elderly people in different income brackets, women, widows/widowers, and part-time or temporary workers;

- the impact on private organizations, such as the partnership between the agencies contracting-out and private organizations, particularly with regard to the relation between various cases and regulations under the supplementary pension plans and other social security schemes;
- technical issues, such as whether the system falls under universal or residual welfare, whether or not asset investigations are required, benefits are linked to inflation or income, the age when benefits begin, rules on the number of years of full benefit payment, and whether or not the system will be based on defined benefit or defined contribution.

Additionally, the examples of various countries show that the planning of pension systems reflects not only the country's population structure (the degree of ageing), economic development conditions, financial soundness, composition of the labour market, relations between the private and public sectors, union strength, and the soundness of capital markets, but more importantly the historical traditions and values of the country concerning social security. For example, Britain has a much stronger tradition as a 'welfare nation' than does the USA, and therefore British pension reforms have tended towards the creation of 'retirement savings funds'. However, there are also many examples of welfare programmes with a public relief tint, as is the case in the Netherlands. In less-advanced welfare states with vigorous capital markets, including the USA, privatization seems to have become a byword for pension system reform. In countries with strong unions and private social organizations, such as Germany and France, the need to secure financing for their pension schemes inevitably forces changes in the system, though only after building consensus with the unions and private organizations through extensive dialogue and negotiation. As far as the systems go, most of the plans discussed here are moving from a PAYG system to a defined-contribution plan. However, in the reform process followed by these countries it is easy to discern that the two exist simultaneously, offering another potential choice.

Concluding Remarks

To conclude, the pension reforms of various countries once again amply demonstrate that the dilemma in this process is one of how to ensure both economic efficiency and social equity. Faced with greying populations, international competition, and concerns over financial viability, the advanced welfare states of Europe and the USA have in recent years turned increasingly to market-based solutions and privatization as the keynote of their pension reform plans. Looking back from the planning of Taiwan's first-phase national pension system in 1993, no basic pension plan has been implemented so far. In comparison with the reforms made by Western countries, the experience in Taiwan can only be considered as 'virtual reform'. Regardless of whether these virtual reforms have been dictated by substantive financial difficulties, or have been the product simply of ideological conflicts between the political parties, if there is anything useful to be drawn from Western experience, it is that the moment responsibility for health-care coverage or old-age retirement guarantees passes from the individual or family to the state or market, it reflects a kind of contractual relation between the people and the state or market. And as with any effective and good contract, this relationship must be built on a foundation of mutual trust. The market or state securing this contract is obliged to make good the guarantees stipulated in the contract. On this level, the planning of Taiwan's pension system at this stage must face at least two pressing issues: First, are the people fully prepared to hand over responsibility for the pension system to the state? (Specifically, has a proper 'trust' mechanism been established?) Second, as the forerunners of the pension system shift responsibility from state to market, will Taiwan continue to insist on the original plan? Both the KMT and DPP plans imply a heavy state role/burden, however, and given the advanced countries' experiences, perhaps it would not be unwise to bypass those plans proposed by both parties and enter directly into 'the third way' which relies more on the market mechanism?

Note

1   Since more than 8 million people are covered under the existing labour insurance programme, therefore, a third version was also proposed, based on the expansion of the existing labour insurance to accommodate all those who are not joining any other existing pension programmes. However, it is likely to become a 'weak' insurance due to its voluntary nature; that is, economically disadvantaged groups may not be able to pay the insurance fee.

References

Chen, Hsiao-hung Nancy (2002). Universal values vs. ideology: dialogue between Taiwan's National Pension Plan and advanced welfare states' pension reforms. Paper presented at Cross-Strait Workshop on Changing Employment Situation and Social Protection, Beijing, China, People's University (in Chinese).

Chen, Hsiao-hung Nancy (2003). A case study of Chinese Taipei. In Chanyong Park and Kye Woo Lee (eds), *Globalization and Social Safety Nets in the Asia-Pacific Region*, Seoul, Korea: KIHASA APEC SSN CBN Head Institution, Ministry of Health and Welfare, pp. 49–86.

Council for Economic Planning and Development, Executive Yuan, July (2002). *Kuo-min nian-chin chih-tu kui-hua chien-pai* (Brief Report on the National Pension System Plan), July (in Chinese).

Council for Economic Planning and Development, Executive Yuan (CEPD) (1998). *Brief Report on the National Pension Plan*, September (in Chinese).

Council for Economic Planning and Development, Executive Yuan (CEPD) (2002). *Brief Report on the National Pension Plan*, April (in Chinese).

Clark, Gordon L. (2001). Age discrimination in financial services. Paper prepared for Help the Aged, London, UK.

Emmerson, Carl (2002). Pension reform in the United Kingdom: increasing the role of private provision? Paper presented at Conference on Pension Security in the Twenty-first Century: Redrawing the Public–Private Divide, University of Oxford, UK.

Examination Yuan and Control Yuan (2002). *An Examination Survey Report on Taiwan's Social Welfare System.* Taipei, Taiwan (in Chinese).

Kuo, Ming-cheng, Zacher, Hans F. and Hou-sheng Chan (eds) (2002). *Reform and Perspectives on Social Insurance: Lessons from the East and West: A Comparative Study of Social Insurance in China, EU, Germany, Great Britain, Japan, Sweden, Taiwan and the USA.* The Hague: Kluwer Law International.

Munnell, Alicia H. (2002). Restructuring pensions for the twenty-first century: the United States' debate. Paper presented at Conference on Pension Security in the Twenty-first Century: Redrawing the Public–Private Divide, University of Oxford, UK.

Palier, Bruno (2002). Facing pension crisis in France. Paper presented at Conference on Pension Security in the Twenty-first Century: Redrawing the Public–Private Divide, University of Oxford, UK.

Riel, Bart Van, Anton Hemerijck and Jelle Visser (2002). Is there a Dutch way to pension reform? Paper presented at Conference on Pension Security in the Twenty-first Century: Redrawing the Public–Private Divide, University of Oxford, UK.

Schmahl, Winfried (2002). A pension system in transition: private pensions as partial substitute to public pensions in Germany. Paper presented at Conference on Pension Security in the Twenty-first Century: Redrawing the Public–Private Divide, University of Oxford, UK.

United Daily News (2002). Financial Series, 24–26 June (in Chinese).

Whiteside, Noel (2002). Historical perspectives and the politics of pension reform. Paper presented at Conference on Pension Security in the Twenty-first Century: Redrawing the Public–Private Divide, University of Oxford, UK.

Wu, S. C. et al. (1998). *Taiwan's Long-term Care Policy under National Social Welfare System.* Taipei, Taiwan: Bureau of Research and Evaluation, Executive Yuan (in Chinese).

Chapter 8

National Policies on Ageing in South Korea

Sung-Jae Choi and Seong-Hoon Bae

Introduction

The rapidity of population ageing in Korea in the first quarter of the twenty-first century epitomizes the experience of developing countries which are ageing far more rapidly than the developed countries. Population ageing at this rate has been identified as a worldwide historical phenomenon which may be equivalent to the experience of globalization in the later part of the twentieth century (UN 2002) and has as great an influence on almost all aspects of social systems and the life of citizens in all countries.

The relatively gradual process of population ageing in the developed countries meant that resources could be accumulated to finance pension schemes and other social welfare policies for the aged. But developing countries that are simultaneously facing much more rapid ageing together with problems of development are likely to encounter greater difficulties in addressing ageing issues. As one of the fastest-developing countries, Korea became known as one of the rising dragons of Asia, but its economic development has lagged since the economic crisis of the later part of 1997, and annual per capita income remains around $US10,000.

Korea has tried to model its social welfare policies for the aged along the lines of Western welfare systems, but with those systems now experiencing many problems, Korea is searching for more effective and efficient measures to deal with her rapidly ageing population. With a number of alternative policies currently under discussion, the outcomes of reforms in developed countries are also being closely watched. As Korea reviews its experience of social welfare policies for the aged to date and examines measures to respond to future rapid population ageing, it may not only learn from the experience of the developed countries, but also provide some lessons for them.

This chapter begins with an account of population ageing and a profile of elderly Koreans. It then describes the policy-making context and details current policies for income support, health care and social services for the aged. Housing policies are not presented, as there has been little development in this field in recent years. In short, compared to other policy areas, housing remains an implicit part of policies on institutional care and this situation is unlikely to change until there is clear definition of long-term care policy *per se*. In concluding the discussion of the latest policy developments and prospects, some lessons from and for other countries are noted.

Population Ageing and the Profile of Elderly Koreans

Demographic Trends

Korean society began to modernize rapidly from the early 1960s when a five-year economic development plan was launched and a family-planning programme was adopted as a national policy. Fertility and mortality have since been in continual decline and life expectancy has increased substantially. In consequence, the absolute number and proportion of older people have increased greatly over the last four decades. Life expectancy at birth for men increased from 51.1 years in 1960 to 71.1 years in 2000, and for women the increase has been from 53.7 to 78.6 years. Life expectancy is projected to reach 78.4 years for men and 84.8 for women in 2030.

Within the population aged 65 and over, the higher the age bracket the faster the rate of increase, as shown in table 8.1. This means that the oldest-old are the fastest-growing segment of the elderly population.

Table 8.1 Actual and estimated number and proportion of aged population in Korea, 1960 to 2030

Year	Total population (000)	Number of elderly (000)			Percentage in older age groups		
		65+	75+	80+	65+	75+	80+
1960	25,012	726	170	59	2.9	0.7	0.2
1970	32,241	991	251	101	3.1	0.8	0.3
1980	38,124	1,456	406	176	3.8	1.1	0.5
1990	42,869	2,195	695	302	5.1	1.6	0.7
2000	47,008	3,371	1,091	483	7.2	2.3	1.0
2010	49594	5,302	1,996	957	10.7	4.0	1.9
2020	50,650	7,667	3,195	1,805	15.1	6.3	3.6
2030	50,296	11,604	4,646	2,571	23.1	9.2	5.1

Source: National Statistical Office (2000).

The proportion of Korea's population aged 65 and over increased from only 2.9 per cent in 1960 to 7.2 per cent in 2000, and is projected to reach 9.9 per cent in 2010,

13.2 per cent in 2020, and 19.3 per cent in 2030. On these projections, it will take only 19 years for the proportion of Korea's population aged 65 and over to double from 7 to 14 per cent. The rate of population ageing is unprecedented compared to that of other countries. As table 8.2 shows, the same doubling of the proportion of the aged took 115 years in France, 71 years in the USA, and 24 years in Japan (UN 1996). The further increase from 14 to 20 per cent will occur in just seven years in Korea, again a much shorter time than in the European countries, the USA or Japan.

Table 8.2 Ageing rates by selected countries

Country	Year by proportion aged 65+			Years taken	
	7%	14%	20%	7–14%	14–20%
France	1864	1979	2020	115	41
Germany	1932	1972	2012	40	40
UK	1929	1976	2021	47	45
Italy	1927	1998	2007	61	19
USA	1942	2013	2028	71	15
Japan	1970	1994	2006	24	12
Korea	*2000*	*2019*	*2026*	*19*	*7*

Source: National Statistical Office (2001b).

Living Arrangements

The proportion of elderly Koreans living separately from their children has increased steadily over the past 20 years. As shown in table 8.3, only 15 per cent lived alone or with a spouse in 1980, but by 2000, 45 per cent lived in single-person or couple-only households; this proportion is expected to reach 60 per cent by 2010. At advanced old age, however, more still live with their children, reaching 80 per cent among those aged 90 and over (National Statistical Office 2002). The latter pattern reflects long-standing family living arrangements of that generation rather than moves to live with family members as age advances, and in future more elderly Koreans can expect to live into advanced old age alone or as couples.

Notwithstanding separate living arrangements, elderly Koreans maintain close contact with their children. A national survey by Kim and others (1999) found that a majority of elderly Koreans living separately from their children saw their children or contacted them by phone at least once a week, 20 per cent did so once a month, and the remaining 13 per cent several times a year.

Economic and Employment Status

The low-income status of the current generation of elderly Koreans is the product of past patterns of retirement at an early age, the underdevelopment of income

Table 8.3   Changes in elderly Koreans' living arrangements

Living arrangement	1980[a]	1985[a]	1990[a]	1995[b]	2000[b]
Living alone	4.8	7.0	9.5	13.3	16.2
Living with spouse	9.9	12.9	17.2	23.3	28.7
Living with children/other relatives	84.8	78.2	71.9	62.6	54.7
Living with the unrelated persons	0.5	1.9	1.4	0.8	0.4

Notes:
[a]2 per cent of census data in each year.
[b]Census data in each year.

maintenance policies, unstable employment throughout life, the pressing need to support the family during the working years, and the burdens of supporting children's education and marriages (Choi and Chang 2002).

Results of a recent national survey (Sunwoo et al. 2001) showed that the monthly average income level of a majority of elderly households was below the official poverty line, which was set at 334,000 won for a single-person household and 553,000 won for a two-person household in 2001. These single and couple elderly households accounted for 45 per cent of all elderly households. The full income distribution of elderly households set out in table 8.4 shows that more than 70 per cent of single and about 50 per cent of couple households are below the poverty line, compared to only 7.7 per cent of those living with adult children. One-third of those living with other unrelated people are below the poverty line, but this is a very small group of the total elderly population.

Elderly Koreans still rely heavily on their families for their income, as shown in table 8.4. The very small fraction of the elderly whose main source of income is retirement benefits or a pension attests to the underdevelopment of income maintenance policies, as discussed further below.

The 2001 Survey of the Economically Active Population reported that just under one-third of the aged were working, as shown in table 8.5. Of those working, about a quarter are doing paid work and the rest are doing unpaid jobs; 55 per cent are engaged in agriculture and fishery, 17 per cent in daily labour, 10 per cent in service jobs, and the rest in a variety of fields. The proportion of those who are economically active, and the employment rate, decrease over the older age range, and work status tends to become increasingly irregular. Older workers are also more likely to be engaged in primary industries in which mandatory retirement ages do not apply.

The income status of the elderly is directly related to the retirement system that operated during the process of rapid industrialization which began in the early 1960s. The Korean economy has been export-oriented, and salary systems for workers in most Korean industries have been based more on seniority than individual capability. These industries therefore preferred to recruit and retain younger workers, who tended to be lower-paid than older workers (who conversely

**Table 8.4 Income distribution and source of income of elderly Koreans'
households (*N* = 3,877)**

	Total	Single elderly household	Elderly couple household	Elderly living with adult children	Elderly living with others
Household income (unit: won)					
Less than 300,000	27.7	72.1	25.1	7.7	32.8
300,000-700,000	24.9	23.5	23.5	14.4	35.4
700,000-1,100,000	17.2	3.2	3.2	24.6	13.1
1,100,000-2,100,000	21.8	1.2	1.2	38.3	14.6
More than 2,100,000	8.4	0.1	0.1	15.1	4.0
Total	100.0	100.0	100.0	100.0	100.0
Main source of income					
Work of elderly person	50.9	21.8	36.5	72.8	30.1
Work of family members	8.2	—	8.3	11.6	9.1
Assets	6.4	6.9	11.1	3.9	7.2
Retirement Benefit or Pension	5.6	3.2	10.8	3.8	9.1
Adults children	20.1	45.8	27.0	4.1	33.5
Public assistance	7.2	20.8	5.0	2.2	9.6
Others	1.5	1.5	1.4	1.6	1.4
Total	100.0	100.0	100.0	100.0	100.0

Source: Sunwoo et al. (2001).

tended to be higher-paid), particularly in manufacturing industries (Tahk 1984).
This is one of the reasons why the mandatory retirement age was set well under 60
in most cases.

Table 8.5 Economically active and employed population aged 15 and over in 2000

	All ages	55–59	60–64	55+	60+	65+
Population (000)	37,139	2,006	1,817	7,218	5,212	3,395
Percentage economically active	59.1	68.7	59.7	48.9	41.2	31.3
Percentage employed	56.7	66.6	58.4	47.9	40.7	31.2

Source: National Statistical Office (2001a).

No mandatory retirement age is codified in law in Korea, and this vacuum has been filled by an almost universal practice in Korean companies to retire their workers at age 55. This retirement age is 'mandatory' only in so far as it exists in the by-laws of companies and industries. In the absence of any national regulation, these customary practices and by-laws became 'compulsory' or 'mandatory' in practice, though not in law. Ministry of Labour figures for 2001 report that just one-half of all employees in enterprises with 300 or more workers retire at 55, and only 13 per cent continue working to 60 or later.

Setting the prevailing 'mandatory' retirement age at 55 is not only contrary to the trend of an increasing lifespan, but also poses a number of serious problems for elderly Koreans, since the pension eligibility age is set at 60. First, the retired workers' home economy may be threatened as family expenditure tends to continue at a high level and often outstrips income when the primary breadwinner reaches age 55 (Min et al. 1993; Choi 1996). Second, many retired workers may experience economic hardship until they become eligible to draw the public pension at age 60, the age stipulated for a normal old-age pension under the National Pension Act. Third, these comparatively young retirees usually have few opportunities to be re-employed or to participate in social activities such as voluntary work, recreational activities or any other meaningful pursuits.

Health Status

Physical functioning and the prevalence of dementia among Korean elders are detailed in table 8.6. It is estimated that 31 per cent of the total elderly population have limitations in instrumental activities of daily living (IADL) and another 12 per cent also have limitations in activities of daily living (ADL). Dependence in IADL and ADL both increase with advancing age. Mental impairment also contributes to the need for care, and the prevalence of dementia in particular increases with advanced age.

On the basis of ADL limitations as reported in table 8.6, it is estimated that around 20 per cent of the elderly may need long-term care (LTC) (Sunwoo et al. 2001), and around 1 per cent are bedridden. When the data in table 8.6 are considered together with the demographic data presented in table 8.2, the impact of increasing limitation with regard to ADL and mental impairment with advancing age on the need for care, is clearly evident. Currently, around one-third of the old population is aged 75 and over, but this will reach almost 40 per cent by 2030, as shown in table 8.2.

Participation in Social Activities

Participation in activities other than work is shown in table 8.7. Almost all the elderly watch TV and listen to the radio very frequently. Around one-half participate in meetings and senior centre activities quite frequently, but participation declines for other activities, with less than 10 per cent reporting participation in learning, volunteer and cultural activities. The national survey from which these data are taken also found differences in participation in various activities by age, rural and urban regions, gender and marital status.

Social Context of Policy-making

Three dimensions of the context in which policies for the elderly are developed are considered here: attitudes towards the elderly, citizen participation in policy-making and the bureaucratic structure in which policies are developed and administered.

Attitudes towards the Elderly

It is difficult to generalize about public perceptions of the image of the elderly in Korea due to a lack of relevant research, but a picture can be drawn from three sets of available information. First, more negative than positive images have been revealed in studies of young people's attitudes, including recent surveys of middle- and high-school students (Kim 2002a) and college students (Seo 1999). An analysis of the content of writings on the elderly in an internet newspaper found they tended to be described in very pejorative terms, such as ill, looking miserable and dirty, past-oriented, introverted, closed-minded, authoritative, lonesome, gloomy, dreadful, low in cognitive and learning ability, rarely contacted by their family, economically poor and jobless (Kim 2002b).

Second, despite the tradition of respect for the elderly and the value of filial piety still upheld quite strongly in Korean society, there is evidence that the elderly are discriminated against in the community. Age-graded norms that have benefited the elderly in the past can be no longer be regarded as a safeguard against age discrimination. Most older workers seeking re-employment experience age barriers; about one-half of the companies responding to one survey limited recruitment to those under 35 (Keum 2002). An exploratory study of elder discrimination (Kim 2002a) concluded that it is emerging widely in Korean society, with 86 per cent of respondents aged over 60 reporting experience of at least one incident of discrimination. The evidence of growing age discrimination poses difficulties when it comes to extending the mandatory retirement age and increasing the employment and re-employment of people in their fifties.

Table 8.6 Physical health status and prevalence of dementia among elderly Koreans

Age Functional Health Status*		Total (65+) (%)	65–69 (%)	70–74 (%)	75+ (%)
Physically independent		57.5	73.9	59.3	35.4
Physically dependent		42.6	26.1	60.7	64.6
Physically dependent	{Limitation only in IADL	30.8	19.8	31.9	43.6
	{Limitation in ADL	11.8	6.3	8.8	21.0
Limitation in ADL	{In part of ADL	10.5	5.6	8.0	18.6
	{In all ADL	1.3	0.7	0.8	2.4

Prevalence of dementia reported by	Total	65–69	70–74	75–79	80+
Park and Koh (1991)	11.3	3.1	7.0	16.2	38.9
Seoul National University (1994)	9.5	3.7	6.7	14.9	27.2
Bae (1999)	7.9	5.2	12.2	17.0	35.2

Notes:
*Sunwoo et al. (2001).

Table 8.7 Elderly Koreans' participation in social and recreational activity (percentage by frequency of participation)

Activity	Never	1–2 times in several months	1–3 times a month	1–2 times a week	Almost every day	Total
TV and radio	3.1	0.3	0.5	5.4	90.8	100.0
Meetings	31.2	10.2	17.3	11.2	30.1	100.0
Senior centres	43.3	1.5	5.9	9.4	39.9	100.0
Religious activities	50.4	16.6	11.3	18.2	3.4	100.0
Drinking (soft and alcoholic)	55.6	1.6	7.3	13.1	22.4	100.0
Games/recreations	56.0	2.8	2.8	14.0	21.7	100.0
Shopping	57.6	4.0	16.3	16.8	5.3	100.0
Travel	68.7	25.6	5.3	0.3	0.0	100.0
Sports activities	77.6	1.8	3.2	4.1	13.3	100.0
Hobbies	84.0	0.7	2.8	3.2	9.3	100.0
Learning activities	93.1	1.1	2.1	2.3	1.4	100.0
Volunteer activities	93.3	2.2	2.2	1.6	0.7	100.0
Cultural activities	97.4	1.0	1.0	0.4	0.2	100.0

Source: Kim et al. (1999).

Third, public attitudes toward the responsibility of children for supporting their elderly parents are changing, with a shift of responsibility towards the elderly themselves and to society. In a national survey conducted by the National Statistical Office in 1991, almost 80 per cent of respondents thought the family was responsible for the economic support of their elderly parents, but in a similar survey in 1999, this proportion had fallen to just under 60 per cent. Another 1999 survey of caregivers of the elderly living in Seoul (Rhee et al. 1999) found that only two-thirds of the respondents said the family had primary responsibility. Some 20 per cent said society had the primary responsibility and 16 per cent said responsibility should be shared between family and society. The lower the caregiver's age, the higher the proportion of those nominating shared responsibility, indicating a likely shift towards this view in the future.

Citizen Participation in Policy-making

One of the major factors affecting formulation of ageing policies in Korea has been citizen participation. Following the model proposed by Kingdon (1997), this participation has been more of an impetus than a constraint, and opportunities for coalition-building have influenced the decision-making process.

Two cases illustrate how citizen participation has influenced the creation and revision of laws relating to the elderly. The process of major revisions of the Elderly Welfare Act in 1989, 1993 and 1997 saw many proposals put forward by interest groups and citizens' groups. In particular, citizens proposed the 'elder respect pension' and negotiated with the government and political parties to have it enacted. In the reform of the National Basic Livelihood Security Act, a coalition of interest groups, citizens' groups and academics made suggestions and submitted their comments on drafts of the bill to the group of congressmen preparing it, and had some influence on the final bill that was passed by the congress in August 1999.

Bureaucratic Structures

The division of responsibilities for policies and programmes for the elderly between different government departments, and between national and local government, reflects the piecemeal pattern of development to date. While almost all of the national policies and programmes are currently planned and implemented by the Ministry of Health and Welfare, some are implemented through the Ministry of Government Administration and Home Affairs, which also deals with government employee pensions. In addition to these two ministries, the Ministry of Labour deals with employment of older workers, the Ministry of National Defence deals with the military personnel pension, the Veterans Administration is in charge of veterans' pensions, and the Ministry of Education and Human Resource Development deals with the private school teachers' pension.

To address this fragmentation, a taskforce was established under the Office of the President, in February 2003, to review and coordinate inter-governmental policies responding to the ageing of society. The presidential commitment to this taskforce signals a concerted effort to achieve more comprehensive policies for the elderly in the future.

National Policies and Programmes

National policy programmes for elderly Koreans can be categorized into three groups: income maintenance, health care and social services. Current programmes in each category are summarized in table 8.8, and their development and provisions are discussed in turn below.

The existence of six categories of income maintenance programmes for older people shows how Korea has sought to deal with the economic problems of ageing through the structure of its national social welfare programmes. Four of the six categories – public pensions, public assistance, the elder respect pension, and the retirement benefit programmes – provide cash payments; and the other two – the senior discount programme and employment promotion – provide in-kind support and assist the elderly to earn incomes through paid work.

Public pensions The four public pension programmes detailed in table 8.9 are all designed to operate as contributory social insurance schemes. The government employees' pension (GEP), military personnel pension (MPP) and the private school teachers' pension (PSTP) cover only people employed in these particular occupations, who account for only 6.2 per cent of the workforce. These pensions provide incomes to only 2.5 per cent of those aged 60 and over. The national pension (NP) is the main old-age pension programme covering the majority of workers and the self-employed, and it provides income to 7.8 per cent of those aged 60 and over.

While pensions for people with special occupations (GEP, MPP and PSTP) were instituted in the early 1960s, the NP was established under the National Pension Act in 1986, and came into force in 1988. As the NP requires a 20-year contribution period, those now aged 60 and over have not qualified as beneficiaries. Until March 1999, moreover, the NP covered only employees and employers of workplaces that have five or more full-time workers, and those employed in agriculture and fisheries, whereas it now covers all those who are not insured under GEP, MPP and PSTP. The main function of the NP is to provide a pension in old age, but it also provides disability and survivor's pensions.

Income Maintenance Policies

The existence of six categories of income maintenance programmes for older people shows how Korea has sought to deal with the economic problems of ageing through the structure of its national social welfare programmes. Four of the six categories – public pensions, public assistance, the elder respect pension, and the retirement benefit programmes – provide cash payments; and the other two – the senior discount programme and employment promotion – provide in-kind support and assist the elderly to earn incomes through paid work.

Table 8.8 Summary of national policies for elderly Koreans

Category	Programmes
Income maintenance	*Cash benefits* *Public pension*: National Pension, Government Employees' Pension, Private School Teachers' Pension, Military Personnel Pension *Public Assistance*: National Basic Livelihood Security *Elder Respect Pension* *Retirement Benefit* *Indirect cash and in-kind support* *Senior Discount*: Discount for admission to parks and museums, public transport, etc. *Employment Promotion*: Elderly Job Placement Centre, Elderly Workshop, Older Workers' Job Bank, Older Workers' Appropriate Job Designation, Older Worker Employment Promotion Assistance, Prospective Retiree's Job Training Assistance
Health care	*Health Care Cost Payment*: National Health Insurance, Medical Assistance *Health Care Services*: Elderly Health Examination, Nursing Home, Home for the Aged, Visiting Nurse, Nursing Hospital, Geriatric Hospital
Social services	*Elderly Recreational Facility*: Multi-purpose Senior Centre, Senior Club House, Senior School, Senior Resort *Community Care*: Home Help, Adult Day Care, Short-stay Care; Meal Delivery, Congregate Meal Service

Public pensions The four public pension programmes detailed in table 8.9 are all designed to operate as contributory social insurance schemes. The government employees' pension (GEP), military personnel pension (MPP) and the private school teachers' pension (PSTP) cover only people employed in these particular occupations, who account for only 6.2 per cent of the workforce. These pensions provide incomes to only 2.5 per cent of those aged 60 and over. The national pension (NP) is the main old-age pension programme covering the majority of workers and the self-employed, and it provides income to 7.8 per cent of those aged 60 and over.

Table 8.9 Coverage and recipients of cash payments under income maintenance programmes, 2002

Programme	Covered persons (000)	Workers covered (%)	Recipients aged 60+ (000)	Total 60+ receiving (%)	Recipients aged 65+ (000)	Total 65+ receiving (%)
Public pensions	17,810	79.7	584	10.3	280	7.2
Government Employees	952	4.3	89	1.6	47	1.2
Military Personnel	150	0.7	38	0.7	22	0.6
Private School Teachers	210	0.9	10	0.2	6	0.2
National Pension	16,498	73.8	447	7.8	198	5.2
Public assistance	1,734	n/a	826	14.5	800	21.2
National Basic Livelihood Security	1,550	n/a	441	7.8	308	8.2
Elder Respect Pension	800	n/a	—	—	800	21.2
Total*	19,544	87.6	1,410	22.3	940	24.9

Notes:
n/a: not applicable as public assistance applies only to those who are not working.
*Percentage of recipients does not sum to totals as some receive more than one benefit; in particular, 308,000 out of 800,000 recipients of the ERP are also recipients of the NBLS and this number has been subtracted from the total recipients in calculating the percentage of those aged 60+ and 65+ receiving each benefit.

While pensions for people with special occupations (GEP, MPP and PSTP) were instituted in the early 1960s, the NP was established under the National Pension Act in 1986, and came into force in 1988. As the NP requires a 20-year contribution period, those now aged 60 and over have not qualified as beneficiaries. Until March 1999, moreover, the NP covered only employees and employers of workplaces that have five or more full-time workers, and those employed in agriculture and fisheries, whereas it now covers all those who are not insured under GEP, MPP and PSTP. The main function of the NP is to provide a pension in old age, but it also provides disability and survivor's pensions.

The conditions of eligibility for a normal old-age pension are reaching age 60 and an accrual of 20 years or more of contributions, although the minimum insured period is 10 years. There are also some special categories of pensions paid to older people with low incomes and to address the needs of those who – because they were already over 45 in January 1988 – have not been able to be insured for 20 years. The NP also provides a disability pension to individuals with physical or mental disability acquired during their insured period, with no minimum period required; and a survivor's pension is provided to surviving dependants of the insured person, without any required minimum insured period. There are also a number of other provisions to cover the divorce or death of an insured spouse.

The benefit paid under the NP is divided into a basic pension amount (BPA) and an additional pension amount (APA). The BPA is designed to provide an income replacement rate of 60 per cent of average monthly income, for a 40-year insured period. The APA is a fixed amount of family allowance paid on the basis of eligible dependants.

The NP is financed from different sources for different types of contributors:

- General workers' contributions come equally from the employee's wages and the employer's liability.
- Individually insured persons, voluntarily insured persons, and voluntarily and continuously insured persons make their own contribution and pay double the normal employee's share.
- Workers in agriculture and fisheries make contributions from their income and a flat rate of government assistance is also contributed.

The contribution rate for the NP is currently set at 9 per cent for the general workforce and 6 per cent for other categories of insured persons. The NP fund is managed by the Committee of National Pension Fund Operations in the Ministry of Health and Welfare, and administered by the National Pension Corporation and its nationwide branches under the supervision of the ministry. As of 2002, about 16.5 million workers, or 74 per cent of the workforce, were compulsorily covered by the NP programme, as indicated in table 8.9. As of 2002, the beneficiaries of the NP number some 447,000 Koreans aged 60 and over, 7.8 per cent of that age group, some 198,000 of whom are aged 65 and over, 5.2 per cent of the older age group.

Public assistance The National Basic Livelihood Security Programme (NBLS) is a public assistance programme designed to guarantee a minimum standard of living for all Koreans. This programme was established by the Livelihood Protection Act in 1961 and re-codified as the National Basic Livelihood Security (NBLS) Act in 1999 and came into effect from October 2000.

The conditions of eligibility for NBLS are that the elderly person's income, calculated as cash income plus the cash value of assets, must be below the poverty line; they must have no one legally responsible for their support; or if there is someone legally responsible, that person must be unable to work.

The NBLS stipulates five categories of benefits for elderly people: livelihood, medical, housing, self-reliance, and funeral assistance. Two more categories of educational and childbirth assistance are provided for non-elderly people. The national government contributes 50 to 80 per cent of the programme costs, with the remaining 20 to 50 per cent shared by local government, with all programme costs drawn from general revenue of both governments. The NBLS is administered through agencies of local governments under the supervision of the Ministry of Health and Welfare.

Elder respect pension The elder respect pension (ERP) was designed to solve the problems arising from the introduction of the NP programme without any interim provision for those who had already reached age 60 and thus could not benefit from the NP. Conditions of eligibility for the ERP are:

• age 65 in the case of the recipient of public assistance (NBLS) or born before 1933;
• household income of below 65 per cent of the average income of individual members of the urban workers' households; and
• household assets below 140 per cent of the assets limit of the household eligible for self-reliance assistance from the NBLS.

The ERP is a non-contributory pension programme financed by both central and local government from general revenue. Costs are shared 50–70 per cent by the national government and 30–50 per cent by local government, with the national government equalizing across variations in the economic level of local areas. The programme is again administered through the agencies of local governments under the supervision of the Ministry of Health and Welfare.

Retirement benefit programme This programme was compulsorily applied to all workplaces under the Labour Standard Act enacted in 1953, even though it is not rigidly enforced. While compulsory application makes retirement benefit (RB) a public programme, it can also be regarded as a private programme in that the system is managed by the workplace. The law requires public and private employers to pay one month's salary per year for each worker into a retirement benefit fund, provided that the worker has been employed for more than one year. The implementation has not been universal or well regulated, and the funds that were to be set aside, in many cases, have not accumulated as might have been expected. About 40 per cent of workplaces setting aside the funds accumulate them at financial agencies outside the workplaces; the other 60 per cent usually invest them in their business. Any full-time worker who has worked for more than one year is eligible for the RB, which is paid as a lump sum when workers leave their workplace on reaching the mandatory retirement age, or for other reasons. This programme is currently the principal income source for most retirees in Korea because the public pension has not yet matured.

Senior discount programme   The senior discount programme (SDP) provides elderly people with discounts for public transport and admission to public facilities such as parks and museums, and also provides a small amount of cash for use as a transportation allowance. This programme is an indirect method of income maintenance and is the only universal provision to all the elderly that is financed entirely by local government.

Employment promotion programmes   There are seven kinds of employment promotion programmes that are designed to help older workers with job-placement and job-training. The Elderly Job Placement Centre and Elderly Workshop are operated under the supervision of the Ministry of Health and Welfare, and the other five are under the Ministry of Labour: the Older Workers' Job Bank, Older Workers' Appropriate Job Designation, Older Worker Employment Quota, Older Worker Employment Promotion Assistance, and Prospective Retirees' Job Training Assistance.

Health Care Programmes

The two streams of Korea's health care programmes parallel the income support programmes, with one funded through social insurance and the other a public assistance programme, but there are important differences in funding principles and coverage. Further, neither of these programmes covers the range of health-care services for the elderly that have developed in recent years and which are as yet funded from general revenue.

Health care cost payment programmes   The main programme for paying the cost of health care is the National Health Insurance (NHI) Programme, which was created by the enactment of the National Health Insurance Act in 1999 and came into effect in 2000. As of 2002, the NHI covered 97 per cent of all Koreans, including 91 per cent of the elderly, and the balance are covered by the medical care provisions of the NBLS. The NHI came about through integration of two separate medical insurance programmes that existed from 1976: the Medical Insurance Programme and the Government Employees' and Private School Teachers' Medical Insurance. Full integration of the two systems was realized in July 2003.

Conditions of eligibility for the NHI programme are that a person should be either the insured or a dependent family member. The insured are categorized into the employee insured, including all employees and employers of all workplaces, public officials and school employees, and the self-employed. The NHI provides in-kind benefits of health care and health checkups, and cash benefits by way of allowances for health care, funerals, compensation for excess co-payment and compensation for the disabled. All ambulatory and inpatient care is covered for the elderly on a year-round basis, but not eyeglasses, hearing aids, dentures and other prostheses. The payment level varies with the medical care system and the kind of treatment. The NHI pays 50–70 per cent of the fees for outpatient care, with a 30–50 per cent co-payment, and 80 per cent for inpatient care, with a 20 per cent co-payment. The only special provisions for the elderly in the NHI are some discounts for outpatient care and pharmaceuticals; the NHI does not cover expenses at nursing homes.

Contributions for the employed insured are shared equally between employees and employers, with the government paying the employer's share for public-sector and military employees. The National Health Insurance Act stipulates a contribution rate of 8 per cent of the standard monthly wage, but as of 2003, the contribution rate of the employed insured was only half that level, with the employee and employer each contributing 1.97 per cent. The self-employed insured currently pay their own contributions, calculated on a means-tested basis, but until 2006, the government will provide some assistance with contributions. The NHI scheme is administered by the National Health Insurance Corporation and its nationwide branches.

The second stream of health-care funding is the Medical Assistance (MA) programme, which covers mainly NBLS recipients but also includes veterans, those prominent in the transmission of traditional culture, and victims of disasters. As of 2002, MA covered only 3 per cent of all Koreans, but 9 per cent of all elderly Koreans. MA pays for the same categories of benefits as NHI, but payment levels vary with the status of the recipient and whether primary or secondary medical care is involved. Deductible amounts are imposed on those who receive self-reliance benefits under NBLS, and if the individual is unable to make payments, interest-free government loans are made, with a reimbursement period of one to three years. This programme is financed by national and local governments and medical fees are paid by recipients, and administered under the auspices of local government.

Health Care Services for the Elderly

Four sets of health care services for the elderly are provided outside the primary and secondary health care services covered by NHI and MA. There are two primary care programmes. First, the Elderly Health Examination Programme provides health checks every two years, but is usually limited to the low-income elderly as it is not compulsory and subject to budgetary constraints. Second, the Visiting Nurse Programme is stipulated in the Community Health Act and Medical Service Act, but not as yet in the Elderly Welfare Act. Visiting nursing services are regarded as one of the major community care services and are provided mainly by general hospitals and community health centres, with some limited provision through the Korean Nurses Association and community welfare centres.

There are two levels of institutional long-term care. Homes for the aged generally accommodate relatively well elderly persons, in free, low-cost and full-fee-charging homes. The Nursing Care Programme covers five categories of nursing homes according to the fee charged and the nature of illness: free nursing homes, low-fee-charging nursing homes, full-fee-charging nursing homes, free skilled nursing homes, and full-fee-charging skilled nursing homes. The Elderly Welfare Act Amendment of 1993 allowed for-profit as well as non-profit organizations to run full-fee-charging nursing homes, but at present all nursing homes are operated by non-profit organizations. Nursing home fees are not reimbursed by medical insurance.

Finally, there are two kinds of hospitals for the elderly: nursing hospitals and geriatric hospitals. Nursing hospitals were introduced by the Medical Service Act Amendment of 1994. These are for medical services for those who need long-term care. Geriatric hospitals were newly stipulated in the amendment of the Elderly Welfare Law of 1997. They are general hospitals for the elderly and have to be approved by the Minister of Health and Welfare.

Social Service Programmes

Social service programmes have emerged to provide a range of social and recreational support and community care in recent years, but they are as yet restricted largely to low-income recipients.

Elderly recreation facility programmes There are four kinds of recreational facility programmes for the elderly, each providing different services to different groups of elders, and supported by different funding arrangements. Senior clubs are the most widely available elderly welfare facilities in both urban and rural areas. Older Koreans come to the clubs for various leisure activities such as watching television, reading newspapers, or playing cards or chess on a daily basis. Most of these activities are casual and there are few organized programmes. Senior clubs are supported by voluntary donations from local communities and central government provides a small amount of operational funds.

The Multi-purpose Senior Centre Programme provides more formally organized programmes with a range of services including health promotion, adult education, recreation, counselling, information and guidance. These centres are built with the assistance of central and local government and their operational expenses are almost fully borne by local government.

Over the past 20 years, senior schools have been established by voluntary organizations and community welfare centres to promote cultural, educational and recreational programmes for the elderly. Government financial assistance is meagre and nominal. The Senior Resort Facility Programme aims to provide facilities for recreation and relaxation, but as fees are relatively expensive, there are few of them.

Community care programmes Korea's community care programmes provide the set of services that form the basis of community care in most countries, but coverage of the elderly with ADL and IADL impairments is limited as yet. The Home Help Programme only provides home help services free of charge to elderly people receiving NBLS benefits. Services are provided by volunteers under the supervision of the voluntary organizations, which receive government financial assistance for recruiting, training and maintaining volunteers.

The Adult Day Care Programme provides adult day care services mainly to low-income elders for a small charge. As private pay services are relatively underdeveloped, higher-income elders do not have opportunities to utilize such services.

The third component of community care is short-stay care services. These care services for the elderly allowing for care in nursing homes for a stay of 2 to 45 days per admission have developed on a very limited scale. Government assistance with fees is available to low-income elders, but fee-charging services are relatively underdeveloped despite for-profit community care services having been made possible with the amendment of the Elderly Welfare Act in 1993.

Finally, there are two kinds of meal services: meal delivery and congregate meal services. The Meal Delivery Programme instituted in 2000 delivers lunches free of charge to low-income elders who experience difficulties in ADL and who are also recipients of the ERP. The Congregate Meal Service Programme provides free lunches to the low-income elderly at multi-purpose senior centres, public parks and other venues.

Recent Policy Developments, Issues and Prospects

Projections of unprecedented population ageing accompanied by warnings of negative effects on society in general have seen the ageing of Korean society become an important agenda for gerontologists, service providers, government bureaucrats and politicians. Nevertheless, the development of almost all policies on ageing has been reactive and piecemeal. Measures aimed at preventing and preparing for the problems of ageing have rarely figured prominently on the policy agenda, yet over the last five years some serious responses have been formulated. As well as describing the content of these debates, the following discussion highlights legislative reforms and formal policy-making structures that have advanced policy development.

Sustainability of Income Maintenance Policies

The necessity of having an effective social safety network was being widely discussed in 1997, around the time that the economic crisis hit all aspects of Korean life, and the need for revision of the National Pension Law – particularly in respect of income replacement rate (IRR), contribution rate, and age of pension eligibility – came to the fore. The NP was originally designed for an IRR of 70 per cent of the average standard monthly income, based on a maximum contribution rate of 9 per cent over a 40-year insured period. That IRR proved too high in relation to the NP contribution rate, and the NP was destined to be insolvent by the mid-2030s. Given the trend of rapid population ageing predicted for early in the twenty-first century, adjustment of the IRR was inevitable.

Accordingly, in 1998 the IRR was revised down to 60 per cent, still based on a 40-year insured period; but the effect of this was only to delay the predicted insolvency of the system to 2048. However, two further measures were introduced along with the lowering of IRR: raising the contribution rate to stabilize the pension fund, and raising the pension age by one year, every five years from 2013, to reach 65 in 2033. Thus raising the pension age, without a plan to raise the customary and 'mandatory' retirement age, may indeed result in there being a widening gap between the prevailing retirement age of 55 and the higher pension age of 65. Raising the mandatory retirement age can thus be identified as one of the critical policy issues for the near future.

Since the revision of the National Pension Act in 1998, the necessity for further reform of the NP has continuously been voiced. The National Pension Act currently stipulates sets of contributions, based on 45 wage brackets, with lower and upper limits, and provides for the recalculation of contributions every five years. The National Pension Development Committee has proposed abolishing this wage bracket system from 2004, thereby raising both the lower and upper wage limits. The committee has recently recommended a more important reform proposal to revise IRR and contribution rates. This proposal offers three options for the combinations of IRR and contribution rates: (1) 60 per cent of IRR and 19–20 per cent of contribution rate; (2) 50 per cent of IRR and 15–16 per cent of contribution rate; and (3) 40 per cent of IRR and 12–13 per cent of contribution rate.

This proposal aims to stabilize the National Pension funds by deferring the expected year of their insolvency from 2047 to after 2070. Yet it will be not easy to get general public consent to the resultant increases in contributions, because Koreans lack confidence in the public pension system. Managing the burden of increasing contributions to pension, health and employment insurances, politically as well as financially, has indeed been identified as the second major issue for the future.

Despite efforts to improve the NP system, the risks of running into deficit have not been fundamentally solved and the risk of a heavy burden on coming generations remains. After consideration of the experience of advanced countries, Chung and others (2001) have argued that a public pension alone cannot maintain an appropriate level of income security in old age for Koreans. Their reform proposals address long-term financial stabilization, affordability, appropriate benefit level, universal coverage, equity within and between generations, and role-sharing between public and private sectors in income maintenance for old age. Their proposals seem reasonable in light of the experience of advanced countries, and so present a third challenge for Korea.

The proposal put forward by Chung and others (2001) has been for a three-tier pension system to be developed mainly by restructuring various components of the present arrangements. The first tier would integrate the NP and the three other public pensions (government employee pension, private school teachers' pension and military personnel pension) to provide a National Pension with an IRR of 40 per cent. The second tier would be a new mandatory occupational pension for employees, combined with the state-approved private individual pension for the self-employed with a new type of public occupational pension for the groups currently covered by the three other public pensions, and converting the current retirement benefit into an occupational pension. The IRR of the second tier would be 25–30 per cent, giving a total IRR of 65–70 per cent for these two tiers. The third tier would be optional private individual pensions, offered by the private financial market.

In relation to this proposal to combine both public and private pension systems, the Ministry of Labour has very recently released a policy plan to convert the retirement benefit into an occupational pension in order to improve income security in old age, to secure workers' rights to the retirement benefit and to ensure equality of access to the retirement benefit on the part of all workers. As mentioned earlier, the retirement benefit system, even though it is a compulsory stipulation of the Labour Standard Act, has not hitherto been well implemented. Many similar proposals have been discussed over the past 10 years, to render the retirement benefit a more effective income maintenance programme in relation to the public pension system. Notably, these proposals have received much attention since the turn of the century, once Korean society entered into the category of an 'ageing society'. The present plan for occupational pensions might seem to be a desirable idea for income security in old age, but it may give pause for thought to government, employers and employees, nonetheless.

It is also desirable that any reform proposal integrates the public assistance programme for the elderly into the public pension system. A further matter to be addressed in any reform is the tendency of the self-employed to underreport their incomes, with the consequence that their contributions tend to be less than the amounts expected. This problem has arisen from the lack of a mechanism to verify incomes of the self-employed; currently the incomes of only 30 per cent of them can be verified and it will take time to have a full verification system in place.

The future of the elder respect pension is not addressed here. The ERP was designed to help the elderly who could not be covered by the NP because they had already reached the age of 60 at the time of its inception. Begun as the elderly allowance in 1991, and converted to the elder respect pension in 1998, the beneficiaries expanded from those over 70 with incomes below the poverty line to include those aged 65–69 below the poverty line and those aged 70 and over with income less than 65 per cent of the average income of urban families. As of 2002, about 16 per cent of elderly Koreans received the ERP. Its original purpose was to be not only an interim pension system that compensated for benefits forfeited because of the late inception of the NP, but also a symbolic expression of respect for the elderly who have made sacrifices for the development of the country. To be faithful to this original purpose, the ERP should have been given to all elderly Koreans, but mainly because of budget limitations it was restricted to low-income elders. The ERP remains one of the main income sources for those elders who cannot benefit from the NP, but as more receive the NP over time, questions arise as to whether the ERP should be phased out, or whether coverage and/or benefit levels should be increased so that more elders can enjoy an improved standard of living rather than a minimum subsistence. Improving the ERP would be an expression of filial piety at the societal level, and resolving its future is a fourth challenge.

A further challenge, one related to the future of the ERP, concerns the balance of responsibility between government, society and the individual for retirement income. A shift to individual responsibility was signalled in 1994 when private individual pensions became available through the private financial market, to help those insured under the NP to save for additional income in old age. These pensions were not attractive to the NP-insured, because the amount of tax exemption on monthly premiums was limited. In response, the government encouraged the market to renew individual pensions by increasing the tax exemption amount in 2000.

The final challenge for improving the economic well-being of the elderly is to provide opportunities for full-time or part-time work to those who want to work after retirement. However, age discrimination, negative images of the elderly and the low age of prevailing mandatory retirement make this a difficult task. One of the proposals to improve the employment prospects of older workers has been to establish a government-backed organization along the lines of an Older Worker Manpower Management Corporation to deal with occupational training, job-placement, development of appropriate jobs for the elderly, and even volunteer activities. This proposal has not been acted on to date, so the challenge remains.

Balancing Health Care and Long-term Care Policies

The problems associated with securing the cost of health care and access to health-care services as the population ages have been aggravated by the substantial deficit that developed in National Health Insurance fund in 2001. This deficit appears to have stemmed from the integration of existing medical insurances into a single NHI system in mid-2000; at the same time the roles of doctors and pharmacists were separated more strictly, a move that was not well received by the public. The Ministry of Health and Welfare has identified an increase in hospital visits by the elderly, together with rapid population ageing, as major causes of the rise in medical expenses (Ministry of Health and Welfare 2001b). From 1985 to 2000, the increase in health-care costs for the elderly was three times the average for all Koreans. While constituting only some 8 per cent of the population, the elderly accounted for some 19 per cent of such costs.

In order to solve the financial deficit of the NHI in the short term, while maintaining a balance between revenue and expenditure for the longer-term development of the NHI system, the Special Act for the Financial Stability of National Health Insurance was legislated in 2002, and will stay in effect until December 2006. This special law provides for a subsidy of 40 per cent of health-care costs and administrative costs for the self-employed insured from treasury funds, and for a further 10 per cent of health-care benefits to be paid from the Health Promotion Funds to subsidize health-care costs for those over 65 who were previously self-employed insured.

The remaining problem concerns the funding of long-term care. As the NHI does not now cover the cost of nursing home care, elderly Koreans tend to stay longer in hospital. Even though almost all elderly Koreans are cared for at home by family caregivers, the cost of long-term health and social care is escalating and the extent of quasi-long-term care occurring in hospitals may disguise the full extent of institutional care in practice. Korea is facing some of the problems that prompted the development of long-term care systems separate from hospitals in advanced countries in the 1950s, and the Korean government has begun to consider various measures.

The Report on Comprehensive Measures for Health and Welfare to Respond to the Ageing Society prepared by an inter-governmental committee in 2002 canvassed the need for long-term care (LTC) insurance. In line with these deliberations, the most likely prospect is that an LTC insurance scheme will be implemented, at least on an experimental basis within three or four years' time. Yet, while creating a separate system for funding LTC would relieve some of the pressures on the NHI, it will not be easy to devise and finance an LTC system that combines social insurance and treasury funding. The tensions between the need to develop the LTC funding and service delivery systems, and the burden of health and social security programmes may discourage the government from taking action on LTC in the near future. In short, LTC funding is set to continue as a critical policy issue.

A further issue for LTC policy is how to integrate the services provided through the health system and the social care services that are emerging outside the health system. The last five years have seen a considerable increase in recreational and social facilities, particularly community welfare centres, provided through local voluntary initiatives. There has not been any particular development in community care programmes to date, but the social welfare centres may serve as a precursor to service development. The report of the inter-governmental committee envisaged that both recreational facilities and community care services would be substantially developed in the near future as elderly Koreans sought to improve their quality of life.

Advances in the Policy-making Processes

The inter-governmental committee which prepared the comprehensive measures came as the third step in advancing the policy process that was instituted in 1999 when the Ministry of Health and Welfare established the Long-term Care Policy Planning Committee. The 1999 committee was charged with reviewing LTC policies in advanced countries, estimating the need for LTC in Korea based on existing studies and recommending a mid-term policy-planning schedule to develop effective and efficient measures for LTC (Ministry of Health and Welfare 2000).

The second step came when in response to the recommendations made, the government commissioned the committee to conduct new survey research to re-estimate long-term care needs more accurately in 2001. The results of the survey were that about 2 per cent of elderly Koreans needed institutional care and about 19 per cent needed community care, and the committee recommended a series of mid- and long-term policies, including methods of financing the cost of LTC (Sunwoo et al. 2001).

The inter-governmental committee's attention to LTC is set within a much broader range of comprehensive polices to address ageing in Korean society, and its report covered income maintenance and employment, health care, educational, cultural and leisure activities, participation of the for-profit sector in services for the elderly, legislation and service delivery systems (Office of the Prime Minister 2002). It seems likely that many of the recommendations of the report will be adopted as policy by the government of President Noh that came to office in February 2003. The Long-term Care Policy Promotion Planning Committee at the Ministry of Health and Welfare that was launched in March 2003 was a sign of adoption of the policy recommendations. The establishment of the Taskforce Team for Population and Aged Society at the presidential office in October 2003 is seen as a positive development, since it appears set to take a more comprehensive and inter-governmental approach. The work of the taskforce will be watched closely to see if policy-making for Korea's ageing society does in fact advance to a new stage.

Conclusion

For the past 50 years, Korea has been among the many developing countries that attempted to adopt Western models in designing their social welfare systems. The slowing rate of economic development, alongside continued rapid population ageing, has called these models into question in developing countries, while escalating costs of pensions and health care for the elderly have led Western societies to attempt to reformulate the structure of their own social welfare systems.

In looking to lessons that developing and developed countries can learn from each other, it is important to recognize that trends emerging in both sets of countries come from different starting points, and may not be heading in the same directions. There are considerable differences between the countries grouped together as developing or developed, and there is no clear evidence that these differences are narrowing. The present balance of responsibilities between individuals, family, community, the state, and the market not only differs between developed and developing countries, but also across the areas of income maintenance, health and LTC, housing, and social services within each country. These balances also change over time. Thus, emerging trends towards more market provision and more individual responsibility, and a decline in family and state responsibility, in advanced countries involve relatively marginal shifts between 'pillars' that are all well established. In the case of Korea and other developing countries, the main pillar is still the family, with a slender state pillar having been built only recently. Construction of the individual, community and market pillars is only now beginning, and will be guided by the role that is envisaged for them in government policies and the effectiveness of any support that is provided for their development.

Korea has already taken on board the experience of advanced countries to encourage individuals and workplaces to prepare for old age, and to foster three or four tiers of income security so that public pensions can be supplemented through occupational pensions or private individual pensions, and other individual preparation for old age. Ensuring that individuals take on these responsibilities requires promotion of awareness and conscious-raising about old age and the ageing process throughout the working life.

Another lesson that Korea has learnt from the experience of advanced countries is the importance of family-centred approaches in delivering community care and social welfare services. The Western welfare state was introduced to buttress the family as the basic unit of welfare provision, but population ageing and social development have brought many significant changes in Western family and generational structures. Welfare benefits and services tended to become concentrated on elderly individuals who lacked family support, and led to the emphasis on institutional approaches that is now being overturned.

Korea's response to providing care in an elderly society begins with a very different balance of individual, family, community and state responsibilities than that found in developed countries now or in the past, and with the market having virtually no role. Rather than having to find alternatives to reliance on the state and a large provision of institutional care, neither of which exists to any substantial degree, responsibility for securing a national minimum level of living standards for all elderly Koreans is seen to lie with government. Responsibility for satisfying needs beyond this minimum lies with individuals or families, working through voluntary agencies and the market, operating within a framework set by government but with little, if any, subsidy.

In considering the balance of responsibilities between government and families, it can be said that the emphasis on the traditional value of filial piety at the familial level has hampered the development of social welfare policy for the elderly in Korea. An over-reliance on filial piety has also been seen as excusing the lack of development of programmes to support the elderly in other rapidly ageing countries in northern Asia, notably Hong Kong (Chi et al. 2002). In a modern society, filial piety needs to be dealt with at the societal level in a way that complements and supports the familial level. Filial piety is expressed at the familial level through provision of economic support and care to parents in order to repay them for their love and care. At the societal level, filial piety takes the form of state provision of welfare to the elderly in order to repay their contributions to the economic and social development of the country. In Korea, this social debt is owed almost wholly to the single generation who built the country in just three decades from the 1960s to the 1990s, and who are now reaching old age with only very meagre savings from their individual efforts and very limited social protection.

The challenges that Korea faces in determining the role of families, how far government responsibility is to extend beyond provision for low-income elderly to other groups, and how far the non-profit and for-profit sectors are to be involved, are very well demonstrated in emerging LTC services. Facilities and services for middle- and upper-class elderly are underdeveloped; the result is that, for example, many elderly Koreans with dementia and their families have difficulties in finding facilities appropriate for their economic level. Although participation of the for-profit sector in service delivery was permitted in the 1993 revision of the Elderly Welfare Law, it has not been widely forthcoming. No particular incentives have been given to attract the for-profit sector, and negative public attitudes toward profit-making from services for the elderly still prevail. The outcome is that despite a considerable expression of demand on the part of those who can afford to pay, they remain without services. It appears that it will not be easy to induce the for-profit sector to participate in the delivery of services for the elderly without government-funded incentives such as tax exemptions and low-interest loans, but it is an open question whether such incentives would be effective or the best use of government funds.

If the Korean welfare state is to advance and respond to the ageing of Korean society, responsibility will have to be shared not only between the individual, the family, the community, and the state, but also between the state and the market. The value base of filial piety can provide the foundation for an increase in government responsibility, not so much in terms of direct provision of cash and in-kind services, but by way of supporting the practice of filial piety at societal level. By developing policies and programme structures that promote the complementary involvement of individuals, families, community and the market, the challenge of the 'Korean ageing society' will become one that engages all Korean society.

References

Aries, P. (1962). *Centuries of Children*, tr. Robert Baldick. New York: Alfred A. Knopf.

Bae, S. S. (1999). Development of a dementia management model: the case of Kwangmyung City. *Journal of Public Health Administration Studies*, 9, 1: 30–71.

Chi, I., Mehta, K. K. and Howe, A. L. (eds) (2002). *Long Term Care in the 21st Century: Perspectives from around the Asia-Pacific Rim*. New York: Haworth Press.

Choi, S. J. (1996). The family and ageing in Korea: a new concern and challenge. *Ageing and Society*, 16: 1–25.

Choi, S. J. and Chang, I. H. (2002). *Welfare of the Elderly*, rev. edn. Seoul: Seoul National University Press.

Chung, K. B., Yoon, B. S., Suk, J. E., Kim, Y. H., Kwon, M. I. and Kim, T. W. (2001). *A Study on the Improvement of Public Pensions*, Research Report No. 2001-23. Seoul: Korea Institute for Health and Social Affairs.

Keum, J. H. (2002). Abolishing retirement age through the legislation of the Age Discrimination Law. Paper presented at the Monthly Meeting of the National Managerial Strategy Research Institute, Seoul, 6 July.

Kim, I. K. (1996). Demographic transition and population ageing in Korea. *Korea Journal of Population and Ageing*, 25, 1: 27–40.

Kim, I. K., Kim, D. B., Mo, S. H., Park, K. S., Won, Y. H., Lee, Y. S. and Cho, S. N. (1999). *Life of Elderly Koreans*. Seoul: Tree of Thought.

Kim, W. (2002a). An exploratory study on elder discrimination in Korea. Paper presented at the Annual Meeting of the Korea Gerontological Society, Seoul, 11 November.

Kim, M. H. (2002b). An analysis of the image of the elderly reported in Internet newspaper (*Oh My News*). Paper presented at the Annual Meeting of the Korea Gerontological Society, Seoul, 11 November.

Kingdon, J. W. (1997*). Agendas, Alternatives, and Public Policies*, 2nd edn. New York: Addison-Wesley.

Min, J. S., Ryu, I. H., Choi, S. J. and Kim, Y. H. (1993*). Ageing Trends of Koreans and Policy Measures for Welfare of the Elderly*. Seoul: Korea Development Institute.

Ministry of Health and Welfare (2000). *A Study on Comprehensive Measures for Long-term Care for the Elderly*. Seoul: Institute for Health and Social Affairs.

Ministry of Health and Welfare (2001). Statistics on recipients of benefit of National Basic Livelihood Security Programme. Mimeographed paper. Seoul: Ministry of Health and Welfare.

Ministry of Labour (2001). *A Report of Survey on Retirement Age*. Kwachun: Ministry of Labour.

National Statistical Office (1991). *Social Indicators in Korea*. Daejon: National Statistical Office.

National Statistical Office (2000). *Population Estimate (1960–2030)*. Daejon: National Statistical Office.

National Statistical Office (2001a). *Annual Report on the Economically Active Population Survey*, Government Report. Daejon: National Statistical Office.

National Statistical Office (2001b). *Results of Population Estimate*. Daejon: National Statistical Office.

National Statistical Office (2002). *Result of Final Analysis of Census of Population and Housing*. Daejon: National Statistical Office.

Office of the Prime Minister (2002). *Report on Comprehensive Health and Welfare Measures to Respond to the Ageing Society*. Seoul: Office of the Prime Minister.

Park, J. H. and Koh, H. J. (1991). A classification of causes of senile dementia and its prevalence rate for the elderly in Myun, Youngil-Gun, Kyungbuk Province. *Neuro-Psychiatry*, 30: 885–91.

Rhee, K. O., Cha, H. B., Chi, S. J., Yoon, H. S., Suh, H. K. and Park, K. S. (1999). Needs of the elderly in long-term care and their families' support burden. Unpublished research report, Yunan-Kimberly Company.

Seo, B. S. (1999). A study on the image that university students have of elderly people. *Journal of Korea Gerontological Society*, 19, 2: 97–111.

Seoul National University (1994). A Development of Mangement System for Demented Elderly Patients. A research report prepared by the Experimental Project Team, Local Medical System Development Group, Seoul National University.

Sunwoo, D., Chung, K. H., Oh, Y. H., Cho, A. J. and Suk, J. E. (2001). *A Study on Long-term Care Needs of the Elderly and Policy Measures for Long-Term Care*, Research Study Report. Seoul: Korean Institute for Health and Social Affairs.

Tahk, H. J. (1984). Current status and problems of the retirement system. In Asan Foundation (ed.), *Industrializing Society and Retirement*, pp. 31–41. Seoul: Asan Foundation.

United Nations (UN) (1996). *Population Ageing in Asia and the Pacific*. Bangkok: Economic and Social Commission for Asia and Pacific.

United Nations (UN) (2002). *Report of the Second World Assembly on Ageing*. New York: United Nations.

Chapter 9

Inter-generational Equity and Social Solidarity: Japan's Search for an Integrated Policy on Ageing

Tetsuo Ogawa

Introduction

Japan has a pattern of welfare different from that of Western industrial countries (Esping-Andersen 1990; Esping-Andersen and Gallie 2002). With the second largest GDP in the world, the country differs from Anglo-Saxon countries in other ways with regard to national development, in particular financial and capital markets, corporate culture and industrial relations (Mishra 1999). Moreover, the level of public social expenditure has been extremely low compared with the EU average (OECD 2001a).[1] Partly due to these factors, Japanese social development is often described as unique by scholars and policy specialists. However, the current issues regarding population ageing with which the country is faced are very relevant to many EU member states. Certainly, in order to harmonize and sustain reforms to ageing policy and to build up public understanding and support, strategic frameworks need to be in place at the national level (Hoskins 2002: 14). In this regard, the Japanese practice can be said to be successful. This chapter will analyse how social policies for older people have been reformed in Japan; and how the reforms are scheduled to be carried out. It will emphasize how ageing policy reforms have had to be coordinated with other policy areas. It will also discuss whether welfare provision for older people can be replaced by ways other than state provision. In conclusion, it will address the policy implications of the Japanese experience for the EU member states.

Population Ageing and Social Protection in Japan

Demographic changes pose a serious challenge to Japanese society. Population ageing will reduce output growth and limit increases in economic welfare in most OECD countries over the coming decades (OECD 1998), but Japan will be particularly affected by the process of ageing. Its population enjoys the greatest longevity, and the share of older people relative to the working population is already among the highest, whereas fertility rates are among the lowest (Faruqee and Muhleisen 2001). Low fertility implies a declining population, and the age distribution will continue to shift rapidly in the coming decades (OECD 1998). As a consequence, by 2025, one older person will depend on roughly two persons of working age, which will leave Japan with a significantly higher old-age dependency ratio than any other country (OECD 1998; MHLW 2001).

Since the early 1990s, the government has prioritized policy reforms in pension, health, social care, employment and family policy in order to respond to ageing issues (MHLW 2002). At the same time, sociologists, legal experts, economists and political scientists have paid much attention to the study of old age and related policy proposals. Long-term policies on ageing require a broad view of the Japanese economy in order to understand the government's capacity to generate resources, and a long-term view of demographics in order to understand the demands that will be placed on the economy (OECD 1997). In reality, in responding to population ageing, the Japanese government has been trying to coordinate this long-term view with economic policy, in order to maintain the low level of social protection expenditure and to avoid excessive financial pressures from ageing (OECD 1997; Faruqee and Muhleisen 2001; Ogawa 2000). However, the economic situation remains stagnant despite Japan's continued pursuit, first and foremost, of economic prosperity. Given these circumstances, the government has begun tackling ageing issues in a new way.

Discussion of ageing in Japan relates mainly to debates about inter-generational equity and social solidarity. A central feature of Japan's demographics is the long-run decline in fertility, which implies a huge future decline in the labour force. The government is also concerned over increases in public expenditure. There is a need to tackle ageing via a series of social policy reforms in respect of pensions, health care, long-term care and employment. The state has addressed these issues by generating debates focused initially around two questions: (1) how to finance the rise in social security expenditure; and (2) to what extent future or current benefits should be cut, if this proves politically feasible (Faruqee and Muhleisen 2001).

Cutting across these questions are two key issues surrounding prospective policy solutions and policy actions. The first concerns whether it is possible to share society's resources between the working generation and its dependants in an efficient way, and how to avoid unacceptable societal and inter-generational unfairness. At the same time, it is important that the contribution of older people to society is sustained, so that economic prosperity can be enhanced (OECD 1999). The second issue relates to the ways in which pension, health and long-term care systems should be reformed in the interests of the beneficiaries themselves. There are also debates about what changes in the financial infrastructure are needed to support the development of advance-funded pension systems. Japan has already taken steps to reform its public pension systems, but the policy solutions might be insufficient to cope with future demands. Public pension accounts in Japan may start to go into sustained deficit in about ten years' time, and the public pension provision of health and long-term care for retirees would further add to costs in the future (OECD 1999).

Several reforms have been embarked on to modify the current contract between the Japanese people and the government, reforms which must be implemented with advance warning if people are to have time to adjust to new notions of generational equity and social solidarity; that is, to begin to anticipate problems only likely to be arising two or three decades down the road. In addition, there is a limit to how fast Japan can move to an advance-funded scheme because of equity considerations: current workers could end up paying twice into their own pension fund – for their own pension and for the pensions of the currently retired.

Table 9.1 confirms the current disparity in incomes between older persons and the general run of the population. Nevertheless, the provision of income in older age should take account of all the resources available to older people, including public and private pensions, earnings and assets. Existing public pension systems, which enable older people to maintain adequate standards of living, are likely to remain the major source of old-age income for many retirees for some time to come. However, other sources may have to play a growing role, in order to spread the social costs across generations and enable individuals to diversify risks between different sources of retirement income. In the context of Japan, such reforms are likely to mean that middle- and high-income earners will want to supplement their public pensions. Hence, it will be important to establish a sound regulatory framework for private pension funds, including occupational pension schemes (MHLW 2002).

Table 9.1 Average annual incomes of households (2000)

	Per household	Per household member
Households of aged persons	JP&¥; 3,289,000 (€26,037)	JP&¥; 2,187,000 (€17,313) (1.5 persons)
All households	JP&¥; 6,266,000 (€49,604)	JP&¥; 2,198,000 (€17,400) (2.85 persons)

Source: MHLW (2000).

According to NIPSSR (1998) figures on the breakdown of social security revenue and expenditure, insurance premiums account for about 60 per cent of the total revenue and government contributions in respect of older people. Social policies for older people involve a number of social service programmes, e.g. pension, labour policy, health care, long-term care, and housing policy. In reality, however, expenditure on the public pension takes up nearly half of the entire expenditure, and that on health insurance accounts for a further one-third (NIPSSR 2002).

Japan's processes of ageing, together with structural changes, are likely to raise a wide range of issues concerning resource allocation (OECD 1989). The Ministry of Health, Labour and Welfare (2000) assumes that the increasing needs of supporting and caring for older people, e.g. the costs of pensions and health care, housing, employment and other related topics, are the issues of an ageing society resulting from successful national development. Certainly, an increase in the older population will escalate the demand for age-related services and health care industries in Japan (Martin 1987: 7; Standing 2000). Solutions may necessitate state policy-making developments and changes, since one consequence of ageing could be a large increase in the role of government in transferring resources from working-age people to elders. Public social spending is very sensitive to the age distribution of the population. In particular, the combination of rising health-care and pension outlay is projected to increase total social expenditures significantly. At the same time, there is public concern that efforts to contain rising health care costs might impact on the quality and quantity of health care services for the older population (OECD 1989; Faruqee and Muhleisen 2001).

The Policy Background

Pensions

Under the current Japanese pay-as-you-go (PAYG) pension programme, the younger generation stands to receive less by way of benefits than they will have paid by way of contributions prior to their retirement. In short, there may be an inequity with regard to the ratio of contribution to benefits between the generations. In order to avoid such a prospect, some academics argue that the pension system should be transformed from PAYG to a funded, 'actuarially fair' system. But the system itself cannot be the solution for equalizing the ratio of contribution to benefits over the generations. Moreover, there is an issue regarding the two meanings of equity in this context: equity with regard to the ratio of contributions to benefits, and equity between the amounts of pension elder recipients receive and the amounts the working population are contributing over the same period. Replacement ratios must be stable but, at the same time, social solidarity must be produced and institutionalized via the redistribution of wealth by institutions of the state, to improve the quality of life of the poorest and the most vulnerable segments of the population.

Figure 9.1 shows the present structure of the pension system in Japan, which has three pillars.[2]

As Japan's population ages, its payments from the current PAYG pension system will increase considerably (Yashiro 1996; Barr 2001; Hatta and Oguchi 2001). This means that social responsibility for the National Pension Scheme (NPS) and the amount of contributions to fund it will also increase. The relationship between pension payments as a proportion of wages, and national pension contributions as a proportion of wages is significant. It emerges that while pension payments have so far been roughly on a par with Western European countries, national pension contributions have been lower (MHLW 2000). In future, while the total costs of NPS contributions in Japan will approach European levels, the rapid ageing of Japan must mean a further increase in contributions, leading to a rapid decline in the payment/contribution ratio (MHLW 2000; Barr 2001). Consequently, the social shares of funding pension payments will increase across the generations, from the current generation receiving pensions at the 'high end' to future generations receiving their pensions at the 'low end'. One of the major issues for coming years is thus the need to find ways of somehow sustaining the current balance – or else of agreeing on a new appropriate balance – between payment and funding, avoiding an excessive burden on future generations (Hatta and Oguchi 2001).

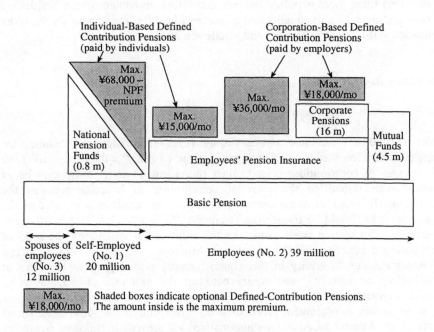

Figure 9.1   Japanese pension scheme structure

Source: NIPSSR (2002).

Health Care

In Japan health care services are financed via a public mandatory health insurance system, which is composed of two types of schemes: occupation-based and region-based. The former is called the Health Insurance. Employers and employees of firms of a certain size and over form a health insurance society (these are collectively called the Society-managed Health Insurance). There are nearly 1,800 such societies. For those who work at smaller firms, the government provides a collective health insurance, which is called the Government-managed Health Insurance. In addition, special professions such as civil servants, day labourers and seamen form separate nationwide professional associations. These occupation-based health insurances cover employees and their dependants. For those not covered by the Health Insurance, there is the region-based National Health Insurance, for which municipalities act as the insurers. The National Health Insurance (NHI) is composed of most self-employed people, farmers, workers in smaller firms and their families. These health insurances together provide almost universal coverage of the population.

With regard to health-care costs, however, the proportion of those who are satisfied is declining (MHLW 2000). National health-care treatment costs (public expenditure plus patient expenditure) were 7.6 per cent of GDP (OECD 2001b). It is certain that one of the causes of the rise in the overall medical treatment costs is the cost for older generations. According to figures for 1997, Japan's total national expenditure on health per capita was €1,588 (Euro Purchasing Power Parity), and this was almost the EU average. However, it should be considered that increases in national medical treatment costs and the old-age dependency ratio will raise Japan's total health-care costs in the future. Until the mid-1980s, national medical treatment costs as a proportion of GDP had risen in accordance with the ageing ratio, and had almost levelled off until 1991, when the proportion began rising again. In Western Europe and the United States, state medical treatment costs have consistently risen in accordance with the ageing ratios. Therefore, since Japanese society is projected to age far faster than any other developed country, it is very likely that medical treatment costs will increase far faster as a proportion of GDP in the future.

So far, the persistence of demand for more appropriate long-term care services has been evident in the excessive use, by international standards, of hospitals to provide long-term care for older people (OECD 1997). The rising costs of medical treatment for older people reflect the long periods many of them spend in hospital when they should be looked after in long-term care services (OECD 1996). Before a policy measure for this was implemented (see below), it had been estimated that the monthly cost of caring for an older person in hospital was about two times higher than that of a social care institution. Nevertheless, there are still not enough home-care services and social-care institutions for older people. Meanwhile, another reason for the extensive use of hospitals as care facilities relates to the payments made by patients. From the users' point of views, health care was seen as less expensive than long-term care. According to figures for 1996, expenditure on inpatient care per capita was €469, whereas expenditure on outpatient care was €649, and that on pharmaceuticals per capita was €200. The proportion of all older people being hospitalized was 4.9 per cent (the proportion of those aged 80 and over was 8.9 per cent) (OECD 1997).

Retirement

Japanese older people have higher labour force participation rates than in the EU member states, which is explained by two factors: a high commitment to work and an insufficiency of retirement systems capable of providing an adequate income in old age.

With regard to men's labour participation rates, 61.0 per cent of those aged 55 to 59 were in full employment, by comparison with 25.7 per cent of those aged 60 to 64 and 12.5 per cent of those aged 65 to 69. Corresponding labour participation rates for women were 24.7, 8.9 and 3.4 per cent, respectively (MHLW 2000). However, the labour participation of those aged 65 and over is on the decline. The relation between the working-age population (aged 15–64) and the older population (aged 65 and over) is regarded as one factor which determines the dynamics of a country. In 2000, it was projected that the ratio of the young population (aged between 0 and 19) will continue to fall, while that of the working-age population (aged 20 to 64) will remain relatively high (Medium Series of Population Projection, NIPSSR 2000). An increase in the old-age dependency ratio[3] will result in an increase in social costs to be shared by the working-age population. Already, in the year 2000 when the old-age dependency ratio was 25.1 per cent, there were only two persons of working age to support one aged person under the current PAYG system (MHLW 2000). Therefore, there have been considerations about raising the retirement age from 60 to 65 and delaying pensionable age, partly by relying on the strong Japanese work ethic. The aim of these policy changes is to prompt older people to opt out from being dependent and to support the present social protection system by their high commitment to work, in accordance with the idea of Active Ageing (Horioka 1998).

Changing Roles of Women in Japan

It is clear that women have tended to be regarded as a potential labour force, but in many cases they are in fact unpaid workers. If they are to be able to offer financial support for the older population, then they cannot remain in the traditional gender role (Beneria 2001). In Japan, women still tend to be disadvantaged financially compared to men, since they tend to have fragmented careers without completely independent pension schemes – although married women are generally better off than widowed, divorced or single women, because of their reliance upon husbands' incomes and pensions. In 1995, about 80,000 women gave up careers to care for a family member at home and, by 2025, about 220,000 women may have to do so if formal care is not provided (MHLW 1995). In the past, it was common for the eldest son of the family to live with his parents; the actual caring was done by their wives, daughters or daughters-in-law (Ogawa 1999). In particular, the care responsibility of daughters-in-law in rural areas was paramount. Such informal carers provided most of the daily requirements of older persons with moderate or severe physical and/or psychological impairments. There appeared to be a severe lack of social care facilities, rehabilitative services and respite care. In addition, there was a stigma associated with failing to provide family members with constant, long-term care at home – a task which typically proved both physically and mentally demanding.

Cumulative Financial Pressures on the Provision of Pensions, Health Care and Long-term Care

It is obvious that Japan's population ageing will have enormous impacts on pension, health and long-term care spending in the future. People are living longer and leading healthier lives. Nevertheless, population ageing means that health and long-term care costs are likely to rise. The central challenge is to see whether such expenditures can be rendered cost-effective and meet the most pressing requirements.

The government has emphasized the achievement of economic growth rather than an increase in social protection expenditure (OECD 1997; Faruqee and Muhleisen 2001). Public expenditure on this remains very low compared with the EU average (OECD 1997). Nevertheless, the government will have to cope with the tremendous costs of social protection caused by population ageing. The overall cost of welfare payments for older people in the form of pensions, medical treatment and social care services is bound to grow with the ageing of the population, with the result that the financial costs to be shared by the whole population will also increase (Takeda 1996: 219; MHLW 2000).

These expenditures must be shared by people who pay contributions, especially for pensions. As a consequence of its low fertility rates, Japan will have to devote an increasing share of its output to support a larger number of older people in future. As the role of government is being expanded, public finances must inevitably be affected.

In the past, care-giving to frail older people was often described as fragmented, due to the underdeveloped state of social policies in the country and, sometimes, its unnecessary costliness to users. As demographic trends point to a particularly large growth in the numbers of people in the oldest age groups, it has been important to develop explicit policies and financial arrangements for care-giving that deliver cost-effective services. Japan is now facing up to the reality of ageing. Material standards of living might be expected to be higher if people live longer. Nonetheless, one of the issues with which Japan is faced is the insufficiency of formal care provision for older people. This concerns both the nature of elder care and its relationship with other social policies in Japan. Realization has been sharpened by the fact that the national pension, medical treatment and social-care systems are independent and not well coordinated in terms of finance, thus lacking capacity for integration in terms of equity and efficiency (Walker 1989).

Reform of Pensions, Health Care and Long-term Care

Necessity for Pension Reform

> Ageing populations in industrial and transition countries have provoked heated debate
> about pension reform – in particular, about the desirability of abandoning pay-as-you-
> go schemes in favour of private, funded pensions. What kind of pension plan would
> best meet the needs of future retirees? (Barr 2001)

In March 2000, the Japanese Diet passed key pension and social security reform
legislation (MHLW 2002). Under the new laws, the pensionable age will rise from
60 to 65. Unfortunately, there will remain an 'income gap' between the age at
which pension payments begin and the mandatory retirement age of 60, which
continues at many firms. Although the law states that firms have the duty to
endeavour to continue hiring and employing workers between the ages of 60 and
65, this will be a financially insecure period for many workers. Therefore, this
provision will not be phased in until 2018, in order to avoid adversely affecting
those workers already nearing retirement (MHLW 2003).

Both Japan's National Pension and the Employees' Pension Insurance are
facing the financial difficulty of accumulating enough funds to meet pension
payments (MHLW 2002). The current reform basically takes care of reducing
benefits, but fundamental problems concerning the financial crisis facing the Basic
Pension – which covers the entire population – have not been adequately addressed
(NIPSSR 2003). At the moment, there are various reform proposals which involve
both cutting back benefits and raising premiums. One solution has been to delay
the age of receipt of pension benefits from 60 to 65 years. But a key issue
surrounding the national pension is that a large number of the population has not
participated in this mandatory scheme. According to a survey by the NIPSSR
(1998), 4.9 per cent of prospective contributors are being dismissed. One of the
reasons for this non-compliance is that Japanese employees now tend to have
fragmented career paths, contrary to the myth of lifetime employment at Japanese
firms. In addition, under the current economic circumstances it is getting even
more difficult for small firms to contribute to the pension schemes, which form
part of the pensions for employees. There is another issue, of a high drop-out rate
among pension subscribers in paying premiums in the National Pension Scheme.
One of the crucial problems with this issue is that many young people are not
willing to participate in the mandatory national pension scheme. Some 73.0 per
cent of subscribers in 2000 were contributing fully to the scheme. There are likely
to be large numbers of non-participants and drop-outs from the national pension
scheme among younger people.

In addition, it is clear that the financing of corporation pensions is a key issue
still to be resolved. It has been difficult for private companies to continue defined-
benefit (DB) corporation pension schemes due to the economic recession, and it is
getting difficult for some corporations to pay employers' contributions to their

workers' pension funds. Some private corporations have actually liquidated their employees' pension insurance.

Furthermore, there have been many changes in employment patterns, away from lifelong employment in a single company to employment in various companies over time. It remains true that women may have more diverse employment patterns than men, because of their various roles in the private and public spheres; this means they are unlikely to be able to satisfy the minimum duration and contribution requirements of either the national pension scheme (22 years and over of contributions in return for full benefit) or their own employees' pension fund. In addition, another area of 'missing duration' of contributions to the pension scheme concerns Japanese people working outside Japan. These are not able to participate in the scheme due to lack of social security agreements with other countries (apart from Germany and the UK, to date).

Various possibilities have been mooted as to how to cut net pension benefits: through reductions in the gross replacement ratio, higher taxation of pension incomes, an increase in the retirement age, or a shift to privately financed pension schemes. Maintaining high benefits at lower contribution rates would require an increase in government transfers to the social security system. However, through pension reform, the government plans to strengthen the pension system by raising contributions for all parties (government, employers and employees), while also cutting pension payments to retirees. First, the government raised its share of the pension burden from one-third to one-half, beginning in 2002. Next, the pension contribution rate is set to rise to 26.7 per cent in 2025 (from the current 17.35 per cent) with employers and employees sharing the burden. Finally, there will be a 20 per cent reduction in the overall lifetime pension benefit under the public pension system, to be implemented gradually over 20 years. Such increased contributions and reduced benefits are deemed crucial to keep the pension system afloat. In June 2001, the Defined Benefit Corporate Pension Law (DBCPL) was enacted.[4]

The benefits for both the employees' pension and the national pension began to be reduced in April 2003 as a result of the application, for the first time in four years, of a price sliding scale, by which changes in consumer prices are to be reflected in pension benefits. In principle, this sliding scale was established to ensure that pension benefits did not decline in value when prices rose. In practice, the government has put a freeze on benefits, as 59 per cent of the income replacement rate, despite the fact that, in a deflationary period, prices have dropped. Nevertheless, because the pension fiscal situation is expected further to deteriorate, this sliding scale has been introduced since April 2003. Since the trends in declining birth rate and ageing of the population are expected to continue, there are likely to be wide-ranging discussions on such issues as the ratios of burden between the active working population and the national treasury, measures to increase the birth rate, and measures to ensure revenue for pensions towards a reform of the pension system scheduled to be implemented in 2004.

In principle the revenue for public pensions comes from the insurance fees paid by the people, although one-third of the basic pension benefits – to which all people aged 20 years or over are enrolled – are covered by taxes (MOF 2002). At

the time of the previous pension system reform in 1999, the government decided
on a policy of raising this ratio to one-half (Hatta and Oguchi 2001). This new ratio
is scheduled to be implemented in fiscal year 2004. As a basis of discussion for the
2004 reform, the Ministry of Health, Labour and Welfare has indicated a new
formula for fixing the insurance premiums paid by the active working population
so that they do not rise above a certain level and paying benefits to elderly persons
within this range. The aim here is to eliminate the concern among younger people
that their share of contributions is simply going to escalate in the future. As a
standard case, the Ministry proposes that the employee's pension insurance fee of
13.58 per cent of annual salary (paid half each by company and employee) should
be raised incrementally every year from April 2002 and fixed at 20 per cent from
fiscal year 2022.

In this case, the concern of the working population that their burden is going to
increase without limit will be eased, but the level of benefits they themselves can
expect is going to decline. At present, the model pension that an average salaried
worker and his full-time housewife will receive in their old age is about 59 per cent
of the annual salary of that employee when working (replacement rate). Under the
new system, this figure is scheduled to decline to about 52 per cent. However, the
new system is premised on there being an increase in the national treasury burden
to one-half in fiscal year 2004. In addition, if the birth rate declines even more than
expected, the level of benefits could drop below 50 per cent of the annual salary
during employment.

In the pension system reform scheduled for 2004, there is a strong possibility
that measures to counter the declining birth rate and ageing of the population will
feature importantly. MHLW (2002) suggests measures to support child-rearing.
Under the present system, people who take childcare leave are exempted from
paying insurance fees for a maximum of one year, and their pension does not
decrease in the future as a result. In the case of a person quitting work for the sake
of child-rearing and having reduced income, however, the pension amount does
decrease. Therefore, an increasing number of women are of the opinion that
quitting work to have children is just not worth it. Bearing in mind the
circumstances that have led to the declining birth rate, the ministry proposes – as a
basis for discussion – to study a mechanism by which, in the case of a person
quitting work for child-rearing, his or her pension would be guaranteed, to an
extent, for a certain period. However, the Ministry points out that the issue of the
declining birth rate should also be discussed in the context of a revision of the
working environment, wherein the first consideration should be to establish an
environment in which people do not lose their jobs or income if they take leave for
child-rearing. Furthermore, from the perspective of securing a viable workforce for
the future, an increasing number of people in business circles are saying that Japan
should consider accepting foreign migrant workers.

In preparation for the pension system reform of 2004, an argument has
emerged from business circles that the consumption tax rate (currently 5 per cent)
should be raised to ensure additional revenue (Japan Brief 2003). The Japan
Business Federation has proposed the so-called *Okuda vision*, suggesting that the

consumption tax rate should be raised by 1 per cent every year from fiscal year 2004, to be fixed at 16 per cent in the 2010s; and that this revenue should be used exclusively to cover social security expenditures, including pensions. The Japan Chamber of Commerce and Industry, and the Japan Association of Corporate Executives, appear to agree with the Okuda vision. Since they would have to share the contribution costs equally with employees, business circles are strongly opposed to making the insurance fee burden any heavier and, in so doing, are closing their eyes to the adverse impact that such a consumption tax hike could have on personal consumption. Raising the national treasury share of the pension burden from one-third to one-half (Japan Brief 2003) will require an additional revenue of JP&¥; 2.7 trillion. Since this sum is equivalent to about 1 per cent of consumption tax, Liberal Democratic Party (LDP) politicians are concerned at the prospect of the economic slump likely to result from such a change in the consumption tax rate.

Health Care Reform

Thanks to the universality of the national health insurance scheme from the patients' point of view, there is no distinction between public and private hospitals so far as the use of services is concerned. Any patient is free to select any health-care service provider. Patients are also guaranteed equal access at an equal price for services anywhere in Japan. According to the relevant laws, the coverage of health insurance and the prices of health services are standardized and equal access to the same services is guaranteed.

As a result of Japan's population ageing, some academics claim that the overall system of health services for older people must be overhauled (NIPSSR 2003). Yet it is not likely that there will be radical reform in the near future. Some also claim the need for reform in extending risk-sharing. This could be done by merging National Health Insurance (NHI) with other systems in municipalities (NIPSSR 2003). The NHI has a larger number of elder subscribers than any of the others. Obviously this has become a financial burden on the system. To be sure, in order to minimize the burden of health-care costs for older people between the different insurance schemes, a new system was introduced in 1983 to separate costs for those aged 70 and over in all schemes from those aged 69 and under. But this was scarcely enough to resolve the underlying problem.

Current medical expenses in Japan total about 30 trillion yen, of which 11 trillion are used for older people (70 or over). Moreover, medical expenses increase every year. Costs for those aged 85 and over are ten times as much as for those aged 30 to 40. So long as high-cost older people increase in number, medical finances face possible bankruptcy. Thus the Japanese government urgently needs to reform its financing of health care. As a first move, since 1 April 2003 there has been a change in the rates of co-payment by salaried workers, to raise the current 20 to 30 per cent of their medical costs (*Economist* 2003).

Requests for health care reform have been especially strongly expressed among health insurance unions. At the moment, medical expenses account for about 70 per cent of revenue collected from the working population. In principle, their companies have paid half of this. Yet in recent years, the burden on the working population has become heavier. Last year a bill was passed and a law will be enacted to raise the co-payment of salaried workers' medical expenses up to 30 per cent of total costs. With regard to the older persons' medical insurance system, the MHLW changed the coverage of insurance from that for those older people aged 70 and over, to that for those aged 75 and over, but it is planned that half of these costs should be paid by public money from 2007 onwards.

There are two further reform proposals in the offing (MHLW 2003).

- Proposal A plans to develop a policy adjustment which can take into consideration the differences in age composition and the differences in income between the various working populations which contribute to elder medical expenses.
- Proposal B proposes to establish an elder medical insurance system to collect insurance premiums from older people themselves.

Proposal A is particularly favoured by the MHLW minister, Mr Sakaguchi, who thinks it necessary to inject additional tax revenues into pension finance. He also thinks that taxes for health insurance might well be restricted in the future. The ruling LDP and the Japan Medical Association (JMA) are in favour of Proposal B. The National Federation of Health Insurance Societies, and National Health Insurance Central Council, have also shown their strong support for it.

The future plan for the older people's health-care system is regarded as one of the major reforms drafted by the MHLW in recent years. The draft plan states that the present health-care system for older people and salaried worker retirees be abolished and new two-tiered systems be introduced according to patient age. The system will be divided into two categories, one for people aged 65–74 and one for those aged 75+, with a new arrangement of premium rates. Once the three ruling parties (the Liberal Democratic, Conservative, and Komei parties) have agreed to the proposal, the draft plan will be sent for decision at the Cabinet Meeting. According to the tentative plan for health-care system reform released by the MHLW at the end of last year, Proposal A was based upon cost-sharing between older people and the working population, differences in the premiums to be adjusted according to age or incomes. Proposal B was for elder health care to be separated from the current system. Interestingly, the latest announcement of new principles would seem to be an amalgamation of these two. The MHLW proposes to introduce a burden-adjustment system in respect of younger older people (65–75), but a conclusion has not yet been reached on establishing a new and separate health care insurance for older people (75 and over) (which would entail the setting-up of a new organization to manage this branch of national health insurance). At the same time, there is a tentative MHLW plan to reorganize and integrate the relevant management bodies in all prefectures, though this plan has so far met with strong criticism.

Reforms Relating to Long-term Care

In long-term care policy there is a demand for system reform to correspond with the needs of users, which are expected to increase rapidly in the future, due to the ageing of society and the increase in the numbers of working women. In addition, as the diffusion of these services to other than low-income group users has increasingly diversified the needs to be served, it has become necessary to raise the quality of the services, including improvement of the living environment in which they operate.

With the launch of the Long-Term Care Insurance System (LTCIS) and enactment of the Social Welfare Law, both in 2000, the system of social welfare, which had been the essential service provided by the administrative authority to citizens as 'the national minimum policy solution', has been reformed, and is based on the free choice of its users, based on the notion of 'contracts' between service providers and users. As a result, the number of long-term care service users has increased dramatically. Nevertheless, the delay of service providers in taking appropriate measures to make good regional gaps in demand is presenting a serious problem.

This is largely attributable to the various tensions arising between the new contract-based system and the old system in which the services were 'the national minimum policy solution'. Even after enacting and enforcing the Long-Term Care Insurance Law (1997) and the Social Welfare Law, the government strictly maintains the interpretation of the Japanese Constitution that welfare, including long-term care and other services, pertains to 'charitable and philanthropic' activities. It also holds that the same kind of public funds as those available to social welfare corporations cannot be provided as assistance to private companies; the regulations and supervision required for maintaining the stable and continuous provision of services cannot be imposed on these. Based on these principles, welfare facilities for long-term care and other purposes, built and operated by social welfare corporations, are regulated much more strictly than those built and operated by private companies.

It has been argued that the current welfare system must be reformed in the direction of securing equal competitive conditions by promoting information disclosure and assessment by third parties. It is the important goal of long-term care policy to dramatically increase the provision of services and to improve their quality by the entrance of various management bodies, including NPOs and private companies, into the social-care quasi-market.

Old Age Care Crisis and its Policy Solutions

The provision of welfare is the product of four sectors and their combinations: the informal sector (such as family, relatives and neighbours); the statutory sector (such as local authorities); the private sector (such as private corporations – for-profit and private) and the voluntary sector (such as charity organizations and

NGOs – non-profit and private). In Japan most older people, for cultural and historical reasons, have relied heavily upon the informal sector. However, the current trend has been away from the traditional to another type of pluralistic welfare production, which seeks an optimal welfare mix (Maruo 1986; Ogawa 1999).

From April 1999 to March 2001, the number of older people who were insured by the LTCIS increased from 21.56 to 22.42 million. As of March 2001, the number of older people needing care whose needs were accredited by the LTCIS was 2.47 million. The number of older people receiving care by the LTCIS was in total 13.6 million. The number of older people in care institutions was 6.64 million. There were 3.14 million in social-care facilities, and 2.41 million in health-care facilities. Analysis of care benefits revealed that older people were receiving various care services from local authorities and the total sum was JP&¥; 3,226,955 million. In addition, it demonstrates the development of the LTCIS as seen in the increase of service users in the system (see table 9.2).

Table 9.2 Development of the LTCIS and its impact on the situation of older people in Japan (as of 1999, 2000 and 2001)

	Monthly average in 1999[a]	November 2000[b]	May 2001[c]
Home-visit long-term care	3,550,000	5,390,000 (52% over)	6,450,000 (82% over)
Commuting long-term care	2,500,000	3,400,000 (36% over)	3,840,000 (54% over)
Short stay	918,000 days	849,000 days (7% decrease)[3]	1,092,000 days (19% over)[3]
Group home for older people with dementia	266 place (number of operating cost subsidies in 1999)	870 place (March 2001)	1,312 place (September 2000)

Notes: Comparison of service usage before and after the implementation of the Long-Term Care Insurance[a]. The figures for home-visit long-term care, commuting long-term care and short stay are taken from autonomy data which is used as the basis for the fiscal year 2000 Map of health and social welfare for the elderly.
[b]Sum of past benefit payments by federations of National Health Insurance Associations.
[c]Past benefit payments by federations of National Health Insurance Associations do not include service use replacement (measurement to replace the remainder of home-visit commuting service benefits to short stay services). Therefore, the data above have been calculated from the results of surveys conducted by 108 insurers.

Source: MHLW (2002).

The most fundamental aspect of the relationship between public, voluntary and private sectors is that the state, in its regulatory role, can permit or deny voluntary and private sectors as service providers in the Japanese social care context. In Japan both voluntary and private sector providers can operate only under a regime of admission and registration (Law on Welfare for the Aged, 1963). A would-be private provider is regulated strictly to provide services according to the relevant laws. Because of these regulations and laws, there are many private care-service providers which still hesitate to enter into social welfare areas. At worst, private corporations may be fined or even shut down. By contrast, the voluntary sector has a long tradition of cooperating with local authorities, while being substantially financed by the local authorities. In reality, the care provision by the LTCIS is to some extent determined by local authorities, which cover half of the cost by collecting premiums. An important way in which the government determines the coverage of care services is in the regulation of service providers and the coverage of services; mainly admitting service providers only into the area of home-based care services (e.g. home nursing care, home help service, short-stay service and day-care service) which the MHLW has emphasized the need for in its Gold Plans (MHW 1990, 1994, 1999). Voluntary and private providers may also be regulated by local authorities as a result of half the costs being covered by the LTCIS (MHLW 2002).

In addition to revenues from contributions through the LTCIS, the government further defines the proportion gained from other tax revenue for long-term care. Implementation of the LTCIS is funded 50 per cent from LTCIS subscriptions and 50 per cent from taxation. Tax relief is not granted on LTCIS subscriptions, and the state does not allow service users to choose services themselves. Care-service provision is decided by a welfare office of the local authority by means of needs assessment and care package plans (LTCIS 1996). LTCIS contributions are paid direct from the local authority to service providers and the central government does not touch these funds. However, the current tax treatment of pensions encourages the development of care services through the LTCIS (Takayama 1997).[5] While the most common providers of care services for older people are local authorities, the development of the Gold Plan (1990) and the New Gold Plan (1994) have had a significant influence on private sector providers by influencing structural links between public and private services. In addition to these Gold Plans, the Gold Plan 21 (1999) can also be expected to encourage the growth of private care providers.

As the Law of the Welfare for the Aged (1963) offered care service which was free at the point of use or at a minimum cost (according to local authorities' charging policy), the difference between the public (including the voluntary sector) and private sectors was very clear. Private providers offered a choice of services, which they sold to users directly without the intervention of government. The principal differences defining the public–private boundary seemed to be the prices charged and the quality of the service. Surveys (MHLW 2000) have shown consistently that a significant proportion of the population is dissatisfied with the public service (this includes that part of the voluntary service which is totally financed by public funding) (ibid.). However, there was no other alternative for those who could not afford to pay. The main aim of the Gold Plans (1990, 1994) had been to make the statutory service sufficient to meet needs and to offer greater care services, in particular in the area of home-based care services, such as home help services, day-care services and short-stay (respite care) services. However, the new Gold Plan 21 (1999) has strongly encouraged private companies to enter into the area of social care.

In addition to their expanding needs, users have expected access to increasingly varied forms of care services (MHLW 2000). In the past, the availability of care services under the statutory services was in a critical state. Choice of care service was extremely limited, and most care users had complaints about the quality and availability of public services – especially in respect of residential care, where about 98 per cent of the services were provided by the statutory and voluntary sectors (the latter financed totally by local authority and central government).

While it is notable that the informal sector – including volunteer groups - has now become a much more influential provider of long-term care services, the areas in which it has entered are still limited, since its care skills and methods of service provision determine the scope of the tasks it can perform. Nevertheless it can be seen that diversification of long-term care service providers is to be observed in each area and that the monopoly of the local authority as single service provider has been reduced to the handling of specific types of care provision in local communities.

To evaluate the appropriateness of the new care arrangements under the LTCIS, it is necessary to bear in mind two main sets of considerations bearing on the mechanism and financing of social care: economic efficiency and social equity (Walker 1989). These together help explain why an unregulated free market in long-term care has not so far emerged, just as they also help identify problems with state involvement and the use of quasi-markets in care provision (Le Grand 1993).

It goes without saying that a free market in older people's care services does not exist in Japan, mainly because it would have produced both inefficiencies in service provision, such as those described above, and problems of equity (MHW 1997). But this is hardly to say that the former social care system, pre-LTCIS, was more efficient. As the old state-financed system did not allocate care service by costs alone, it used other non-price mechanisms (such as the use of limited coverage for certain care services and strictly limited standards of service in terms of costs) to ration needs and provision, and operated within-budget only thanks to social-care expenditures from government. This had not given rise to economic inefficiency, but some service users had different preferences. The services which they demanded were, in most cases, the high-quality, expensive ones. So, in the face of differing preferences among older people, the most economically efficient system is that which allows those who wish to, to choose private care, the costs of which can be supplemented by the standard payment offered by the LTCIS (Tochimoto 1997). Such users may have to pay more than the capped amount of LTCIS take-up payment for care services, and hence it effectively sustains the same level of resources available in the limited coverage under the state care system for other users.

However, access to social care has special social and ethical considerations not pertaining to other, commercial, goods. In short, access to social care is not to be distributed by costs alone, because it represents something basic and essential to human life and civil rights (Titmuss 1970; Wistow 1994). The public has a strong perception that there is something special about social care for older people (Wistow 1994: 93). This leads to the conclusion that the form of social care must be central to the equity debate as well as to the arguments about pursuing a new inter-generational contract (Svetlik 1996). Thus the objective of the LTCIS with respect to old-age care should be to aim for particular core outcomes and fundamental long-term objectives in social and economic organization, for example by promoting notions of social justice (Figueras 2002).

So, can the Japanese long-term care system meet the two required elements of equity and efficiency (Walker 1986)? As suggested above, the government's role seems to be more residual than was historically the case, since the diversification of service providers has resulted in a decrease in the government's role in direct provision. Without the LTCIS, such a situation might have polarized service users into two kinds of older people: those who could afford care and those who could not. In addition, older people with less spending power might have been excluded from choosing the care they needed, if other policy measures had not been institutionalized. This still might be the case, since co-payments of 10 per cent for long-term care services have been introduced into local authorities, which may lead to the exclusion of some service users and their dependency upon informal care, since total government funding for care provision is still insufficient. This is clearly against the principle of equal access to elder care in Japan, in contrast to the ideal of LTCIS. Already some local authorities have reputedly not been able to offer various care services, due to a lack of budgetary resources (MHLW 2001).

Meanwhile what of efficiency? Total care needs are predicted to expand continuously over the coming decades. The government's care provision may not be able to catch up with the pace of the expanding needs of an ageing society and, while efficiency in care is surely significant, dedication purely to efficiency considerations will not ensure an adequate and sufficient supply of care for every older person. Although the ideal is for everyone to be able to receive the care they really need, regardless of their age, gender, social class or geographical location, the current care structure with the LTCIS and the level of care provision may not be able to reach an entirely satisfactory standard. By 2025, an estimated 5.7 million older people will need care. In such a situation, it is presumed the government will have to fill the gaps in provision in various communities by some other means – such as by using more community resources, for example volunteer carers, which come free of charge to the government.

Japanese society itself has meanwhile changed to the extent that it now acknowledges the need for volunteering in communities. However, the need for care over the next few decades will be extremely urgent, as the overall care provision from all sectors is insufficient, and it is clear that the Gold Plan 21

(1999) is not going to be able to meet the needs of present generations of older people.

The LTCIS and the new care system in Japan have been introduced with the emphasis on home-based services in local communities as an alternative to informal care. The primary aim has been to supplement informal care by family members in private household settings and to replace informal carers with formal carers. In accordance with family culture, the most popular form of care in Japan is in many cases family care, where older people live in their own homes and are cared for by their family. Therefore, the concept of community policy under the new funding system is favoured not only by the public but also by the government, since it is geared to restraining care costs for older people without further expanding institutional care budgets. It seems clear that the idea of Japanese community care is suited to the preferences of both the public and central government.

Within this system, private care services under the quasi-market have been growing because of significant shortcomings in public care provision in Japan. In the past, statutory care services and private care services had developed in such a way that the systems were parallel, but seemed increasingly complementary. Now, however, the introduction of the LTCIS has become a threat to voluntary sector management, which was hitherto totally financed by local authorities. It has been pointed out that the cost-effectiveness of the current care system does not make the voluntary sector an alternative to the private sector's care service, and in fact makes it less attractive than at first thought. Since the implementation of the LTCIS has presented wider opportunities for private companies, a clearer basis for allocating resources and available services through the LTCIS has resulted in a major opportunity for private companies to provide additional services, best geared to meeting the previously unmet needs of public care users.

The long-term care system has seen the entrance of wide-ranging operating bodies, including private companies, into the field of community care services (MHLW 2002). As a result, it has promoted competition among service providers and expanded service options for users. In the field of institutional care, such as special nursing homes for older people, the regulations have so far prevented the entrance of private companies (MHLW 2002). In the field of care facilities assisting the daily lives of older people, however, there is scope for private facilities, nursing homes, and group homes providing similar services to long-term care insurance facilities – like special nursing homes for older people on long-term care insurance benefits – as an extension of home-care services. At present, there remains a great shortfall in this area of provision (MHLW 2002).

While accommodation and meals (the so-called hotel costs) are covered by the long-term care insurance in the case of special nursing homes and other facilities – classed as residential long-term care services – 'hotel costs' are not covered by the benefits in the case of private paid homes or nursing homes, whose long-term care services are defined as home-care services 'provided at a residence independently selected by users'. In the long run, it is true there is a plan to finance establishment costs and maintenance fees in such private facilities, via the long-term care benefit, just as is done in the case of health-care insurance benefits. Even under the current law, social welfare corporations recognized as charities are allowed to procure part of the necessary funds by taking out loans against establishment and maintenance costs, and to reimburse these loans from long-term care benefits. Under the long-term care insurance system, which is dependent on the users' choice to contract, users themselves are also able to select which service to use between facilities, such as special nursing homes for older people or private paid homes for older people. Therefore, it is very important to create appropriate qualification systems for this range of facilities, to establish regulations geared to different business styles and also to standardize the constituent parts of long-term care services. In fact, regulations that govern complete information disclosure, the supervision of contracts and third-party assessment – are being established (MHLW 2002).

Social welfare corporations (charity organizations), the core providers of long-term care, are still contributing to the continuous and stable supply of high-quality welfare services, and it is certain that they will continue to play an important role in the future. However, at present, since the insurance system has been launched on the premise of competition among service providers under the same conditions regardless of the type of management body (statutory, voluntary and private sector), it may be necessary to utilize private companies in various ways – including management of a public facility by the private sector. Although deregulation measures have already been taken in respect of social welfare corporations, further efforts should be made in this area in order to promote even-handed competition among the various types of management body, including the existing social welfare corporations.

Policy Implications for the EU and its Member States

Exploring the impact of population ageing on Japan's social protection is quite relevant to policy debates over appropriate social protection and production systems within and between EU member states. Japan's unique experience in this regard could provide a perspective that will shed light on the current and future socio-economic environments within which the EU member states have to operate.

Population ageing, retirement saving, medical practice patterns, and entitlement to income, health and long-term care support after age 65 – all these factors largely define the economic environment and well-being of the Japanese at the beginning of the twenty-first century. First of all, the ageing of the population has furnished a powerful incentive for reforming the overall social protection system. The country has also tried to coordinate the nation's production system of goods, capital and services. Over the past 30 years, life expectancy has increased from 71 to 81.3 years, while correspondingly the most common age of retirement[6] has gradually been increasing from 60 to 65 (MHLW 2003). Retiring at age 65, the typical Japanese today faces another 16 years of living, consuming and, at one time or another, in many cases regularly, needing health care or long-term care services. These situations have placed significant financial pressure on the public and employer-sponsored programmes that provide pensions and health care to Japanese elders. Nevertheless, the government has been reluctant to increase public social expenditures.

Meanwhile, the second factor prompting reform has been the empowerment of older people, along with pressures from business groups and NGOs. Such changes have also been influenced by the perception that Japanese people must regard the ageing population not as a problem but as a new opportunity for the country. There is a consensus that older people should be included in society as social contributors and/or potential consumers after their retirement.

This kind of societal motivation has facilitated the discovery of fresh human capital in civil society and also the development of hitherto unmarketed areas in the market economy. For example, to the extent older people are now regarded as influential and wealthy consumers in private markets, particular markets have been built especially for them. In addition, many new NGOs, from the smallest grassroots to the largest undertakings, have been established in accordance with the new opportunities introduced by the NGO Related Laws (1999). This scheme has taken advantage of those NGOs as influential social actors in a civil society. Many older volunteers have begun to get involved in non-profitable activities to sustain their zest for life, which can perhaps be viewed as a typical case of Active Ageing (OECD 1999). Moreover, older people themselves have shown strong interest in working either part-time or full-time even after their retirement, as is also encouraged in the concept of Productive Ageing (Sigg 2002). These changes in Japanese society may give pause for thought in some EU member states.

The debates over pensions in the EU member states have mainly been concerned with poverty in old age, adequacy of pension levels and gender equality in pensions. Questions are asked about the financial sustainability of pensions. Can they be maintained in ways that sufficiently address social justice and solidarity between the generations? The Japanese experience can speak usefully here. As evidenced in this chapter, the Japanese approach to coping with the increasing social costs of an ageing population is regarded as unique, in terms of its efforts to adjust the benefit level of current, to that of future, elder cohorts in the year 2025. In that sense, the benefit level of current cohorts is being balanced with that of the 2025 cohorts in terms of generational equity. Generational equity here does not necessarily mean inter-generational equity. The majority of Japanese people hesitate to agree to an increase in taxes and social security contributions. The rationale of several social policies has been to keep the equity of incomes and wealth between the current and future elder cohorts, and to minimize the imbalance of contribution and benefit levels over the generations. Another rationale is related to the concept of social solidarity that is employed to minimize inequality of incomes. Since this concept attaches importance to equality among people and the necessity to maintain social cohesion, it aims to avoid people having a disincentive to work, as a result of disparities in income and wealth within society. There are some policy implications here for the EU.

- Firstly, any policy lesson – particularly in respect of pensions – should be related to its work incentive compatibility (Yashiro and Oshiro 1999).
- Secondly, while Japan has had an efficient PAYG defined-benefit (DB) system for social security and pensions, the system and its management have been quite successful only so long as the Japanese economy was also enjoying rapid and huge growth, plus a youthful population.
- Thirdly, the methods employed in the system have been very effective for ensuring a reduction in poverty among older people, and for providing them with a stable standard of living after retirement, compared with the situation of some of those in other industrial countries. In addition, thanks to the system's efficient operation, the administrative costs have been relatively low.

According to Takayama (2003), there may be important policy changes still pending in the social security system with radical reforms geared to future sustainability already under preparation. These forthcoming potential shifts in the Japanese social protection system include:

- switching to a notional defined-contribution plan;
- partial funding shift to a consumption-based tax;
- possibility of reducing benefits;
- reducing earnings gaps between husband and wife;
- shift to income-related contributions for non-employees; and
- extension of the coverage of part-time employees.

These are all concerned with the issues and solutions of individual-based actuarial fairness, gender equality and anti-discrimination for part-time employees from pensions and social security (Yashiro and Oshiro 1999). With these changes and reforms in the air, it is worth noting that people are being encouraged not to rely so much on the social security system and to become self-reliant in advance of retirement. In other words, the ideology behind these policy changes is to encourage people to be self-supporting and to avoid relying upon future generations or their families. While these changes have the advantage of actuarial fairness over the life course, the distribution of old-age income will in due course also be quite different from the current situation.

It would be interesting to see whether some parts of the Japanese Model for Social Protection can ever be taken on board by individual EU member states, or can be useful for the European Model of Social Protection (EC 1992). Japan's own experience of establishing its comprehensive social protection system has largely drawn upon individual EU member states' experiences, since the European Commission itself started to take a more active approach to social protection from 1992. Debates over ageing policy in the EU have been of considerable relevance to Japan's preparation for the further ageing of its population. While the EU has concentrated on pensions, health insurance and the financing of health care for older people, Japan has paid attention rather to issues regarding social protection. It has been trying to balance production and protection through new social policy decisions. This Japanese practice may be referred to by the EU member states and the EU itself to make their pension plans and systems sustainable (EU 2003).

One of the most crucial policy implications is to assess which markets, or government actions, can best generate efficient inter-generational risk-sharing (Campbell and Feldstein 2001). Both markets and the government have the potential to promote risk-sharing, markets via the trade in financial instruments, and government via taxation and social insurance. Each has potential on the inter-generational front since there are financial instruments and some social insurance programmes – such as pensions and social security – that last for many generations, and can transfer resources across generations. However, it must be acknowledged that markets have problems generating optimal insurance, and self-interested voters may defeat government efforts to overcome market failures (Campbell and Feldstein 2001). Governments have a more legitimate power to transfer resources between generations to implement optimal generational risk-sharing than markets do.

The Japanese case is radical to the extent that the government has recently decided to cut current rather than future levels of pension benefits (MHLW 2003). This may be the very policy decision to keep current tax rates unchanged, but it does not necessarily mean that future benefits will be lower than under the current governmeit arrangements (Gustman and Steinmeier 1998). Nevertheless, it does confirm that these benefits may be a little uncertain, bearing in mind the life expectancy of future retirees and the levels of future wages. Any promise to maintain benefits at the same level in the future as under current relevant laws ironically raises the expected level of future tax rates, and so threatens additional risks for future taxpayers (Campbell and Feldstein 2001). In this case, future tax rates would have to be raised by more than the 'internationally expected' amount – since Japanese retirees generally live longer, and the rate of growth of wages is lower than has been currently projected. Japanese retirees and taxpayers are also subject to the political risk that future administrations might change these rules, by either reducing benefits or increasing taxes. In the case of the Japanese National Pension Insurance, there is already about 40 per cent non-compliance for current pension schemes, and this has been a very serious issue for the Japanese social protection system. In reality, many people are opting out from the national schemes; many of them are still insuring themselves in private pension schemes. In this sense, this issue is concerned with the credibility of government policy and people's preferring private insurances to long-term governmental safeguards.

This bleak warning aside, the main arguments within Japan have been about ways of avoiding inter-generational conflict and offering solutions for future elder cohorts (Hatta and Oguchi 2001). The debate over social protection has deliberately been extended over several generations. There is still argument as to the extent of resources for older people to be equitably allocated, and how every elder cohort should be able to reach its own consensus on resource allocation (Faruqee and Muhleisen 2001). Because of the combined impact of Japan's population ageing and its current economic stagnation, it has been argued that the government must pursue a more pluralistic strategy for social protection than it has done in the past (Faruqee and Muhleisen 2001).

Discussions regarding social protection expenditures are concerned with the balance between the working population and needy people. The analysis of policy imperatives behind the development of social protection systems in Japan is related to the fundamental changes in welfare transfer patterns and responsibilities which have been accompanying socio-demographic changes in Japanese society. In terms of social policy reform lessons, the case of Japan seems comparable with those of EU member states, which are also seeking better social policies in respect of their ageing populations.

Notes

1   Japan's public social spending was 14.7 per cent of GDP in 1998 compared with the average of 24.2 per cent for EU countries (OECD 2001). Under Japan's social protection system, the current national burden rate as a percentage of national income is 36.5 per cent (13.9 per cent of social security contributions and 22.6 per cent of taxes – fiscal year 2000). This rate is extremely low, like the United States rate of 35.8 per cent (9.7 per cent of social security contributions and 26.1 per cent of taxes), compared with those of European welfare states, cf. 48.3 per cent for the United Kingdom, 55.9 per cent for Germany, 65.3 per cent for France and 70.3 per cent for Sweden (MHLW 2001; MOF 2001).

2   The multi-pillar pension system is widely adopted as the *first-tier pension*, intended primarily to provide poverty relief. Though normally set up as a public PAYG system, it can take other forms, including finance through general taxation. The *second tier* provides consumption-smoothing; it can be publicly or privately managed, funded or PAYG, and integrated into or separate from the first tier. The *third tier* is private, funded, and voluntary (Barr 2001).

3   Kono (1994: 159) argues that 'the old age dependency ratio is particularly relevant in as much as this indicator roughly quantifies the weight of social costs that the current working-age population has to bear in order to support social security and medical expenses for older people'.

4   In the past, Japan had three forms of private pensions for employees: (1) Employees' Pension Funds, (2) Tax Qualified Pensions, and (3) individual pension plans, including those offered by life insurance companies. The first two are provided by the employer, and thus are called 'corporate pensions'. They are under strict regulation and enjoy tax-preferred treatments. The first (Employees' Pension Funds) have a portion of the public pension, since they take a portion of the premium for that pension and manage that portion of it together with the additional 'private' part. This was done because the 'private' portion of the funds was small, and in order to get a good rate in the market a bulk sum of funds was thought at the time to be necessary. The Tax Qualified Pension also gets a preferential treatment in taxes, but less so than the Employees' Pension Funds (NIPSSR 2002).

5   Since April 1999 (the original plan was from April 1997), care insurance contributions have been collected by several means, one of which is the local authority's responsibility to levy JP&¥; 2,500 per month from those aged 40 to 64, and JP&¥; 1,250 to 3,750 from those aged 65 and over, according to each local authority's decision for the levying rates. These rates are under revision (MHLW, 2002).

6   In Japan *retirement* means that people retire from the primary firms in which they used to work, and is not meant to refer to retirement from the labour market. It was usual in Japan for older people to continue to work after mandatory retirement from the primary firms, moving to smaller firms with no mandatory retirement (Yashiro and Oshiro, 1999: 240).

References

Barr, N. (2001). *The Welfare State as Piggy Bank: Information, Risk, Uncertainty, and the Role of the State*. Oxford: Oxford University Press.

Beneria, L. (2001). *Changing Employment Patterns and the Informalization of Jobs: General Trends and Gender Dimension*, Working Paper. Geneva: ILO.

Campbell, J. and Feldstein, M. (2001). *Risk Aspects of Investment-based Social Security System*. Chicago: University of Chicago Press.

Economist (2003). *The Ecomonic Data*. London: *The Economist*, Economic Intelligence Unit.

Esping-Andersen, G. (1990). *The Three Worlds of Welfare Capitalism*. Cambridge: Polity Press.

Esping-Andersen, G. and Gallie, D. (2002). *Why We Need a New Welfare State*. Oxford: Oxford University Press.

European Commission (EC) (1992). *Convergence of Social Protection Objectives and Policies (Recommendation)*. Brussels: European Commission Official Journal L 245.

European Union (EU) (2003). *Strengthening the Social Dimension of the Lisbon Strategy: Streamlining Open Coordination in the Field of Social Protection*. Brussels: EC/COM.

Faruqee, H. and Muhleisen, M. (2001). *Population Aging in Japan: Demographic Shock and Fiscal Sustainability*, Working Paper No. 1/40. Washington, DC: IMF.

Figueras, J. (2002). *Trends in Evidence-based Health Care Reform in Europe since the 1996 Ljubljana Charter on Reforming Health Care in Europe*. Parliamentary Colloquy on the Reform of the 'reform of health care systems in Europe: reconciling equity, quality and efficiency', Paris. Paris: Council of Europe, Parliamentary Assembly, Social, Health and Family Affairs Committee.

Gustman, A. and Steinmeier, T. (1998). Privatizing social security: first-round effects of a generic, voluntary, privatized US social security system. In M. Feldstein (ed.), *Privatizing Social Security*. Chicago: University of Chicago Press.

Hatta, T. and Oguchi, N. (2001). *Switching the Japanese Social Security System from Pay as You Go to Actuarially Fair*, Working Paper 13. Oxford: Oxford Institute on Ageing.

Horioka, Y. (1998). Japan's public pension system: what is wrong with it and how to fix it. *Social Security Reform*, Conference Proceedings, June, pp. 174–86.

Hoskins, D. (2002). Thinking about ageing issues, *International Social Security Review*, 55, 1.

Japan Brief (2003). *Declining Birthrate and Ageing of Population Necessitate Pension Reform*. Tokyo: Foreign Press Centre.

Kono, S. (1994). *Ageing in Japan*. Tokyo: Japan Ageing Research Centre.

Le Grand, J. (1993). *The Theory of Quasi-Markets*. London: Macmillan.

Martin, L. (1987). The graying of Japan. *Population Bulletin*, 44, 2 (July).

Maruo, N. (1986). The development of the welfare mix in Japan. In R. Rose and R. Shiratori (eds), *The Welfare State: The East and West*. Oxford: Oxford University Press.

Ministry of Finance (MOF) (2001, 2002). White Paper on the National Lifestyle. Tokyo: Ministry of Finance Printing Bureau.

Ministry of Health and Welfare (MHW) (1990). *Annual Report on Health and Welfare*. Tokyo: Japan International Corporation of Welfare Services (JICWELS).

Ministry of Health and Welfare (MHW) (1994). The implementation of a new Gold(en) Plan. In *The Latest Information for Retirement Life*, Series 12. Tokyo: Akebi Syuppan. pp. 4–60.

Ministry of Health and Welfare (MHW) (1995, 1997, 1999). *Kousei hakusho* (White Paper) Annual Report on Health and Welfare. Tokyo: Gyousei.

Ministry of Health, Labour and Welfare (MHLW) (2000, 2001, 2002, 2003). *Kousei Roudou hakusho* (White Paper) Annual Reports on Health, Labour and Welfare. Tokyo: Gyousei.

Mishra, R. (1981). *Society and Social Policy: Theories and Practice of Welfare*, 2nd edn. London: Macmillan.

Mishra, R. (1999). *Globalization and the Welfare State*. Cheltenham: Edward Elgar.

Mishra, R. (2003). Globalisation and social security reform in East Asia. In L. Weiss (ed.), *States in Global Economy*. Cambridge: Cambridge Unversity Press.

National Institute of Population and Social Security Research (NIPSSR) (1998). Low fertility and family policy – in an international comparative perspective. Tokyo: *Journal of Population and Social Security (Population)*, Supplement to Volume 1.

National Institute of Population and Social Security Research (NIPSSR) (2002). *The Cost of Social Security in Japan*, IPPS Statistical Report No. 13. Tokyo: NIPSSR.

National Institute of Population and Social Security Research (NIPSSR) (2003). *Social Security in Japan 2002–2003*, Research Paper. Tokyo: NIPSSR.

OECD (1989). *Ageing Populations: Economic Effects and Implications for Public Finance*, Working Paper No. 61. Paris: OECD.

OECD (1996). *Caring for Frail Older People – Policies in Evolution*, Social Policy Studies No. 19. Paris: OECD.

OECD (1997). *Ageing in OECD Countries: A Critical Policy Challenge*. Paris: OECD.

OECD (1998). *Maintaining Prosperity in an Ageing Society*. Paris: OECD.

OECD (1999). *OECD Economic Outlook*. Paris: OECD.

OECD (2001a). *Ageing and Income*. Paris: OECD.

OECD (2001b). *Maintaining the Economic Well-being of Older People – Challenge for Retirement Income Policies*. Paris: OECD.

Ogawa, T. (1999). Decentralization and diversity in the delivery of social care services for older people in Japan – the development of community care policy and social care markets. Doctoral thesis, University of Sheffield.

Ogawa, T. (2000). Japanese women and elder care – changing roles? *Journal of Asian Women*. Seoul: Research Institute of Asian Women, 13: 135–67.

Sigg, R. (2002). The future of pensions and retirement. In *Etudes et Dossiers*. Geneva: Geneva Association (International Association for the Study of Insurance Economics).

Standing, G. (2000). *Globalization and Flexibility: Dancing Around Pension*, Working Paper. Geneva: ILO.

Svetlik, I., with A. Evers (1996). *Balancing Pluralism: New Welfare Mixes in Care for the Elderly*, Aldershot: Ashgate.

Takayama, N. (1997). *Proposals for Reforms of the Pension System*. Tokyo: Jihyo.

Takayama, N. (ed.) (2003). *Taste of Pie: Searching for Better Pension Provision in Developed Countries*. Tokyo: Maruzen.

Takeda, H. (1996). *Koureisya Fukushi no Zaisei Kadai* (Financial Issues of the Welfare for Older People). Tokyo: Akebi Syobou.

Titmuss, R. (1970). *The Gift Relationship*. London: Allen and Unwin.

Tochimoto, I. (1997). *Kaigo Hoken – Fukushi no Syakai Ka* (Care Insurance – the Socialization of Welfare). Tokyo: Ieno Hikari Kyokai.

Walker, A. (1986). The political economy of privatization. In J. Le Grand and R. Robinson (eds), *Privatization and the Welfare States*. London: Hyman and Unwin, pp. 19–44.

Walker, A., with Qureshi, H. (1989). *Caring Relationship: Elder People and their Families*. London: Macmillan.

Wistow, G., with M. Knapp, B. Hardy and C. Allen (1994). *Social Care in a Mixed Economy*. Buckingham: Open University Press.

Yashiro, N., with M. Hurd (eds) (1996). *The Economic Effects of Ageing in the United States and Japan*. Chicago: University of Chicago Press, National Bureau of Economic Research Project Report.

Yashiro, N. and Oshiro, T. (1999). Social security and retirement in Japan. In J. Gruder and D. Wise (eds), *Social Security and Retirement around the World*. Chicago: University of Chicago Press.

PART III
THE LESSONS

Chapter 10

Ageing in East and Southeast Asia

Paul Wilding

There is always, of course, a danger in generalizing about 'Asia' or even 'East and Southeast Asia'. The terms embrace societies very different in terms of size, levels of economic development, urban–rural balance, history, religious and cultural tradition, and in this particular case responses to ageing populations. Two features these societies have in common, however, is that they are at once part of the world's most rapidly growing sector of the globe, economically, and part of its most rapidly ageing sector, demographically (Phillips 2000a: 14). The extent to which such commonalities constitute the makings of a coherent *region*, as opposed to a loosely regionalized collection of roughly comparable trading nations in competition as much with one another as with the outside world, remains for outsiders, as much as insiders, to adduce for themselves.

Thus it is that the national case studies raise such a number of key issues for analysis and reflection.

The Particular Background Problems of the Region

To understand both the nature of the problems posed in the region by ageing populations and the way the different societies have responded to them, it is important to pinpoint some essential and distinguishing aspects. These will recur in different places in the course of this overview, but it is useful to see them in the round at the start.

First, and perhaps most important, is the sheer speed of the ageing that has been taking place. Increases in expectation of life have been dramatic – from 60/65 in Singapore in 1957 to 76/80 in 2002, for example – as have been increases in the size of the elderly as a percentage of the total population – in Hong Kong, for example, from 4.5 per cent of the population aged 65+ in 1971 to 11 per cent in 1999 (Chow 2000: 159). As we have seen in the case study chapters, changes which may have taken many decades or even centuries in the West have been happening in Asia within two or three decades. The pressures for policy development are, by the same token, both strong and urgent.

Second, concern about ageing is emerging at a time when economic growth has slowed dramatically and when the 1997 Asian Financial Crisis has badly dented economic confidence. For example, while arguing strongly for the need to expand caring services in Hong Kong, Nelson Chow has concluded that in the current economic situation the government has no choice but to limit expenditure (Chow 2003: 420–1). Joe Leung takes the same view in his chapter in this volume following a doubling of expenditure in the territory on services for elderly people between 1997/8 and 2002/3. Pressures for policy development are combined with equally strong pressures for public expenditure restraint.

Third, ageing is being accompanied by significant and highly relevant social changes. Four stand out as of particular importance. The role of women – the traditional caregivers – has changed and is changing throughout the region as more women move into paid employment. Smaller families mean that there are fewer children available to care for the previous generation. Co-residence, which was traditionally the basis of family care, has declined sharply in recent years, even though it remains at a comparatively very high level. Families are becoming more nuclear. Malaysia, for example, neatly illustrates all these trends. Children's financial support for elderly parents has also declined (Kwon 1999: 11). Predictably there are 'ambivalences' and tensions between the generations about family responsibilities between more 'Western' approaches and traditional Confucian patterns (Teo et al. 2003), but the family simply lacks the capacity to perform the kind and level of caring functions it performed in the past. While clearly aware of these changes, governments continue to stress the social value and virtues of reliance on family care in a way which is not always conducive to a rounded assessment of the problem.

Fourth, all these societies have deep anxieties about Western-style welfare state policies. They face the issues raised by ageing populations without an established ethic of collective responsibility. Their approach to public welfare provision is essentially 'productivist' (Holliday 2000). There is concern about the extent to which state welfare might allegedly create dependency. There are also deeply held beliefs about the economic benefits of low taxation and low rates of public expenditure. Such a mindset militates against the acceptance of public responsibility for the needs of an ageing people.

Fifth, in the West when populations began to age significantly there was already a basic institutional structure for service provision which was capable of expanding incrementally to meet new or increasing needs. However, within East and Southeast Asia, the infrastructure and the institutions have had – or still need – to be created almost *ex nihilo* to meet the rapidly emerging needs. Policy has to be initiated rather than simply refined and extended.

Sixth, formal retirement ages in the region have, until recently, tended to be low – 55 in South Korea, Singapore and Malaysia, for example. Retirement ages are now being raised in many countries. This has not so far produced the levels of protest generated by comparable proposals for change in Europe; nevertheless, it does generate opposition. Such changes are, however, absolutely crucial to the production of effective and sustainable pension provision. Myles has shown that raising the age of retirement by even relatively small amounts can bring huge cost savings in benefit expenditure (Myles 2002: 154). Realistic retirement ages need to be established, before unrealistic expectations solidify into notions of rights. They also need to be linked to ages of access to pensions – which is not always the case at present.

Does the particular nature of the process of ageing in the region suggest room for what Phillips calls an 'Asian way' of ageing (Phillips 2000: 5)? There may be such room but what is striking in societies which are, in many ways, so different from the West, is the similarity of the issues and dilemmas to those faced by Western societies. Similar, too, is the way governmental responses in the region mirror Western patterns of service provision.

The Unresolved Debate about Responsibility

In most societies in the region, there is still no consensus about the appropriate location and balance of responsibility for financial support and care in old age. Family has traditionally been the front line of support in both spheres but, as we saw above, that is changing as circumstances and values change. Filial piety remains strong but changes in families and changes in the circumstances of elderly people make it more difficult for families to care as in the past. They may be more geographically dispersed. Financial support in retirement is likely to be required for longer. Caring may well be more demanding and require more skills than in the past. But many people still believe strongly in family responsibility – and governments in many countries in the region place great emphasis on this responsibility both as a way of reducing public expenditure and, as they see it, as a way of reinforcing and maintaining social stability.

There are pressures on governments to assume greater responsibilities for the organization and funding of pension schemes and for the provision of care. But the limited nature of organized grey power – except in Japan – together with the absence of a strong, unified labour movement or of social democratic political parties, limits the pressures on governments to expand their role in this direction. Rather, governments remain ambivalent. Leung aptly captures the state of play in his judgement that most countries in the region are not prepared to face the increasing need for government intervention in the care and support of older people (Leung 2000: 82). Confucianism is a key element here. It has been the philosophical and cultural basis of the pattern of family relationships and care which has come to be defined as the bedrock of the good society. State action can be seen as undermining family responsibilities (Kwon 1999: 3). Ishikawa and Maeda, for example, suggest that the introduction of Long Term Care Insurance in Japan will have a revolutionary impact on traditional value systems (Ishikawa and Maeda 2000: 156). So, apart from government concerns about increases in public expenditure at times of economic uncertainty, there are also significant concerns about the possible broader social implications of any extension in government responsibility.

There are other issues – the extent of the responsibility of individuals for providing an income for themselves in old age; the role and responsibility of employers in the organization and provision of pension schemes; the role of the

182 *Ageing Matters*

community and the voluntary/not-for-profit sector in the provision of care; the potential of the market as provider of services in societies possessed of a prosperous middle class, for example South Korea and Malaysia.

The future is very clearly a mixed economy of welfare with responsibilities shared between individuals, families, the state and civil society. Neverthless, how to achieve that mix and how to establish the best balance between the different elements remains to be worked out on the ground. Choi argues convincingly and challengingly that the future must be one of shared responsibility between state, community and family, and the development of a modern sense of filial piety involving a collective sense of responsibility for all members of society (Choi 2000: 240–1). This is perhaps overly optimistic. But the issue of responsibility has to be resolved, whether or not the decisions are explicit or merely implicit, as conveyed in the policies which emerge from the smoke-filled rooms.

Income

The countries of the region are all struggling with ways to secure an adequate income in old age for rapidly increasing elderly populations. All face similar dilemmas and decisions – which parallel decisions which all societies will have to face at some point about ageing. Six stand out.

First, in many countries there is a serious and urgent problem of old-age poverty now – among women. Elderly people are frequently excluded from the formal labour market because of age or infirmity. They are often not covered by existing schemes of support. For example, in Taiwan, as we have seen, more than one in five elderly people had no old-age benefits of any kind. In South Korea again, pensions made only a small contribution to the incomes of currently elderly people. Elderly people with no other sources of income generally receive only very low benefits from very residual assistance schemes.

Second, there is the question of the future of family support. Currently, children are the main source of income for elderly people – for example, for 40 per cent of elderly people in South Korea and over 50 per cent in Taiwan (Kwon 1999: 11). In Singapore seven out of ten elderly people rely on family members, particularly children, for financial support in old age (Asher 1998: 19). There is evidence that such support is declining. What regard should the policy-makers give to this matter?

Third, what is the best balance of responsibility – and for what – between individual, family, state, employer and private financial institutions in what is clearly going to be a very mixed economy of provision? And what are or should be the contributions of compulsory and voluntary schemes to this policy mix?

Fourth, what should be the age of retirement? Most countries in the region now have plans to raise this age. That certainly offers scope for major savings on pension and assistance costs if the elderly can be persuaded and/or be allowed to remain in full- or part-time employment for longer.

Fifth, how is the short-term/immediate problem of gaps in coverage and limited benefits, because of limited contributions, to be best dealt with? This is a real issue even, for example, in Malaysia and Singapore where Provident Fund schemes have been in existence since the 1950s. In Singapore, one in five men and one in three women retiring in 2000 had no CPF coverage (Lee 1998: 302). Other countries' schemes, for example South Korea's, are too new to generate anything approaching adequate retirement incomes for many years to come. Elsewhere – for example Taiwan – schemes with universal coverage are still, even yet, under discussion.

The result of all this is a serious problem of securing an adequate income in old age for the current generation of elderly people. Policy-makers have been preoccupied with the more exciting policy problem of putting in place the right scheme for the longer term. However, for the shorter term, assistance schemes will have to be expanded in terms of both coverage and generosity of benefits, if hardship in old age is to be avoided. South Korea's Elderly Respect Pension shows one way forward on this front.

Sixth, enormous policy-making energy has been devoted to trying to get the right scheme for the long term – in spite of all the evidence from the West that few pension schemes turn out to be durable, however carefully they are planned. Funded schemes take years to mature and are always at risk from a government's borrowing requirements. Pay-as-you-go schemes depend on the resilience of the intergenerational contract. Compulsory savings/Provident Fund-type schemes – even with large contributions from both employees and employers – simply do not deliver adequate incomes in retirement (Asher 1998: 19; Ramesh 2000: 255). Obviously, countries need to establish schemes with a careful eye to the future, but a robust pragmatism about the limitations of long-term ideal-type planning is clearly a vital element in the pension-planning process.

Care

All societies in the region have very limited formal caring services – even Japan which is the richest, with a long tradition of social policy programmes including a long-term care insurance scheme. An ageing society means an increasing problem of care – more older elderly people in need of care and in need of more care and care for longer periods of time. How care has been provided in the past is a poor guide to the future, both because of the changing nature of the problem and because of social changes. Changes in family patterns and changes in culture and in the status of elderly people all raise questions about the resilience and future of family care. However, governments generally continue to define ageing as a personal/family problem rather than as a broader social problem (e.g. Shin and Shaw 2003: 338). This inhibits effective policy development, and caring services are generally underdeveloped.

Some commentators are more realistic than their governments. Nelson Chow, for example, argues that 'the community can no longer be assumed to be effective in performing its caring functions' (Chow 2000: 161). Not because of wilful family failure so much as because of increased life expectancy and the resulting increase in the demand for care that only formal services can realistically be expected to meet (2000: 169). Vasoo and colleagues make the same point in relation to Singapore (Vasoo et al. 2000: 182).

What is very clear is that there is a need in all our societies to develop formal caring services. Equally clear are the obstacles in this particular case: Confucianism, filial piety and faith in the family; the stigma for the family associated with an elderly member entering institutional care; the relative novelty of the issue; the orientation of health services to cure rather than care; the traditional productivist hostility to any state welfare provision which seems unconnected to economic development; the economic uncertainties in the wake of the Asian Financial Crisis. All these societies in the coming decades will face the issue of how to provide and finance long-term care to fill the gaps exposed by ageing and societal changes which are reducing the caring capacity of the family and informal sectors. Predictably, Japan has advanced furthest in reviewing how such needs might be met and funded, but work has also been done elsewhere – for example in Taiwan and in South Korea – and similar issues face, or will soon face, all societies in the region. In every case such changes will involve conflicts – or at best tensions – with traditional values and ideas of family responsibility (Kao and Stuifbergen 1999). And the development of services can only challenge such values.

The Complexity of It All

Coping with the problems and opportunities presented by an ageing society represents a multiple challenge for policy-makers. Such problems have been clearly illustrated in the case studies presented here. Disentangling the elements in such complexity can be illuminating and helpful in inducing a constructive humility about realistic possibilities.

* Difficult though it is, there needs to be an integrated approach which tries to look synoptically at income, health and care needs and how these might best be met.
* There needs to be a carefully planned incremental integration of the various elements, systems and institutions which constitute the necessary, inevitable and desirable mixed economy of care – state, market, family and community.
* Services must be developed to complement and strengthen rather than replace or supplant traditional caring systems.
* An infrastructure for service development, provision and delivery has to be established nationally and locally.
* Integration of income security / pension policies and employment policies to raise employment among elderly people and/or delay retirement is vital.

- Policy-makers have to work with and take account of changing values. In an interesting analysis of value change in Singapore, for example, Teo and colleagues use the concept of 'ambivalence' rather than conflict to capture the implications of value change (Teo et al. 2003). The nature and significance of that change is open to argument, but change there certainly is and policy-makers must be sensitive to it.

The challenge posed by ageing in East and South East Asia is both multidimensional and urgent. These case studies illustrate that. What they also reveal is a continuum of responses in different countries, ranging from a myopic reliance on traditional mechanisms in the face of dynamic social changes to attempts to engage actively with emerging issues. Clearly, there is no one right way to a better future but reliance on past practice is not a realistic option.

References

Asher, M. G. (1998).The future of retirement protection in Southeast Asia. *International Social Security Review*, 51, 1: 3–30.

Choi, S. J. (2000). Ageing in Korea. In Phillips (2000b).

Chow, N. (2000). Ageing in Hong Kong. In Phillips (2000b).

Chow, N. (2003). New economy and new social policy in East and Southeast Asian compact, mature economies: the case of Hong Kong. *Social Policy & Administration*, 37, 4: 411–22.

Holliday, I. (2000). Productivist welfare capitalism: social policy in East Asia. *Political Studies*, 48: 706–23.

Ishikawa, H. and Maeda, D. (2000). Development of LTC for elderly people in Japan. In Phillips (2000b).

Kao, H. F. and Stuifbergen, A. K. (1999). Family experience related to the decision to institutionalise an elderly member in Taiwan: an exploratory study. *Social Science and Medicine*, 49, 8: 1115–23.

Kwon, H. J. (1999). *Income Transfers to the Elderly in East Asia: Testing Asian Values*. London: Centre for the Analysis of Social Exclusion, London School of Economics.

Lee, W. K. M. (1998). Income protection and the elderly: an examination of social security policy in Singapore. *Journal of Cross Cultural Gerontology*, 13: 291–307.

Leung, E. M. F. (2000). Long term care issues in the Asia Pacific Region. In Phillips (2000b).

Myles, J. (2002). A new social contract for the elderly. In G. Esping-Andersen with D. Gallie, A. Hemerijck and J. Myles, *Why We Need a New Welfare State*. Oxford: Oxford University Press.

Phillips, D. R. (2000a). Ageing in the Asia Pacific region: issues, policies and contexts. In Phillips (2000b).

Phillips, D. R. (ed.) (2000b). *Ageing in the Asia-Pacific Region*. London: Routledge.

Ramesh, M. (2000). The politics of social security in Singapore. *The Pacific Review*, 13, 2: 243–56.

Shin, C. S. and Shaw, I. (2003). Social policy in South Korea: cultural and structural factors in the emergence of welfare. *Social Policy & Administration*, 37, 4: 328–41.

Teo, P., Graham, E., Yeoh, B. S. A. and Levy, S. (2003). Values, change and intergenerational ties between two generations of women in Singapore. *Ageing and Society*, 23: 327–46.

Vasoo, S., Ngiam, T. L. and Cheung, P. (2000). Singapore's ageing population. In Phillips (2000b).

Chapter 11

Lessons to Be Learnt

John Doling, Catherine Jones Finer and Tony Maltby

Introduction

This book started from the proposition that Europe might take policy lessons from the East (Asia-Pacific) on matters to do with ageing. The very idea was arresting in its novelty (cf. Doling and Jones Finer 2001: 293–305). Its practical usefulness, however, depended on the selectivity and sensitivity with which it was applied.

Accordingly, chapter 2 introduced the subject of two-way 'lesson-trading' – between countries and/or between regional blocs – as a matter for academics and policy-makers to approach with circumspection and discrimination, to the extent that they were interested in the best practicable results as opposed to, maybe, the best political effect. The inclusion of Asia-Pacific as a notional policy-trading *partner* for an EU-sponsored social policy research project was a move of potential political significance in itself. Chapter 3 completed the preparatory picture by setting out the EU's own range of concerns. Understandably, but strikingly, this latter presentation concentrated on those matters of prime importance to the European Commission: namely pensions and employment. Other issues, to do with the promotion of health, social and family care, were allocated relatively little space – not because they were seen as less urgent in the scale of ageing matters, so much as because their operation had so far remained very much the business of the individual member welfare states.

This in itself raises a point of significance for the purpose of this book and that of the research project behind it. To what extent were we concerned above all else with potential policy lessons for the EU itself, as opposed to some or all of its member states? By the same token, to what extent were we interested in learning from the experience of individual countries in Asia-Pacific, as opposed to learning from the questionable generality of 'the East Asian Welfare Model'? (cf. White and Goodman 1998: 3–24). In practice, we have endeavoured to do justice to all our contributors by steering a maximally inclusive path between individual country concerns and ostensibly regional interests and issues, at both ends of this spectrum. The extent to which the countries of Asia-Pacific, as here included, are to be considered a potentially organized equivalent to the countries of the EU, for social policy purposes, remains to be seen.

Meanwhile, there remains an immediate practical question in need of an answer. It is not merely the notional 'East Asian Model' but the reputation of successive individual East and Southeast Asian states which has imbued Western welfare states with the idea that these systems and peoples are somehow 'other' from anything Westerners can comprehend or feel comfortable with. So who is conceivably to learn from whom in these circumstances? On what terms, and at what cost? Might globalization already have made a cultural difference-reducing difference? Might respective local forms of 'political correctness' already have reached their sell-by date?

Europe has the world's longest experience in evolving social policies to cope with ageing. It has the longest traditions of NGO activity dedicated to the interests of older people, as well as the longest, best-established traditions of giving older people (at least notionally) a democratic say in the treatment they should be entitled to receive from the state. The leading NICs (newly industrialized countries) of Asia-Pacific, by contrast, have an unrivalled experience (some of this still forecast, yet to come) of *high-speed* population-ageing as a result (in part) of unprecedented high-speed economic development. Hence they also have experience of determined attempts to shore up and reinvigorate traditional family systems of support as a first line of defence against what could otherwise, it is feared, prove communally and politically crippling burdens of public care provision. The prospect of older people as a potential voting block within these states (as opposed to within their families, maybe) remains as yet more possible than actual.

Just what might these respective sets of predicaments be able to learn from each other? The following sections of this chapter review the issues raised, broad topic by broad topic, before concluding on prospects for the future.

Pensions and Employment

It is clear from the contents of the previous chapters that two linked concerns – the adequacy and sustainability of (retirement) pensions – dominate debate in this area and constitute a shared concern for governments, policy-makers, academics and older people themselves in both East and West. The case studies presented in chapters 4 to 9 have documented various attempts at their solution.

Common to all of them is the initial adoption of some aspects of an original Western model – be these forms of public assistance (Japan, Taiwan, Hong Kong), compulsory savings (provident) funds (Singapore, Malaysia and the latest Hong Kong initiative), or cumulative experiments in social insurance (Japan, South Korea, and – still potentially – Taiwan). It is striking, in particular however, that it should be the compulsory savings fund – a 1950s imposition, intended to be cost-saving (for Britain), on the colonial likes of Singapore and Malaysia – which has since been hailed as such a key to their success. It was not merely to be emulated by the introduction of the Mandatory Provident Fund to social insurance-suspicious Hong Kong (see chapter 6 above), but also to inspire Western political leaders with the idea of trying to import such self-financing imperatives somehow into their own longer-standing pensions systems, which had been organized (whether on

Bismarckian or Beveridgean lines) on such a very different, risk-pooling, basis (see, e.g., Jones Finer 1997, in respect of British Prime Minister Blair's stance).

Manifestly, nothing has stood still, least of all in respect of any original imported Western models for income provision. There has increasingly been a shift towards the state supporting a solution reliant on the primacy of the market, but subject to state regulation and supplemented, to a greater or lesser extent, by continuing systems of family support. Given the rapidity with which their societies are ageing, Japan and Korea, in particular, are adopting their own models, which reflect both their respective cultural inheritances and the dominance of the particular forms of work ethic prevalent within these societies. Nevertheless, they are building on the experiences of the West, in particular of Europe, whose countries are considered to have more experience of operating a 'welfare state' than they themselves seek to achieve. Thus, given the lessening influence of filial piety (see below), these new pensions structures are being premised on a more individualistic notion of self-help.

Nevertheless, the strongest (and socially the most potent) demonstration of the capacity for self-help remains the older person's capacity to continue in employment, at however reduced a level. Paradoxically, it is the least developed economies (or the least developed sectors of any economy) which offer the greatest scope for older people's continued economic involvement. There is nothing to prevent older people (however old) from seeking or continuing in employment in the likes of Hong Kong, Taiwan, South Korea, Singapore or Malaysia. But the situation has long been more formalized for some, in the case of Japan. Here the institution of a compulsory executive retirement age of 55 was humanitarianly linked to the parallel institution of a separate 'grey' jobs market, run by the same grand employers, for the sake of both their domestic distribution systems and their long-service retired employees.

Chapter 3 confirmed that the policy focus on ageing within the EU has largely been upon retirement pensions, particularly in their relation to employment policy. As one commentator (Von Nordheim 2004) has recently observed, the EU has set itself two strategic targets: to boost the (otherwise declining) employment rates of older workers up to 50 per cent, and to delay the 'early exit' of workers into pensioner status by five years. Inevitably, these two policy areas and objectives have become inextricably linked. Actions taken to reduce the 'early exit' of individuals have been tied to policies relating to the sustainability and adequacy of pensions across the EU. So it is interesting that a similar linkage (between retirement pensions and employment policy) is to be discerned in the East Asian countries discussed in this book. In Japan, the age from which a pension can be claimed is being increased from 60 to 65. Nevertheless, differences of culture and working practices between Japan and the EU15 countries have meant (as indicated above) that some private companies in Japan (e.g. Matsushita Electrical Industrial Co. Ltd) have continued to employ people anyway, after the mandatory retirement age. This, paradoxically, may have contributed to embedding age-discriminatory practices among those over 60 years of age, since they are treated differently in human resources management terms, for example by easing older workers into publicly subsidized but low-paid jobs (Taylor 2004). Might this prove to be a lesson for the taking?

Meanwhile, for Malaysia and Singapore the pension (and indeed the retirement) age remains at 55, which is, of course, low by European standards. In the EU, reducing the average retirement age was seen as a threat to pensions and to wider employment policy. However, in Malaysia and Singapore, the concern is about not only increasing the pension age but, linked with this, questioning the adequacy of the pensions actually being received. As yet, in sum, it is difficult to discern who is learning what from whom. Perhaps a mutual sharing of ideas and policy recommendations might be the best description of our prospects here.

Another important theme, if not one directly discussed, running through chapters 4 to 9 is the higher levels of poverty experienced by women in retirement and, linked with this, their inferior social status throughout these patriarchal societies as they age. Additionally, in all the East Asian countries here considered, an overt form of *familism* exists which acts to reinforce their status as the primary carers. Even so, the status and economic position of women in this respect also remains a central concern within EU states, as Maltby and Deuchars noted in chapter 3, despite many years of attempts to reduce the structural effects of such a social division. With the increasing incorporation of women into employment (a point raised by Paul Wilding in chapter 10) as one of the results of the globalization of trade – and with it a less gendered approach to employment structure and practices – the sharing of policy ideas between the EU and East Asia may increasingly be possible. On this issue alone, the lessons that could be learned on both sides are a solid argument for the continuation of this dialogue started with the APPLE project.

Social and Health Care

The material presented in this book has confirmed and reinforced the evidence that, among the populations of states with advanced economies, the greatest demand for health and social care is being exerted by the older age groups. The chapters on both South Korea and Japan, for example, indicate the rising health-care expenditures consequential on the ageing of their populations. The precise needs of older people, moreover, can be very wide-ranging. In health care, they cover services for primary and secondary, preventative and curative, and chronic and critical care. In social care, where the services may also relate to the health conditions of individuals, they include the provision of adapted housing, mobility aids, meals and social contact. For all of them, in all countries, the same two challenges apply:

- On the one hand, there is the challenge of ensuring that the care received by all is of high quality, the definition of which includes the ability of those receiving care to make choices about the nature of such care.

- On the other hand, whatever the units by which the resources used to deliver the care are measured, there is the question of who, precisely, is supposed to be paying for it.

The case of Malaysia illustrates some of the issues. Traditionally, the family – backed by the community – has performed a major role, alongside that of state-provided health-care institutions. However, with strains appearing in both systems, the state has attempted to shore up family commitments through tax subsidies (see below), while encouraging the private sector to expand its own forms of health-care provision. This may have reduced the potential impact on the public purse of meeting the health-care needs of older people, but it has done so by re-asserting the responsibility of the family. The advantages afforded to the general population by private sector provision have largely accrued to those who are relatively well-off and living in urban areas.

By contrast, the evidence from Japan and South Korea suggests that the issue in these places is less about which sector actually provides care, and more about who pays for it. Specifically, the issue is about whether the cost falls directly and solely on the user (and their family) or is met through a social commitment.

In every (other) Asian country included in this book, the transition to an ageing society has proceeded further than in Malaysia. Although the extent to which their governments have reacted is variable, the reaction has in all cases resulted in the efforts directed at improving the well-being of older people being more concerted than has often been the case in European countries. In Hong Kong, for instance, the main emphasis has been on the 'ageing in place' policies, i.e. home and family first; followed by informal and then formal community care; with full-time institutional care (whether provided by public, non-profit or for-profit organizations) as the very last resort. Meanwhile, in South Korea a task force has been established under the Office of the President with the objective of coordinating policies responding to the ageing of society. The Korean and Japanese cases also identify the involvement of wide interests, including business and community groups, in the relevant policy debates. It is in Japan, however, that there has been the longest and deepest consideration of the issues concerning inter-generational fairness. One message for Europe, therefore, is the possibility of policy formation that is more comprehensive both in its application across the range of issues arising from ageing populations and in its involvement of all sectors of society in their resolution.

It is also clear from the surveys of each of these six Asian countries that, notwithstanding the strong traditions of family members providing care directly, or indirectly through financial support, this tradition is being eroded. In an opposite direction, there is a comparison here with European perceptions of the desirable future of pensions, away from sole reliance on the state towards a multi-pillared model in which the social protection of the state is allied to resources derived from the workplace and the individual. By contrast, the recognition in Asian economies, in respect of health and social care, is that it is the single pillar of the family which needs to be balanced by other pillars, of which the state must be one. So, if the general picture in Europe is for the state to withdraw from, adapt, and recalibrate its role in the provision of all types of welfare and social spending, the general picture in Asia is the withdrawal from, adaptation and recalibration of the role of the family.

The Family as a Bulwark under Threat

Cultural distinctions between East and West with regard to the family – however prominent in the mass media at either end – should not be overstated. Prior to the emergence of dedicated social services in developed and developing parts of the world, the family, backed by the immediate community, had an obligation to provide, as best they could, whatever income support, health, education or social care provision most people in the world were ever likely to receive, *wherever* they were brought up. Furthermore, the role and importance of the family – especially of parents and parentage – has long been sanctified in Western as well as in Eastern tradition.[1] The fact that family norms vary as much, nowadays, between parts of northern (more developed) and southern (less developed) Europe, as they do between Asia-Pacific and Europe itself, says as much about the concomitants of economic development, as about the rival qualities of social philosophy being propounded by respective governments. Furthermore, the degree of vigour with which such philosophies are openly promoted differs markedly between governments within as well as between East and West.

The fact that it should be the most explicitly eulogized *Confucian* family tradition (*pace* Malaysia) which is now being exposed to economic and demographic change at a pace and on a scale never experienced in Western (as opposed to Central–Eastern) *Judeo-Christian* Europe may strike Western observers as ironic. More to the point, however, the fact of its being the proclaimed strongest family tradition, which is now apparently facing the greatest socio-economic threat, strengthens the possibility of there being potential lessons for the taking elsewhere, with regard to how best (or how not) to try to control, sustain or even resurrect the family as a supportive institution. It is in their selective assessment of the feasibility, suitability and acceptability of such material for application elsewhere, that the skills of policy-makers – and/or the adequacy of their policy-making processes – will be tested.

As is evident from the earlier chapters of this book, as well as from the earlier pages of this chapter, the family in Asia-Pacific – just as previously in Europe – has been witnessing a steady diminution in the scale of both its collective obligations and its permitted freedom of manoeuvre. How far the concomitant increase in the provision of government-backed specialist services – in respect of pensions, public assistance, housing, health care, professionalized community care and long-term social care – has rendered this a *zero-sum game*, rather than adding to the total of available provision in support of increasingly aged populations, remains to be seen.

It is striking, however, that there has been no single advance in public policy provision or regulation within Asia-Pacific, which has, explicitly sought to *replace* the underlying, backstop responsibility of families to take care of their own. Thus, there exists no pensions or public assistance system in Asia-Pacific, as here reviewed (or even systems still in the pipeline, as in Taiwan), which specifically lets families 'off the hook' of financial responsibility for their elder members. In any case, pensions systems are mostly far from complete in their coverage; nor are they adequate (so far) in the scales of protection they offer. Meanwhile, forms of remedial public assistance (or approved voluntary charity for needy cases) are typically framed in terms which involve at least the entire immediate family – not merely what may be the *co-resident* members of this family – in the assessment of an older person's eligibility for outside assistance. In Singapore, South Korea, Taiwan and Japan, children are legally bound to support their parents financially, to the best of their ability. However, the authorities in Hong Kong seem content to rely on traditions of family shame to take their full 'assistance-rationing' effect.

By contrast, a family's potential capabilities with regard to the accommodation of its older members would seem to have been *increased* as a result of the extent of state involvement in mass housing provision, at least in Singapore and Hong Kong. The housing requirements of families in Singapore are under apparently constant review by the Housing and Development Board, with the well-being of their older members – requiring at least accommodation near to the rest of the family – a major allocatory factor. Meanwhile, in Hong Kong the inclusion of an older person within the family list guarantees a shorter waiting time (as laid down in government regulations) for either the rental or purchase of government-financed accommodation.

The modernizing emphasis in public or government-backed health-care provision continues, from the top down, to be entirely Western-'curative'-oriented in Asia-Pacific. By definition, this allocates little save a supporting role for the families of patients. Set against this, however, the persistence of family support for forms of traditional medicine chimes increasingly with the preferences of discriminating Westerners, interested in equivalent forms of holistic, minimally invasive, treatment for themselves and *their* families.

Meanwhile, modern East Asian families, driven by the work ethic of success-dedicated Asia-Pacific – young wives and mothers especially – are not going to find it easy to combine traditional family obligations with distinctly non-traditional commitments to the labour market. Governments, as in the case of Hong Kong and Singapore, have responded to this challenge by instituting forms of 'Family Life Education' to help 'culturally deprived' immigrant generations to catch up with what should have been their heritage all along. Other governments, such as that of Malaysia – not so far down the line of socio-demographic 'advance' – hope to stem, if not reverse, the latest trends in extended family disintegration by the provision of tax breaks to encourage children to share the same house as their parents and to purchase appropriate forms of care and care equipment for their benefit. Yet others, further down this line, such as South Korea and Japan, agonize over how far whole societies – as opposed to individual families – should be obliged to carry the cost of these 'interim generations': those who have contributed to their societies' success without themselves being in time to benefit from any eventual long-term, self-funding pension or insurance arrangements. In the case of Japan this amounts to a new *collective* version of Confucianism, whereby the whole society is expected to take responsibility for the well-being of – and just relations between – the generations within it. Nevertheless, even Japan's institution of long-term care insurance – itself an idea borrowed from Germany for potential re-export in this case to elsewhere in the West – would not seem to have resolved all the underlying matters of family conscience on this score, quite apart from its practical complications.

Conclusions

This innovative project and book have raised questions as much about the feasibility and acceptability of lesson-learning between East and West, as about the particularities of each or any separate lesson-learning possibility. So there are in effect two levels of findings to be reflected on here. Paradoxically, it remains the most general – rather than the most particular – indicators which are easiest for this level of policy undertaking (as opposed, say, to a field-level practitioners' workshop) to deal with most effectively (cf. table 2.2, above).

Being formed from a group of nation states, which in number is scheduled to expand to 25, the European Union has considerable opportunity within its own borders for cross-country policy-learning. However, what from a perspective inside the EU looks to be considerable diversity in the potential lesson-givers – from the social democratic Nordic states to the *familism* of the countries bordering the Mediterranean, let alone to the former state-socialist countries of Central and East Europe – constitutes only a fraction of the global spectrum to everyone else. To be sure, the countries of North America as well as Australia and New Zealand, all with their European legacies intact, meet one of the requirements identified in chapter 2 for successful lesson-learning and potential exchange: namely cultural proximity. However, the evidence of this book is that the East Asian parts of the spectrum furnish another set of experiences no less ripe for another set of exchanges.

To be sure, there are elements in the East Asian mix which are clearly removed from Western cultures, the dominance of Confucianism in particular. However, there are also long-standing points of East–West interaction, some of them with an origin which is nowadays embarrassing. British colonial traditions in Singapore, Malaysia and Hong Kong (as well as earlier Portuguese and Dutch influences) have been matched by late twentieth-century American influences in Japan, Taiwan and South Korea. None of these have turned out to be propitious for the even-handed exchange of lessons thereafter. Nevertheless, some of the social welfare arrangements, such as the provident fund systems in Singapore and Malaysia, however moulded to and by local conditions, remain, as outlined in earlier chapters, European in origin. So, even if they are different, the policies themselves are not necessarily remote or lacking in relevance to European situations.

Meanwhile, there remains the larger case for taking an interest in Asia-Pacific. With the exception of Japan, over the last century or so, the major industrial economies have all been Western. But over the last half-century, in comparison with the European economies, the NICs of East and Southeast Asia have, in economic terms at least, been outstandingly successful. On GDP per capita Singapore has now overtaken all EU member states, while the others in our group are comparable to those currently joining the EU. Just as their economies have been transformed very quickly, so have elements of their social and political circumstances. As earlier chapters have shown, the rate of change in populations, for example, is more rapid than in Europe. Whereas in the past, the West has been looked to by those in the East determined to catch up, it is at least possible that the future will be one in which the West looks more to the East to see how the newcomers are rising to the challenge of ageing populations. The so-called teacher perhaps becomes the so-called pupil in the end – before they both ideally agree to dialogue, if only still to differ.

It is this final unresolved, but at least better-defined and appreciated, question which points at once to the value of the APPLE project, such as it was, and to the scope for further exchanges, building on this experience and the contacts established. The next steps could include at once:

- widening the geographical scope of debate and lesson exchange to include an (increasingly Asia-conscious) Australasia;
- deepening the socio-philosophical scope of the debate by facing up to the sorts of family/gender/community/individual rights-based issues with which every 'globalized' population and government is going to have to contend.

It is on the basis of such a continuing, underlying, mutual investment, that the exchange of more immediate 'practical' policy lessons between East and West stands a decent chance of success.

Note

1   For example:
    - the Judeo-Christian Ten Commandments (13th–12th century BC): 'Honour thy father and thy mother, that thy days may be long in the land which the Lord thy God giveth thee (Church of England *Book of Common Prayer* (1642) adapted from Deuteronomy 5:16).
    - *Confucius (K'ung-fu-tzu)* (6th-5th century BC): Filial piety (*Hsiao*) as the first step towards moral excellence.

References

Doling, J. and Jones Finer, C. (2001). Looking East, Looking West: trends in orientalism and occidentalism amongst applied social scientists. In C. Jones Finer (ed.), *Comparing the Social Policy Experience of Britain and Taiwan*. Aldershot: Ashgate.

Jones Finer, C. (1997). The new British social policy. Social Policy & Administration, 31, 5.

Taylor, P. (2004). Age and work: international perspectives. Social Policy and Society, 3, 2.

Von Nordheim, F. (2004). Responding well to the challenge of an ageing and shrinking workforce: European Union policies in support of member state efforts to retain, reinforce and re-integrate older workers in employment. Social Policy and Society, 3, 2.

White, G. and Goodman, R. (1998). The search for an East Asian welfare model. In R. Goodman, G. White and H.-J. Kwon (eds), The East Asian Welfare Model: Welfare Orientalism and the State. London: Routledge.

Statistical Appendix:
Ageing Matters in Figures

Li Kan

Table A1 Demographic characteristics

Country	Population (million) 2001[1]	Aged 0–14 (%) 2001[1]	Aged 65+ (%) 2001[1]	Life expectancy 2001[2] M	F	Healthy life expectancy 2001[2] M	F	Average household size 2000[3]	Birth rate (per 000) 2001[1]	Rural population (%) 2001[1]
Asia										
Hong Kong	6.7	16.7	11.2	—	—	69.3[5]	72.4[5]	3.1[6]	7	0
Japan	127.0	14.5	17.6	77.9	84.7	71.4	75.8	2.7[7]	9	21
Malaysia	23.8	33.7	4.2	69.2	74.4	57.6	63.2	4.2[8]	22	42
Singapore	4.1	21.5	7.3	76.5	81.1	67.9	69.5	3.7[9]	12	0
South Korea	47.3	21.3	7.0	71.2	78.7	64.5	70.3	3.5[10]	13	18
Taiwan	22.5[4]	20.8[4]	8.8[4]	—	—	—	—	3.3[8]	12[4]	31[4]
Europe										
Austria	8.1	16.5	15.7	75.9	81.8	68.9	73.0	2.4	9	33
Belgium	10.3	17.2	16.6	74.8	81.2	67.7	71.8	2.4	11	3
Denmark	5.4	18.4	14.9	74.8	79.5	69.3	70.8	2.2	12	15
Finland	5.2	17.9	15.0	74.5	81.2	67.7	72.5	2.2	11	41
France	59.2	18.7	16.1	75.6	82.9	69.0	73.5	2.4	13	24
Germany	82.3	15.3	16.4	75.1	81.1	68.3	72.2	2.2	9	12

Greece	10.6	14.9	18.1	75.5	80.8	69.0	71.9	2.7	11	40
Ireland	3.8	21.5	11.2	73.8	79.2	67.6	70.4	3.1	15	41
Italy	57.9	14.2	18.4	76.2	82.2	69.2	72.9	2.6	9	33
Luxembourg	0.45	18.9	14.1	74.9	81.8	68.6	72.7	2.6	12	9
Netherlands	16.0	18.5	13.7	75.8	80.7	68.7	71.1	2.3	13	10
Portugal	10.0	17.1	15.2	72.7	80.1	64.3	69.4	2.9	11	34
Spain	41.1	15.0	16.9	75.3	82.6	68.7	73.0	3.0	10	22
Sweden	8.9	17.9	17.5	77.7	82.3	70.5	73.2	2.0	19	17
UK	58.8	18.6	16.1	75.1	79.9	68.4	70.9	2.3	11	10

Sources:

[1] World Development Indicators 2003: ⟨http://www.worldbank.org/data/wdi2003/index.htm⟩
[2] http://www.who.int/country/aut.en/
[3] Eurostat Yearbook (2002).
[4] Law, C. K. and Yip, P. S. F. (2003), Healthy life expectancy in Hong Kong Special Administrative Region of China, *Bulletin of the World Health Organization*, 81, 1: 43–7.
[5] Taiwan Yearbook (2003).
[6] Hong Kong Population Census 2000: ⟨http://www.info.gov.hk/censtatd/eng/hkstat/fas/01c/cd0122001_index.html⟩
[7] Japan Population Census 2000: ⟨http://www.stat.go.jp/data/kokusei/2000/kihon1/00/zuhyou/a008.xls⟩
[8] Encyclopaedia Britannica Book of the Year (2002).
[9] Singapore Population Census 2001: ⟨http://www.singstat.gov.sg.keystats/c2000/handbook.pdf⟩
[10] South Korea Government, National Statistics Office: ⟨http://www.nso.go.kr/eng/index.shtml⟩

Table A2 Economic and pension characteristics

	GDP per capita (US$), 2001[1]	GDP annual growth rate 1990–2001[2]	Public pension spending as % of GDP, 2000[3]	Age at which entitled to old-age benefits, 2002[4]		Contributors per working-age person, mid-1990s[5]
				M	F	
Asia						
Hong Kong	25,000	3.8	—	65	65	—
Japan	27200	1.3	7.9	65	65	92.3
Malaysia	9,000	6.5	6.5[5]	55	55	37.8
Singapore	24,700	7.4	7.4[5]	55	55	56.0
South Korea	18,000	5.7	1.4[5]	60	60	43.0
Taiwan	17,200	—		60	55	—
Europe						
Austria	27,000	2.2	14.5	65	60	76.6
Belgium	26,100	2.2	10.0	65	60	65.9
Denmark	28,000	2.4	10.5	67	67	88.0
Finland	25,800	2.9	11.3	65	65	83.6
France	25,400	1.9	12.1	60	60	74.6
Germany	26,200	1.5	11.8	63	60	82.3
Greece	17,900	2.4	12.6	65	60	73.0
Ireland	27,300	7.7	4.6	66	66	64.7
Italy	24,300	1.6	13.8	65	60	68.0
Luxembourg	43,400	—	7.4	65	65	—
Netherlands	25,800	2.9	7.9	65	65	75.4
Portugal	17,300	2.7	9.8	65	65	80.0
Spain	18,900	2.7	9.4	61	61	61.4
Sweden	24,700	2.1	9.0	65	65	88.9
UK	24,700	2.7	5.5	65	60	84.5

Sources:
[1]CIA World Factbook (2002).
[2]World Development Indicators 2003: (http://www.worldbank.org.data.wdi2003/index.htm)
[3]The Global Retirement Crisis-CSIS Report: Pension, Health Care Spending Threaten World Stability: (http://www.csis.org/gai/global_retirement.pdf)
[4]Social Security Programs Throughout the World 2002:
(http://www.ssa.gov/policy/docs/progdesc/ssptw/2002/asia/)
[5]International Patterns of Pension Provision (The World Bank Group Social Protection Discussion Paper No. 0009): (http://www.worldbank.org/pensions)

Index